CW00417956

THE REBEL
WHO LOST HIS
CAUSE

THE REBEL WHO LOST HIS CAUSE

The Tragedy of John Beckett,
MP

FRANCIS BECKETT

LONDON
HOUSE

First published in Great Britain in 1999 by
LONDON HOUSE
114 New Cavendish Street
London W1M 7FD

Copyright © 1999 by Francis Beckett
The right of Francis Beckett to be identified as author
of this work has been asserted by him in accordance
with the Copyright, Designs and Patents Act, 1988

This book is sold subject to the condition that it shall
not, by way of trade or otherwise, be lent, resold, hired
out or otherwise circulated without the publisher's
prior written consent in any form of binding or cover
other than that in which it is published and without a
similar condition including this condition being
imposed upon the subsequent purchaser.

A catalogue record for this book is available
from the British Library

ISBN 1 902809 04 1

Edited and designed by DAG Publications Ltd,
London.
Printed and bound by Biddles Limited,
Guildford, Surrey.

CONTENTS

Preface, 7

ONE
Ashes to Ashes , 9

TWO
The Yeomen of Cheshire, 13

THREE
A Glimpse of the Glittering Prizes, 40

FOUR
A Complicated Life, 63

FIVE
Burning Boats, 80

SIX
Dying on Stage, 108

SEVEN
Following the Bleeder, 126

EIGHT
The Anti-War Faction, 153

NINE
Mr Morrison's Prisoner, 175

TEN
The Outcast, 197

A Note on Primary Sources, 217
Bibliography, 218
Index, 220

PREFACE

There are many people without whose help this book could not have been written, or would have been much poorer. I have tried to acknowledge them in the text, or in the brief notes at the end of the book. But there are a few special debts which I want to identify here.

The Society of Authors gave me a generous grant from one of their funds, and without that I could not have cleared enough time to do the work properly. The value of these funds is not sufficiently recognised. Without them, many important books would not get written, because the economics of publishing means that writers cannot be paid enough to keep their families while they are writing them.

Professor Colin Holmes, late of Sheffield University and the author of, among other works, *Anti-Semitism in British Society*, wrote, many years ago, a profile of my father for the *Dictionary of Labour Biography*. He has been generous with his knowledge and recommendations, and has also read and commented on three chapters. His help and advice, and the introductions he provided to his own contacts, have been invaluable, and I am looking forward to his forthcoming biography of William Joyce.

The Board of Deputies of British Jews have opened their archives for me and given me every help. I would like to thank especially their volunteer archivist Monty Kolsky, who not only gave me permission to use the archive and guided me round it, but also offered me his own very considerable knowledge and wisdom.

The Friends of Oswald Mosley, which still exists and publishes a newsletter, have also helped me in every way they can, in the full knowledge that they were going to dislike pretty well everything I wrote, and I thank them sincerely for it, especially John Christian (not his real name), Bob Row and several others.

I have also been helped by the late Fenner Brockway, Barbara Castle, Michael Foot, the late Fr. Brendan Fox A.A., the late Douglas Hyde, Colin Jordan, Heather Joyce (daughter of William Joyce), Daphne Stone and Jeffrey Wallder.

My sister Clare Beckett has given me her insights, as well as her academic's passion for getting it right, and my late half sister Leslie Beckett contributed knowledge, understanding and common sense.

And I have benefited greatly from contacts with researchers and academics, some of whom came to consult me and ended up telling me more than I told them. Graham Macklin certainly falls into this category, and I eagerly await his study of fascism post-1945. Others include Stephen Dorril (whose forthcoming biography of Oswald Mosley may do something to put the record straight), the late David Englander, Simon Fowler (without whom my Public Record Office visits would be much less productive), Jeremy Gibson (who, among many other things, introduced me to the Collin Brooks diaries), Professor David Howell, Professor Brian Simpson, Nigel Todd, David Turner (whose e-mails always enlighten) and Peta van den Bergh.

I am fortunate to have an exacting and creative literary agent, Julian Alexander, and to have met, at the publishers, first Peter Day, who loved the idea of the book and commissioned it at once, and then his successor Roderick Dymott, who made it one of the first batch of books to appear under the new non-fiction imprint of London House. I am grateful to Ruth Winstone for her editorial help with the book, which, like a previous book of mine, has benefited from her care and knowledge of political history.

And I must not forget to thank Gordon Marsden, who commissioned me to write a study of my father when he was editor of *History Today* (he is now a Labour MP). He took endless trouble to make sure I got it right, and then invented so clever a title that we have re-used it as the title of this book.

CHAPTER ONE

ASHES TO ASHES

During his last illness, my father raved only once.

Mostly, he was lucid. Lucid enough to tell me he was dying, and to tolerate with patience and kindness my squirming, stilted nineteen-year-old response, which was to look longingly through the hospital window at the traffic circling Hyde Park Corner and say tonelessly that I would miss him. He answered, without a hint of irony, that it was kind of me to say so. But there was one day when he was not lucid at all. Against medical orders, he was sitting bolt upright in his bed when my mother and I arrived. He almost shouted to us: you could hear, for the last time, the dim echoes of the huge voice which had quelled hundreds of great meetings in that Indian summer of political oratory between the two world wars. 'They've seen it at last, they've admitted I was right all along.' I knew at once what he meant. He meant: right about Ramsay MacDonald, right about Mussolini and Hitler, right about war and peace.

My mother tried to say something soothing, but he was not a man to be soothed when in a passion. 'It's all over the papers. Haven't you seen the papers?'

I walked swiftly out, leaving the full burden of his unhappiness to fall on my mother, which was where I usually dumped unwanted burdens. I knew now, and wished I did not, what went on during those long, solitary walks in the countryside. As I left I heard him ask where I was going, and my mother told him I was going to get the papers. The next time I saw him, he was lucid again, and for the few weeks of life remaining to him, he never again allowed himself the indulgence of dreaming in public.

Perhaps it was at that moment in 1964 that I decided to write this book. Or perhaps it was twenty years later, when my mother at last gave me a telephone number for my half-sister Lesley, the child of my father's first marriage, born in 1920 on the top floor of Clement Attlee's Limehouse home, whom I had not seen since I was a tiny child.

'What I could never understand about our father,' Lesley told me the first day we met, 'was how he could make speeches against the Jews when he loved his mother so much.' I said I knew how desperately he loved his mother, but I didn't see the link, and Lesley said: 'You know she was Jewish, don't you?'

I didn't, but I should have realised. He once told me that cunning Jews would change their names to hide their origins. If you met someone called Salmon, he said, bear in mind that you are probably talking to a Jew whose real name is Solomon or Salaman. His mother's maiden name was Salmon. I knew that she died in 1932, because after his death I found a faded photograph of an elderly, dignified lady, on the back of which my father had written: 'Daddy's mother, died 1932.' And I knew that my father had refused to join Sir Oswald Mosley when Mosley founded his fascists in 1931, but had agreed to join in 1933, by which time everyone else was starting to leave.

Perhaps this book started much earlier, during my childhood. I was born in May 1945, four days after VE day and a little more than a year after Home Secretary Herbert Morrison released my father from prison, in the small Berkshire village of Chenies, 21 miles from the centre of London. It was exactly that distance because the dangerous fascist John Beckett was still under a sort of house arrest, not allowed to travel more than five miles from his home nor within twenty miles of London.

I do not remember a time when I did not know, at least in broad outline, about the extraordinary life he had lived for the 51 years before I entered the world.

He was elected Labour's youngest MP in 1924, still only twenty-nine. In those far-off days he was seen as one of Labour's rising stars, with his strong platform presence and his gift for organising campaigns. I knew that he had been on intimate terms with the greatest political names in the land. When in my teens I sang 'Lloyd George knew my father' with other cheerful young men on the way home from a party, I reflected that I was the only one whose father Lloyd George really did know.

I knew that in the 1920s he had been the friend and confidant of all those who were to run the 1945 government, and especially its Prime Minister, Clement Attlee. By 1929 he had become the whip for the rebel left wing MPs of the Independent Labour Party group, and the most extreme, most newsworthy left wing Labour rebel of his day.

I knew that he was famous as 'the man who stole the Mace'. He was more than once physically thrown out of the House of Commons, and in 1930 he seized the Mace from the Speaker's table – the first person to do so since Cromwell – shouting 'Mr Speaker, these proceedings are a disgrace', and was forcibly relieved of the burden on his way to place it head first in the gents' toilet.

In the early 1930s he managed London's Strand Theatre, knew all the leading actors of his day, and made a good deal of money. He lost all of it, every penny, on a failed theatrical venture which left him a bankrupt.

My mother, Anne Cutmore, was his third wife. A whirlwind First World War romance ended in marriage to Helen, Lesley's mother. His second wife, Kyrle Bellew, was a famous actress of the time, the widow of the great actor manager Arthur Bourchier. One of the many things I did not know until years after his death was that Kyrle Bellew refused to divorce him, and that for the first eighteen years of my life, my father and my mother were not married.

He spent three years running the British Union of Fascists' propaganda machine, leaving after a bitter quarrel with Sir Oswald Mosley. He and his friend William Joyce (who was to broadcast for Germany during the war, becoming famous as Lord Haw Haw, and who was hanged after its conclusion) founded the National Socialist League. He left that after a few months and founded the British People's Party – a tiny group on the right-wing fringe of British politics – with the Duke of Bedford.

His career, which had looked so promising in 1924, ended in summer 1940 in the squalid wastelands of neo-Nazi politics, and in Brixton Prison, where fascists were interned during the war. He was released in late 1943, on conditions that amounted to house arrest, and was nearly sent back to prison when he was found secretly holed up with Anne in a tiny Victoria flat.

When I was born, in May 1945, he was 51, and had no home, no money, and, with one of the most hated names and faces in Britain, no prospect of getting any work. He and my mother were living on what she could earn as a secretary.

My mother suggested that he revive an old ambition and train for the bar, or that they emigrate to New Zealand where she had relatives who might help them to make a new life. But the arrival of a son must have scuppered those ideas. He knew then that he must earn money in any way he could, and he went back to the only work he could get, reviving the British People's Party, still living on its wealthy patron.

What could make a man like my father put on a black shirt and call himself a fascist? He was the most unlikely fascist you could imagine. He was irreverent, spontaneous, funny. He loathed accepting orders. He spoke and wrote with fluency and humour – the weapons of a democratic politician, not a demagogue. He had no time for the 'heel-clicking and petty militarism' of fascism. He did not have the fascist reverence for The Leader. He was shocked by the people who were attracted to fascism because it enabled them to strut about self-importantly in a uniform. He does not seem to have realised that all this was an intrinsic part of the creed he had embraced. This fascist – for that is what we must call him – was intelligent, sincere, noisy and very human. Thirty years after his death, I still miss the noise.

The one lesson we can surely learn from history is that we have to eliminate the causes of despair, not just attack the symptoms. We may not have a lot of time. My contemporaries grew up knowing that fascism was something dreadful, for its results were part of our childhood. That memory ensured that most of us managed to avoid blaming people of another race for our troubles. But knowledge decays. The conditions that bred fascism are returning just as we are raising a generation which knows nothing of the holocaust.

CHAPTER TWO

THE YEOMEN OF CHESHIRE

On 18 September 1893, at St James's Church in Islington, north London, William Beckett married Dorothy Salmon according to the rites of the Established Church. William was a draper, and the eldest son of a Cheshire farmer.

As for Dorothy, years later their elder son John claimed that her family were 'fisher folk on the east coast'. One of the pieces of wisdom John picked up in a strange and turbulent life, and passed on to his own son, was that while it is of course better always to tell the truth, if you have to lie, you should give your lie as many elements of the truth as possible. It helps to keep track of it. So I imagine they had some connection with fishing and the east coast.

The truth was that Dorothy was the daughter of a Jewish jeweller. None of her ultra-orthodox family attended her wedding, and she was declared dead for marrying out. So far as anyone knows, she never saw any of her family again. She could not have dreamed that her son would one day be among of the three best known anti-Semites in Britain.

Dorothy was tall and slim, with a huge mass of golden hair, and by all accounts heart-rendingly beautiful. The only surviving picture of her shows a lady of 60 or so, her face already marked by the pain of the cancer that was to kill her at 62, but even in that picture you can catch a glimpse of the grace and dignity which was to endure in the minds of both her sons for as long as they lived. John's love for her was, I think, almost too great for him to bear. 'If a boy really loves his mother, he'll choose a woman just like her,' he would say, though his own attempts to do this were not marked with conspicuous success.

William was short, thick-set and emphatic, and John, born on 11 October the year following their marriage, had little affection for him. William held Conservative political opinions and prided himself on his Englishness and his patriotism. John grew up in an atmosphere of lower middle-class jingoism, learning his poetry from Rudyard Kipling and his history from G. A. Henty. Henty was a very popular late Victorian historical novelist. His central character was always a brave clean-cut Englishman who, after tremendous adventures, always won through, defeated the foreigners and the infidels, and saved the situation for everyone.

The family lived in King Street, Hammersmith, west London, above William's draper's shop: William, Dorothy, John and their second son, born in 1899 at the start of the Boer War and christened, with a rush of patriotic fervour which seems to have been typical of William, Cecil Rhodes Beckett. Turning William into a draper was the Cheshire Becketts' idea of placing him on the first rung of the ladder which led to gentility. Dorothy's family seems to have thought the same, and William and Dorothy met when they were both being turned into lower middle-class gentlefolk in a Manchester draper's shop.

Small shopkeepers in the twilight of Queen Victoria's long reign were an intermediate class somewhere between manual workers and professionals like lawyers, doctors and clergymen. They worked hard, their hours were dreadfully long, and they sweated their labour – or, if they could not afford labour, they sweated themselves and their families. They were, as social historian Paul Thompson puts it, 'drawn to the standards of respectability of their clients and customers ... yet without the income and security to maintain them'.

They lived constantly on the edge. If the business failed there was nothing, and they would join the one-third of the population which lived in real poverty, unable to feed themselves or their children properly, or to rely on a roof over their heads.

Thurlwood Farm, in the village of Rode Heath near Alsager in Cheshire, where William had been born and where most of his eleven brothers and sisters still lived and worked, might have been less genteel, but it was almost certainly a lot happier and more secure. The Becketts had worked Thurlwood Farm for generations. To the day he died John still talked proudly of his 'yeoman ancestry', a phrase which was starting to sound very odd by the 1960s.

Each summer the four of them – William, Dorothy, John and Cecil – decamped to the family farm. These long summer holidays were the happiest memories of the boys' childhood.

John's grandfather, also called John Beckett, ran the farm. He was a mountain of a man, big and broad and fat. He lived until he was 80, and from the age of 40 he was unable to see his feet or tie his own shoelaces. 'A goose is a fool of a bird,' he would say. 'Too big for one and not big enough for two.' Some of his sons helped him work the farm. One of them – yet another John Beckett – was the landlord of the village inn. John and Cecil played, watched the men work the fields, and helped a little. In the evenings they sat round the huge kitchen table while their grandfather played host to a good number of his twelve children and grandchildren, as well as his workers, and everyone would eat gargantuan quantities of food which his wife Hannah had spent the whole day preparing. Hannah's maiden name was Billington, and the Becketts, Billingtons and Warburtons had lived, farmed and intermarried in that part of Cheshire for generations. It was a rough life on the farm, far removed from the fragile gentility which William and Dorothy knew in the city. The amenities included a vast outside lavatory, designed for two people to sit companionably side by side. The seat was simply a polished plank of wood with two holes cut into it a few inches apart, allowing for easy conversation between the users. It was considered a mark of favour if, after a huge supper washed down with plenty of beer and cider, Uncle George invited you to 'have one with me'. Dorothy, a nicely brought up Victorian city lady, was permanently terrified that one day she might be in favour with Uncle George.

Yet that, as it turned out, was nothing compared to the troubles that overtook her at home in Hammersmith. She had cut herself off forever from her own family, not only 'marrying out' but marrying in a Christian church. Perhaps she did not realise how much this made her dependent on the character of the man she married. Among the Cheshire Becketts, William was considered irresponsible and feckless, and there seems to have been a determination that he should not get his hands on any more of the family money. He was considered to have frittered away a £500 legacy from his mother's brother, and his father's will decreed that the sum should be deducted from his share of the estate, and that two of his younger brothers, rather then he, should be trustees.

In 1909 he proved them right by speculating all he possessed on the stock exchange, in one of the many schemes proposed by that great politician and confidence trickster Horatio Bottomley, who offered the irresistible combination of the chance to invest in something patriotic and the chance to make loads of money. William lost half of his capital in one wild speculation, and went angrily to Bottomley's shareholders' meeting, from which he emerged having invested everything he had left in another of Bottomley's schemes. That, too, he duly lost.

So at fourteen, John's childhood came to a sudden end. There were no more leisurely summer holidays at Thurlwood, and he was forced to leave the Latymer School in Hammersmith at once. He was heartbroken. He enjoyed school and seems to have been doing rather well. The son of a shop-keeper could grow up with expectations of becoming a professional man: but the son of a bankrupt could have no expectations but grinding labour until he was too old and weak to do any more, and then a pauper's grave.

The boy who had become a boy scout at the age of ten and an officer in the First Middlesex Territorial Cadet Battalion at twelve became, at four-teen, a draper's errand boy. He was part of the child labour on which London's prosperity was based, working every waking hour and sleeping on the job – 'the victim', he wrote, 'of the twin horrors of a Welsh draper and the living-in system in Willesden'. It must have been harder to bear than if he had never had any other expectations.

Fortunately for him, his mother had taken with her a few of her own father's precious jewels. For the rest of her life, she pawned them on the frequent occasions that her husband fell on hard times, and reclaimed them when things improved. By this method she enabled John to gain some qualifications at correspondence courses and night schools.

For she too came from a family which hankered after that elusive quality, gentility. She seems to have defined gentility in a traditional Jewish way; she hoped that her son would be a lawyer. He certainly had dreams of following that profession, but when the chance came, he rather negligently tossed it aside, for that was how he lived his life.

His misfortunes did not change John's conviction that he lived in the finest nation on earth, and that its values and its prosperity were forever. Few people who reached the age of twenty by 1914 ever quite freed them-selves from a secret and unacknowledged wish that the pre-war world might return – even those, like John, who were most loudly to repudiate its values once the earthquake of the First World War had blown their world to pieces.

Half a century later, in the 1950s, he could still sigh, only half humor-ously, for an age when people did not call you by your Christian name unless they were very close friends indeed. 'If someone you hardly knew came up and said, hallo John, you buttoned up your pockets and moved away,' he would chortle to people who had never seen pockets with buttons. In the fifties he could still mourn that young men no longer seemed inclined to address older men as 'Sir'.

There was pleasure, and for John, as for many young men in London, that pleasure was mostly to be found in the music hall, with its entertainment, laughter and girls to fall in love with. To the end of his life he remembered the songs he heard there. Not just the ones everyone remembers, though he sang those too:

'I'm Burlington Bertie, I rise at 10.30 and saunter along like a toff.
I walk down the Strand with my glove on my hand, and walk back
    again with it off ...'

but also long-forgotten ditties:

'We're Cholly and Dolly
We're two of the very best.
We are specimen of the dressy men
You meet up west.
And when in the morning down Bond Street we trot
Every Molly and Polly
Says "Golly, how jolly.
It's Cholly and Dolly. What what?"'

He also understood what they meant, and I like to think of him sitting in the gods, laughing his loud, cracked laugh at the glorious Edwardian euphemisms in Burlington Bertie:

'I've just had a banana with Lady Diana,
I'm Burlington Bertie from Bow.'

He recalled standing outside the Hammersmith Lyceum, aged perhaps fifteen, waiting for a chorus girl with whom he had fallen desperately in love. Falling in love became a habit which he never lost.

Another habit he never shed was that of thinking of something one minute and doing it the next, without pausing to consider the consequences. So on the day war broke out, 4 August 1914, he rushed to enlist, filled with boyish jingoistic enthusiasm. Three days later, the night before he was due to put on his uniform, he celebrated with a massive pub crawl. At last his friends left him sleeping on the pavement, to be awoken in the small hours by a policeman. He started his military training with the mother and father of all hangovers, and never got that drunk again.

The First World War left the whole of his generation irredeemably scarred. Some opposed the war, to be abused and assaulted daily by men, and spat on and handed white feathers by women. Others saw things in the trenches which would haunt them all their lives, and lost nearly all their friends.

Quite what John saw, I do not know, for he never talked about it except to tell funny stories. Although he did not experience the worst horrors of the war, for the rest of his life the war was with him, every day, and his dead and horribly maimed friends were with him too. The burning anger that rich men should send poor men to suffer and die in pain and without dignity never left him. It was the scar he carried around, the goad that drove him.

He enlisted in the 9th Middlesex Battalion, but quickly transferred to the King's Shropshire Light Infantry because Shropshire was closer to the ancestral home in Cheshire. There he served with G Company, recruited (apart from himself) entirely from Ludlow in Shropshire.

These early decisions almost certainly saved his life. While other regiments were sent to France, to be mown down like flies in the squalor of the trenches, and others to Gallipoli to die at the hands of Turkish guns amid the sand and the ferocious insects, the King's Shropshire went to India to hold down the Empire. On 23 January 1915 John found himself in Rangoon. It was by far the safest place to be. He served for just four months in India and two in Singapore. He entered the regimental boxing tournament and reached the final because all the best boxers were in the other half of the draw. In the final bout he was blasted to the canvas in the first round. He remembered getting lost and separated from his comrades, and walking for hours trying to find them, terrified by footsteps behind him. When he arrived at the camp he found that the footsteps belonged to the native water-carrier, who, possessing no boots, found it less uncomfortable to step in John's footprints. One of his favourite war poems was always Rudyard Kipling's 'Gunga Din', about a native Indian water-carrier:

'Of all them blackfaced crew,
The finest man I knew
Was our regimental bhisti, Gunga Din ...'

and especially the lines

'Though I've belted you and flayed you,
By the livin' Gawd that made you,
You're a better man than I am, Gunga Din!'

But, as so often with John, the truth about his war, as he afterwards presented it, does not quite hang together. It is not true, as he sometimes claimed, that he lied about his age to get into the army. A young man of nineteen did not have to lie in 1914, and his army record gives his age accurately. He was released in 1916, with heart disease. 'Dyspepsia on slight exertion. Palpitations with faintness and giddiness, loud systolic murmur, considerable enlargement of heart, result of active service and climate', records his discharge certificate. It would be 'permanent and semi-disabling' and he was 'no longer physically fit for war service'. He had been a soldier for less than two years. I suspect that, perhaps unconsciously, he never quite recovered from a feeling of shame, not only that he survived, but that he had a comparatively easy war.

He was in hospital for about a year, and a semi- invalid for some time after that. He emerged from hospital without teeth. The war revealed that most working class people's dental care was rudimentary or non-existent, and by the time they reached the age of twenty their teeth were in such a rotten state that they could only eat pulped-up food. John's teeth must have been a real mess, because they pulled the lot out, and he wore dentures for the rest of his life.

The oddest thing of all is that he seems to have been a very good soldier, though he always suggested he had been a thoroughly insubordinate one. In the ex-servicemen's movement which he helped found, his two court-martials became the stuff of legend. He told me that every time he was promoted, he did something disorderly and was demoted again. Yet his discharge papers say that his character in the army was 'exemplary' and he was swiftly promoted to corporal and became signals instructor to his company.

I think he may indeed have shown insubordination, despite his attested character, because for all his talk of discipline, he was himself highly undisciplined, and because ever afterwards, among his many hatreds, he voiced his contempt for petty army regulations and those who imposed them. Forty years later, as a child in the 1950s, I found it hard to understand the pleasure and gusto with which he sang the First World War song:

'If you want the sergeant major, we know where he is,
We know where he is,
We know where he is.
If you want the sergeant major, we know where he is,
He's hanging on the old barbed wire.'

He told me what the song was about, and why he liked it. 'The barbed wire was between the trenches. When you went over the top, you'd get shot as you tried to climb over it, and then you'd hang there till you were dead. No one liked the sergeant major, that's why they all laughed when they sang the last line.'

I think he saw himself, in the first of many fantasies, as a G. A. Henty hero, doing brave and unconventional things on behalf of God and his king; and that it took him rather longer than it should have done to realise that the harsh, cynical, class-ridden British army was no place for swash-buckling.

A single man, handsome and fancy-free, entered the army in 1914. A married man emerged from it. On leave one week, he had met a tall, beautiful woman named Helen Shaw on Monday, married her on Wednesday, and returned to his company on Friday.

The married man who was discharged from the army was very different from the man who had rushed to enlist two years earlier. When the war started, John believed, with all his irresponsible, spontaneous, passionate heart, in the things his father believed: Britain ruling the waves, Conservative government, the moral value of material success. By 1918, 'I had completely lost the old views, and thought God and the politicians equally to blame for international strife and inequality of opportunity at home.' Twenty years later, he wrote sadly of the idealism of his generation in 1918: 'Proud of having conquered our inherited inhibitions, in our innocence we believed there was little else to conquer.'

He had a new name. In a family full of John Becketts, he had always been called Jack, and it was Jack William Beckett whose service record begins with a medical certificate on 8 August 1914. Soon after the war, Jack William Beckett seems to have ceased to exist, and in his place was a clever young man with a brilliant future in front of him, whose name was John Warburton Beckett.

He was given the middle name Warburton, he always explained, in deference to his yeoman ancestors. This, it appears, was not quite true. He simply assumed the name, typically without going to the trouble of registering the change, after he left the army. Formalities such as registration never seemed important to him – as at least one of his wives was to discover.

By the time the armistice was signed he had 'a reasonably good job' in Sheffield. He was handsome and fluent, with a loud voice full of absolute certainty which he did not always feel, and six feet tall – exceptional in those days, when people were not as tall as they are now, and the working class suffered stunted growth from bad diet and malnutrition. He had also found socialism, after the most intense period of reading of his whole life and a road to Damascus experience on a night in 1918, when the Labour MP for Sheffield Attercliffe, W. C. Anderson, came to speak at the Ethical Society.

Anderson was then 41, from a Scottish family of crofters. At the turn of the century he had been a radical and effective trade union organiser, and he was an Independent Labour Party MP who was thought of as a future Labour leader. He was, as John was to become, an effective campaigning journalist and platform propagandist. He had also been a pacifist during the war. 'Across the roar of guns, we send sympathy and greetings to the German socialists,' he had written in 1914, the year he became an MP. 'They are no enemies of ours but faithful friends. In forcing this appalling crime upon the nations, it is the rulers, the diplomats, the militarists who have sealed their doom.'

John went to the meeting and badgered the speaker with a constant barrage of questions. He carried on after the meeting had closed, until Anderson invited him back to supper at his lodgings. There John blurted out the worst accusation, he thought, that you could hurl at any man – that Anderson lacked patriotism. He waited to be thrown out.

According to the *Dictionary of Labour Biography*, Anderson's 'open manner and handsome appearance all served to disarm critics', and it certainly worked wonders on the 24-year-old ex-soldier. Anderson answered quietly and clearly, and 'for the first time I realised that foreign affairs were not so simple as the daily press had led me to believe, and that the war had other origins beside the lunacy of the Kaiser. I left my mentor at dawn and walked across the city to my own lodgings, hardly noticing the tiredness of my body for the turbulence of my mind.'

A few days later Anderson sent him a huge pile of pamphlets and a reading list: Marx, Engels, Ruskin, John Stuart Mill. For the next few months John spent all the hours he could spare from work devouring the reading list and attending meetings on politics and economics.

Anderson did not live to see the results of his persuasiveness. He died suddenly and unexpectedly the next year, 1919. John's mentors had a habit of dying and leaving him rootless.

By then, John was back in London, this time in the East End, in Hackney. He had lodgings at 9 St John's Mansions, Clapton Square, a job and a new, raw, exciting religion. He was certain now that only a revolutionary change in the way society was run would be good enough for those who had been ground down and exploited for generations; certain that he must devote his life to making an end to the system that enabled one man to amass huge wealth while another could not earn enough to feed his family. It seemed a betrayal of his dead friends to accept the injustices he found at home.

He saw around him an explosive mixture. Liberal Prime Minister David Lloyd George had called a snap election in 1918, the 'khaki election', which was a triumph for the Conservatives and produced a coalition government dominated, in a memorable phrase which John used often, by 'hard faced men who had done well out of the war'.

Britain in 1918 was probably closer to armed revolution than at any other time in its history. The Communist Party was founded in 1920, and on the day of its foundation the editorial in the Labour-supporting *Daily Herald* expressed, not wild optimism, but something like conventional wisdom: 'The founders of the new Party believe – as most competent observers are coming to believe – that the capitalist system is collapsing.'

The reasons were the same as those that motivated John. The *Herald* reported a commonplace story. 'An ex-serviceman was turned out of a job to make way for a girl, his pension temporarily withheld. One of his three children, owing to the effects of malnutrition, was sent to a poor law institution, and the father received a bill for 24 shillings for four weeks' maintenance in hospital. Then another child was taken ill and in hospital seven weeks, and, with empty pocket and barely a crust in the house, the father received a demand for another 28 shillings.'

John was ready for his first cause.

British socialists, unlike those in Europe, had never taken the army seriously. Soldiers were, by their nature, considered reactionary. The biggest socialist group – the Independent Labour Party, led by Ramsay MacDonald – had adopted a pacifist policy, and many ILP leaders had gone to prison for it. 'The socialist left in Britain,' writes historian David Englander, 'in so far as it considered the subject at all, regarded the army with a mixture of fear and contempt.'

The ILP, even in 1915, had rejected the idea of military trade unions on the grounds that it might make soldiering into a respectable occupation. It was an early example of the British left doing what it has spent most of the twentieth century doing: acting as though it lived in the world it wanted, rather than the world as it is. Soldiers, as much as pacifists, had bitter grievances against the existing order. In their view, unemployment of former servicemen seemed to show the treachery of the civilian population. Their disability pensions were niggardly, and were meanly and inefficiently distributed. Fearfully maimed former soldiers begged for their bread on the streets of London, while war profiteers drove past them in splendid motor cars to the best restaurants, throwing up dust and mud from the un-tarmacked streets on to the already filthy war heroes.

John started by joining the Comrades of the Great War, but quickly decided that this government-encouraged organisation was simply a ruse to trick his old army comrades, to persuade them to take jobs at low wages which they had to subsidise with their war pensions, and to try to prevent them from joining trade unions. George Bernard Shaw wrote despondently in September 1918: 'Already employers openly ask what pension a man has, and make him an offer accordingly.'

So, early in 1919, John Beckett and Ernest Mander founded the National Union of Ex-Servicemen (NUX), to show the former soldier that his interests lay with the Labour movement, and that he should resist efforts by the Comrades of the Great War to persuade him to be a strike-breaker. Mander was general secretary, and John became president.

The union stood for a better deal for ex- servicemen and the families of those who had been killed:

We aim to maintain that spirit of comradeship which existed among us while we were together in the Services. And to reinforce it with that sense of comradeship which should inspire us who are still fighting together, but this time for political and industrial aims at home ... We are ex-Service men, but we are also citizens ... We shall therefore support the Labour Party in its efforts to improve the conditions under which all the people ... must live ... We shall there-

fore support the trade unions ... We did not fight to save the country
for the capitalists, but for the people ...

It campaigned for better pensions, jobs for ex- servicemen and a root-and-branch reform of the hated court martial system which had summarily condemned so many men to death. It demanded back pay for former soldiers at the much higher rates given to Australian, New Zealand and Canadian troops. This would have meant a huge lump sum for all former soldiers, and the NUX proposed that it should be paid for by a land tax which would hit war profiteers.

Within six months the NUX grew from one branch with 50 members to over 100 branches with almost 100,000 members. The Ministry of Labour was seriously concerned. The British Legion (according to its official history) saw the NUX as 'a bitter brooding group of militant Marxists'.

The Labour Party supported the NUX and brought its leading members on to its relevant policy committees. But it refused to support its proposals on back pay for soldiers, and when Major Clement Attlee, a prominent Labour Party activist from East London, proposed amendment of the court martial system, John, on behalf of the NUX, submitted a memorandum demanding much more draconian reform than Major Attlee contemplated. John demanded that the Labour Party should completely reconstruct the army along democratic and classless lines. But this, too, never became Labour Party policy.

The NUX also acted as the ex-serviceman's 'trade union', and John represented dozens of men denied their pensions, or shell-shocked men who were being treated as 'pauper lunatics'. He saw all the human misery created by a country which had won a war and seemed neither to know nor care about the human cost, and it filled him with anger.

Mander sold his home to finance the NUX, and from the pacifist wing of the ILP, Fenner Brockway and Ramsay MacDonald both worked to secure money to supplement the one shilling a month membership subscription. Brockway and MacDonald used their influence to persuade the ILP to underwrite £150 of a £400 overdraft which the NUX ran up, and to donate £50, and Brockway helped to get some private finance. But it was nothing like enough, especially with the NUX now producing a monthly publication, *New World*.

The newly formed Communist Party offered money, but the conditions were onerous. John and Mander both had to join the CP and become paid

Party officials. Their executive was to be confined to members approved by the CP, and they were to accept the principle of democratic centralism which would oblige them to obey instructions issued by the Comintern, the Moscow-dominated Third International.

The communists' conditions were put to the two NUX leaders at a meeting with the CP national executive at their headquarters in Maiden Lane, where the union received, so John claimed, 'the kind of greeting which the Millionaires' Federation might offer to a deputation of office boys'. It was the beginning of John's lifelong loathing for the Communist Party. 'We did not trouble these autocratic "proletarians" with a further visit,' he wrote later.

The money, however, was not found from anywhere else: and money was not the only problem. Special Branch seems to have reported that the NUX was the seedbed of revolution, and the government gave Lord Haig £2 million profit from the services' wartime canteens so that he could build an organisation which would put all other ex-servicemen's groups out of business. As a result of the foundation of the British Legion, with Lord Haig as president, and its own chronic shortage of money, the NUX was forced to wind up and offer its branches either the choice of carrying on independently or throwing in their lot with the ILP, the Labour Party or the Communist Party. Special Branch was distressed to find how many of them chose the Communist Party, and so, no doubt, was the NUX president

Mander emigrated to New Zealand. John seriously considered going with him, and only his ILP work kept him in Britain. Almost a decade later, in 1928, Mander was heard of again – as National Organiser for the New Zealand Conservative Party. Labour Party headquarters asked John for any information which New Zealand's Labour Party could use against him, and got their heads bitten off. 'I knew nothing to his discredit. Mander was a loveable man with a fine brain and few things would give me greater pleasure than to hear good news of him,' he told them, and added, just to rub it in, 'From what I have seen of the Dominion Labour Parties I do not blame anyone for opposing them.' Visceral loyalty always meant more to John that the bloodless loyalty of political party.

Mander was John's first political hero. There were to be many more – charismatic, clever, passionate men who could inspire his fierce loyalty and his fertile fantasy life, the romantic hero to John's swashbuckler, the fellow musketeer, the joint hero of a Henty novel. Labour leaders Ramsay MacDonald and Clement Attlee, socialist leaders John Wheatley and Jimmy

Maxton, fascist leaders Oswald Mosley and William Joyce, all were to have spells in Mander's shoes. Unlike Mander, they lacked the good taste to emigrate before their clay feet became so obvious that even John could not avoid seeing them.

It had been a turbulent two years. John had found a faith, a love for his fellow man, and a loathing of injustice. Others took decades to accommodate all of that. John did it fast, and in his usual untidy, haphazard way, he took in alongside it some very undesirable baggage.

The meeting at the Communist Party headquarters put in place the last of the trio of prejudices which were to sit and fester in the back of John's mind until, under the pressure of events, they fatally coalesced.

He disliked communists because they were receiving huge sums of money from Moscow. The Party denied it, but everyone on the political left knew it was true, and documents which have come to light since the fall of the Soviet Union show that the sums were greater even than the Party's enemies dreamed of. He thought communists were rich, showy and trendy, and worst of all, unpatriotic. 'Almost all political Bloomsbury belongs to the Party,' he said, and he knew few worse insults.

He still considered pacifism unpatriotic, and intellectually snobbish. And anti-Semitism was even more common in John's new home on the political left than it was in his old home on the right. Historian Colin Holmes has pointed out that, in the years before the First World War, it was largely Jewish businessmen who made the City of London pre-eminent in finance, and that anti-Semitism was common on the left because Jews tended to be identified with capitalism. There was a widespread feeling that war profiteers were mostly Jews, and such profiteers were the class of people towards whom John displayed the most blinding, disabling hatred of which even he was capable.

For the moment, these bitter feelings were locked safely away, smothered by the excitement of the times and the dream of creating a better world which he shared with the best of his generation. The notorious pacifist Fenner Brockway could become a close friend. Pacifists, communists and Jews, all saw in John simply what everyone else saw – a very able, very energetic young man with an acute form of the revolutionary socialist fervour which his generation had brought out of the war; a fine platform performer with a loud voice, a strong personality and massive self-confidence.

After the demise of the NUX, all John's energy went into the Independent Labour Party. The ILP had been founded in 1883 by Keir Hardie in order to get independent parliamentary representation for working men, and its title implied independence of the Liberal Party. In 1900 it came under the umbrella of the newly formed Labour Representation Committee. The LRC was an alliance of trade unions and socialist societies, including the ILP, formed to return Labour MPs who would form an independent party in the House of Commons.

In 1918 the LRC ceased to be a loose federation of trade unions and societies and became a political party with branches in each constituency. In short, it became what we now know as the Labour Party.

Before 1918 you could only join the Labour Party by joining an affiliated society like the ILP, or an affiliated trade union. Now anyone could join the Labour Party directly. In the long term this destroyed the ILP. Yet no one would have predicted that in 1918, when the ILP seemed to be the inspiration of all Labour's activities, as well as the keeper of its socialist conscience.

John joined the Hackney branch of the ILP in 1918. ILP leader Ramsay MacDonald, knowing that he needed the support of ex-soldiers, to whom he was suspect because he was a former pacifist, invited the well-known ex-servicemen's leader to meet him at the ILP head office in Johnson's Court, off Fleet Street. So John, still only in his mid-twenties, and just two years out of uniform, found himself moving in elevated political circles.

For a short time, MacDonald took Mander's place as his political hero. 'The handsome face behind the heavy black moustache, the organ-like voice and the graceful gestures seemed to good to be true. It took me a year to learn the ability behind this God-given exterior, and more than five to discover the vanity and cunning.'

MacDonald was favourably impressed, and told the new secretary of the London Labour Party, Herbert Morrison, likewise a pacifist, to make use of John. So John found himself invited to a vegetarian meal at the home of another important political figure. Here are his first impressions of the man who, twenty years later as Home Secretary, was to hold the keys of his prison cell:

Herbert Morrison was under 40, a small, unprepossessing looking man with one almost blind eye and a queer expression of furtive pugnacity mainly engendered by a stubborn jaw and an unruly forelock spreading over a low but well developed forehead. Son of a London policeman, he seemed, except for his vegetarian, non-

27

smoking and prosaic manner, a typical smart-alec cockney, and while his businesslike manner and shrewdness suggested sound organising ability, there seemed no sign of any real statesmanlike qualities.

Vegetarians always rather puzzled John, who was, like his Cheshire ancestors, a hearty carnivore, and he worried all evening about how he was supposed to handle 'the extraordinary meal I was kindly invited to share'.

The political importance of the evening lay in the decision that Labour could win Hackney, even though it had not at that time a single representative on the borough council. John explained the problems of the Hackney branch, and they planned how to overcome them.

There was, he told Morrison, a group of malcontents in the branch led by the Secretary, who would need to be sidelined. 'This man,' he wrote later, 'was the type of socialist Bernard Shaw must have had in mind when he declared that "only Socialists have prevented the coming of socialism". Small and inoffensive, with vague features, a wispish gingery moustache and a weak, peevish voice, he and two doctrinaire Jews, who spoke voluble and incoherent English, attempted to dominate the meetings and thought themselves real revolutionaries. They had not strength, kindness or charity, and many promising faces faded out after an evening spent listening to the diatribes of these incorruptible nuisances.'

With help and guidance from Morrison, John took the Hackney party in hand. He held three open air meetings every week, generally attracting six or seven hundred people. He ran indoor meetings and lectures. John spoke at least once a week and the ex-servicemen always came out to hear him. The result was a sensational victory in the November 1919 borough elections. Labour, which had not previously held a single council seat, obtained a majority of one. This was a shock to everyone, especially the newly elected Labour councillors who, suddenly finding themselves expected to run the borough, at once co-opted Herbert Morrison as an alderman, and elected him leader of the council, so that he could tell them what to do.

As council leader, Morrison's policy was ultra-cautious, and Hackney's left-wingers quickly became very restive, none more so than John Beckett. Two months later there was a by-election for a council seat which Morrison considered unwinnable. When John pushed through a decision that a candidate would be fielded whether Morrison liked it or not, Morrison took his revenge by nominating John as the candidate. John did not want to be a councillor – he probably already had his heart set on Parliament – but in the circumstances he could not refuse without embarrassment, so he put his heart and soul into the fight. His greatest strength was always his energy and vitality as a political campaigner. He could drown out an opponent's message and at the same time capture hearts and minds with the sheer force of his own convictions. To everyone's surprise except his own, he won.

He at once became the leader of a group of five left-wing councillors opposed to Morrison's rule. This group, because of Labour's tiny majority, could hold up the work of the council whenever it chose to do so.

The big issue was unemployment. Morrison, unlike George Lansbury in neighbouring Poplar, refused to commit council money to unemployment relief. But a much smaller issue brought the conflict to the boil. Some council employees threatened a strike over a fairly modest pay claim. John was for paying, Morrison was against. But many Conservatives also wanted to meet the claim, and Morrison knew he faced defeat in the council chamber. He moved a half-hour adjournment and in an adjacent room, he raged at his rebel councillors. He was forced to give in.

Neither man ever forgot or forgave. As we shall see, both were still talking about it more than a quarter of a century later, after the Second World War, after the dangerous fascist Beckett had finally been released from prison by Home Secretary Morrison.

And more than half a century later, in the 1970s, Labour councils were still playing out precisely the battle that John Beckett and Herbert Morrison fought in Hackney in 1919. No one has yet found a way of reconciling Labour's ideals with the desire of its leaders to appear moderate and unthreatening. John summed it up in words that could have been used about almost any Labour council at any time in the last 60 years:

A Labour majority on a local authority may make a determined effort to implement its lavish election promises, which will mean increased rates and eventually a sharp conflict with the national government; or it may throw aside its promises and endeavour to prove that Labour majorities are safer, more economical and more efficient than their opponents. The personal beliefs and ambitions of the leaders do not allow the first course, and the rank and file make the second impossible.

The same battle was fought out in neighbouring Poplar but with very different results. There, George Lansbury and his colleagues imposed high rates so as to keep the unemployed from starving, and the government surcharged the borough. The councillors cheerfully went to prison for their refusal to commit the borough to paying the surcharge. While Lansbury was in prison, Morrison savagely attacked him for breaking the law.

John had by then spent more evenings in Lansbury's 'comfortable old home in Bow Road' than he ever spent in Morrison's vegetarian household, and sprang to Lansbury's defence, concealing from no one his wish that Hackney had a courageous and committed leader like Lansbury, and his extremely low opinion of its present leader. He organised a conference of London Labour parties which, with Clement Attlee from Limehouse in the chair, passed a unanimous vote of censure on Morrison.

John's heart was in Brixton Prison with Lansbury. The memory must have returned to haunt him when he entered the same prison in 1940. 'Only twenty years after did I realise the full weight of the enmity I had incurred,' he wrote after the Second World War. He meant that he was convinced Morrison took a terrible revenge for his humiliation in Hackney by keeping him in prison when the committee set up to advise the Home Secretary was recommending release.

The notoriety attached to a rebel left-wing Hackney councillor ensured that John lost his job. And in this way, the first fateful decision of his life was made. He had agonised for months about whether to throw up a promising career in advertising to become a full-time politician. Now there was no more agonising to be done. It was the first of four luminous careers which he threw away, without regrets yet also without real intention. That was the way he lived his life.

He became one of the small army of full-time ILP speakers who toured the country, from one draughty meeting hall to another, selling the socialist message. He lived by taking modest fees from the local parties whose meetings he addressed. He loved the hard work, the comradeship, the discovery that he had the ability to lift an audience.

He relished the stories and told them all his life, for he had, as Colin Cross put it, 'a schoolboy delight in elaborating an anecdote'. 'We've 'eard the greatest socialists in this 'all,' enthused one local chairman. 'We've 'eard Brother Keir 'ardie in this 'all, we've 'eard Brother Ramsay MacDonald, and tonight we're honoured, brothers, to 'ave with us Brother ... what did you say your name was, Brother?'

An elderly trade unionist, standing for Labour in a mining constituency, faced a young Conservative candidate with a beautiful, patrician wife, and on the eve of the poll he told his audience: 'I hear Lady X has told you that tomorrow she will be going away with the Member for this Division. You know old Tom well enough to know that he will defend his honour with his life.'

There was only one rule, he said. You must make sure you finish in good time for the audience to get a pint in the pub afterwards. Whether this was for the benefit of the audience or the speaker was not always clear. Sometimes a long-winded chairman would make it impossible. He told the story of a speaker who listened to a chairman's long introduction. When the speaker finally got to his feet he said, 'Well, now, comrades, I think we should all thank our brother chairman for that long and interesting address, and now let's get round the pub, before we all die of thirst.'

He loved the people he met, the rough and ready accommodation he stayed in. He wrote: 'In every town there were a number of good comrades who possessed a spare room, or at any rate a spare bed. The same folk put up all speakers who visited their districts, and usually at supper on Sunday evenings, the leading local members were invited to meet the visitor. Such evenings are a source of many happy memories. These men and women on small wages were financing the propaganda for a great movement. Fierce arguments were carried on until the small hours of the morning.'

In Maidstone he set up camp with Ernest Hunter, later political editor for the *Daily Herald*, and Seymour Cocks, later an MP, and there the three of them were witnesses in one of the great mysteries of Labour movement politics.

They held an outdoor meeting just outside Maidstone prison. After John closed the meeting, a tall man approached him and said, 'That was a fine speech, sonny. I used to give them just the same stuff.' He took them to the nearest pub, bought drinks, told stories of Irish politics, and said he was connected with the Irish secret service, and that his name was Victor Grayson.

The name meant nothing to them, which showed how little they knew of the history of the movement they served. Victor Grayson, MP for Colne Valley, had been the great romantic hero of socialist politics before the First World War. He had disappeared suddenly, and no one ever saw him again. If this man was really Victor Grayson, they were the only people known to have met him since before the war. John always believed that it really was Grayson, and so did Grayson's biographer, Reg Groves.

John was humorous and extrovert, with enormous energy, and he specialised in a rough, knockabout platform style which was very popular on the ILP circuit. Some full-time speakers lived like that for years, and brought up their families as part of the ILP 'family', but John was a young man and seemed to have a brilliant future ahead of him. A better opportunity swiftly presented itself. Major Attlee, Labour candidate for Limehouse, put it about in the 1917 Club that he required a secretary and election agent.

The club, founded in 1917 by Ramsay MacDonald and some other Labour and Liberal pacifists, was based at 4 Gerrard Street in London's West End, and was where the political and literary left met, dined and talked the excitable radical politics of the time. John was introduced to the club, of which Attlee was a committee member, in 1918, often lunching there several times a week.

John had heard a lot about Major Attlee, all of it good: a left-winger, a soldier, and a charming and witty man. Attlee, too, had heard of John. While John was waiting to be interviewed by the Limehouse Party Executive, a member came out and told him his appointment had already been settled because 'the Major wants you'.

Attlee had that precious political asset, an inheritance which gave him a modest income, though not as large as had been rumoured. John needed real money for propaganda work, not just the pennies you could collect from impoverished members. The only money Attlee could offer was earmarked for John's first year's salary of £6 a week. So John made a proposal.

Attlee had bought a big old house, Norway House, in the constituency. The ground floor was used as a club for the Labour Party. Attlee lived on the first floor, with his former army batman to look after him. There was a flat on the top floor, and John proposed that he and Helen should move into it rent-free, and he would therefore take no salary, raising his own living expenses by part-time work for the ILP, to which he could add some journalism and a few advertising commissions.

Attlee noted in his terse way: 'November 1920. Jack Beckett came to act as secretary and agent and subsequently lived at Norway House with his wife and little girl who was born there.'

There, in Attlee's rambling East End home, John found the first stability and contentment he had known since he was fourteen, and the last he was to know for many more years. Attlee was eleven years older and had received the university education which John seemed now to crave. The two men spent long, calm evenings puffing on their pipes together and talking about God, politics and the state of the world. They made a complete genealogical tree of the Forsytes some years before it was published in the complete edition. I am sure this project was Attlee's idea, for he loved precise, detailed work, and Galsworthy's *Forsyte Saga* was a favourite of his. John, left to himself, could not have sat still long enough, but he loved the company of his gentle, witty, Oxford-educated friend.

If Attlee provided the learning that John lacked, John liked to think he could give his less outgoing friend some instruction in the ways of the world. Attlee's childhood had been spent with his rather protective family in Putney and at a boys' boarding school. He was painfully shy, and probably knew even less about women than the average unmarried former public schoolboy in 1920. John, on the other hand, was thoroughly extrovert. If he ever suffered from shyness in his life, no one ever noticed, and he had discovered early that he was very attractive to women. He wrote of his friend with amused affection:

> The few occasions when his humour became caustic were in his discussions about feminine methods and their effect on masculine life. Never a young woman came near a friend without his instant realisation that she was 'gunning for poor old so-and-so ...' It was therefore a great surprise when [Attlee] went off for a continental tour with a man friend, and returned completely absorbed in his friend's sister who, by some strange chance, had been, with her mother, on his line of route. In response to a query whether she had been 'gunning', he spent some time telling me how difficult his task was, and how fortunate he hoped to be.

When Attlee married the friend's sister and moved to the suburbs, 'I missed our regular talks very much'. Attlee's friendship was a deep happiness to John, and it was nearly a decade before he smashed it to pieces.

All the lessons John had learned in the advertising business, and all his flair for a phrase, a slogan, a propaganda method, went into selling Attlee to the electors of Limehouse. One of his most successful innovations was a free advice service. He spent each morning listening to people's troubles. If anything could be done he promised to 'see the Major about it'. If he was sure that nothing could be done, the case never reached Attlee. 'I was the

Hyde to Clem's Jekyll, and there were many who lamented that if only I had let them go to the Major, things would have been different.'

The *East London Pioneer* was another propaganda success, and the first of a series of newspapers which John founded regularly over the next four decades, and through which he disseminated his gospel of the moment. It set the pattern for all the rest. John was editor, business manager, despatch clerk – he *was* the paper. It lasted two years, reached 5,000 people in Lime-house, Mile End and Bow and Poplar, and even paid its way. This was partly because of its success at attracting advertising. Attlee as mayor managed to ensure that some of the borough's advertising went into it, trade union branches took space, and some Labour supporters owned shops which they advertised in its columns.

The journalistic style is unmistakably John's, with big headlines and little restraint in the writing, but also with a real news sense. In November 1921 he was writing about the failure of the transport strike of that year, attacking 'the noisy and dangerous people who urged all sorts of impossible cures' on the one hand, and the right-wing union leaders on the other: 'Those masterly recruiting agents for the Communist Party ... The lesson is: avoid bad leaders.' TURN THE WASTERS OUT was the lead headline just before the borough elections in March 1922. Hearing that railway magnate Sir Eric Geddes was being paid huge sums of money to recommend cuts in public expenditure (the so-called Geddes axe) he wrote under the headline BRAZEN IMPUDENCE OF A SHAMELESS PARASITE:

> Sir Eric is eating up the share of twelve families. So the other eleven families must starve. And Sir Eric has the brass face to be Chairman of a Committee which calls upon the other eleven families to economise.

Attlee and John worked together on a small committee which wrote a new policy for the ILP. It was adopted by the 1922 conference and served the ILP until 1933 – and by then the four men who drafted it were in four different political parties.

These four could only have come together in the extraordinary conditions of the immediate post-war years, when everything seemed possible. There were two ex-soldiers – Attlee and John – and two ex-'conshies', Fenner Brockway and Clifford Allen. In 1922 the divide between soldiers and 'conshies' was still bitter, the wounds still raw. John already knew and liked Brockway, but he instinctively disliked and distrusted Clifford Allen, and the feeling was almost certainly mutual. Yet in 1922 they must all have felt that they were creating a new world together. None of them could have imagined that by 1933, the Labour Party and the ILP would have split: Attlee would be in the Labour Party; Brockway would remain in the ILP; Allen would have followed Ramsay MacDonald into the National Government, having, for practical purposes, turned Conservative; and John would have become Sir Oswald Mosley's propaganda director, bringing to fascism the skills which, in 1922, he was using on behalf of Attlee.

It was Brockway who brought the four of them together in a flat in one of those splendid mansion blocks in Prince of Wales Drive, Battersea, which Clifford Allen shared with Bertrand Russell. John, impressed that he was about to meet the great philosopher, was terribly disappointed to find the two flatmates squabbling over some minor domestic matter.

The final detailed draft was left to John and Attlee, which must have been a relief to John. Never good at being polite to someone he disliked, there was something about Allen which roused all his anger and contempt. He wrote of him: 'His gentle "charm" had gained him great popularity among the wealthy Quakers and pacifists who provided ample means for the lavish anti-war campaign of the No-Conscription Fellowship of which he had been Chairman.'

John was a good hater. His hatred of Clifford Allen deepened over the years as the latter linked himself with the treachery of Ramsay MacDonald, until John could write, only half humorously: 'I am against war because it is a blind and expensive way of weeding out the population. It takes your Rupert Brookes and leaves your Clifford Allens, and that is an extremely bad thing.' Three years after they drew up a policy together, we find him at an ILP conference, furiously opposing the minimum wage proposal put forward by 'Clifford Allen and his little band of middle class intellectuals … well known writers and thinkers who could pass Allen's standards of gentility'.

In October 1922 Lloyd George's unstable coalition government was brought down by his Conservative supporters. The new Conservative Prime Minister, Andrew Bonar Law, called a general election the next month. In Limehouse, Attlee faced a sitting member with a 6,000 majority, yet there was a sense of victory about his campaign from the start. The Liberal split already looked terminal, and the 1918 Representation of the People Act had changed the electorate radically. For the first time, women could vote (though only if they were over 30) and so could many more working men. Attlee engaged an additional agent to handle the detailed work so that John could concentrate on propaganda and publicity. John thought his candidate needed careful handling, writing in 1938:

> Even now he is far from being an orator, and in those days his best friends could not have called him even a tolerably good speaker. His strongest cards were his erudition and wit, both of which were over the heads of a Limehouse audience which needed fireworks and crudity. I was able to supply them with both.

They hired an old two-seater car. 'Look out for the little yellow car,' said the election literature. Every day, with supporters clinging to it, they drove through the narrow streets. They would pull up in the middle of a street and make as much noise as possible while supporters knocked at the doors, inviting electors to appear at windows and doors and listen to the Major. When an audience had gathered, John would speak for five minutes and introduce Attlee, who would answer questions and exchange friendly greetings before they drove to the next street. John loved it, but sensed that his candidate was never quite comfortable:

> Once we met a number of Conservative canvassers, and as one of our men rang a bell loudly to attract attention, a resident thrust his head out and asked if we were selling muffins. Like lightning a Tory woman replied 'No, mate, pups', a retort which the crowd, seeing my shy and miserable companion, were not slow to appreciate.

The election address has John's finger marks all over it. To the end of his life, Attlee was proud that his election speeches contained the same policies – he was telling electors the same things in 1950 that he told them in 1922. That was true, but his later election addresses never again had the same fire, the same short, direct sentences, the same bite-size chunks, the same heavy headlines, or the same extravagance of abuse. Attlee never again found anyone with the same talent for forceful over-the-top propaganda.

John produced a tabloid newspaper, *Limehouse Election News*. Half the front page was taken up with a picture of the scene outside the Hotel Cecil when the Conservatives decided to dump Lloyd George and make Bonar

Law Prime Minister. In 1922 the idea of taking up half the front page with a picture would have seemed revolutionary. A huge headline went with the picture:

THE ROLLS ROISTERERS

Our picture shows the parade of Rolls-Royce cars which blocked up the Strand when the Tories elected Bonar Law as their leader at the Hotel Cecil.

A Rolls-Royce costs about £2,000. This would provide £5 a week for a family of five or six workers for over seven years – Or it could be used to build four decent houses. Yet when the worker asks for a living wage or somewhere to live, the Rolls Roisterers shout: 'We can give you nothing; we are crushed by taxation.'

Inside was a strip cartoon of an ugly war profiteer clutching his bag of gold, finally despatched by the heroic figure of organised Labour. To modern eyes, the war profiteer looks uncomfortably similar to those caricatures of Jews which the Nazis produced ten years later. The cartoon was accompanied by a rhyme. We do not know who wrote it, but it was almost certainly either Attlee (whose passion was poetry, though his own was indifferent) or John (who wrote hearty doggerel.) My money is on John, because Attlee's poetry was generally more subtle.

'My name is Mr Profiteer
And talk of taxes makes me queer.
I made my millions in the war,
That's why your living costs you more.
Let homeless heroes starve in ditches,
But don't make levies on my riches.
And if the Empire needs a tax
Well – shove it on the workers' backs.
The Tory-Libs, they love me so,
They'll never make me pay, I know.
But oh! when Labour wins, I fear,
It's good-bye Mr Profiteer.'

They produced a leaflet in Attlee's name:

THE GREAT BETRAYAL

Like many of you I took part in the Great War in the hope of securing lasting peace and a better life for all. We were promised that wars should end, that the men who fought in the War would be cared for and that unemployment, slums and poverty would be abolished.

ALL THESE PROMISES HAVE BEEN BROKEN

In every way the conditions of the workers are worse than before.
Wars and threats of war continue.
Your wages are still falling and many of you are unemployed.
You pay high rents and live in overcrowded hovels.
Ex-soldiers are found lining up for unemployment pay or
outdoor relief.
The wounded and widows have to struggle on a starvation dole.
Men made insane in the War are sent to pauper lunatic asylums.

On election night, 15 November 1922, John joined an excited throng at the 1917 Club. It was the turning point, the night Labour replaced the Liberals as the principal opposition to Bonar Law's Conservative government. Attlee won by 9,688 votes to 7,789, a majority of 1,899 – a considerable achievement since the popular sitting Conservative had held the seat for sixteen years.

But it seemed to John and his friends even better than that. It was not just Labour which was on the verge of government. Between 1918 and 1922, ILP left-wingers such as John, Attlee, Brockway and Allen had put their heart and soul into efforts to ensure that ILP candidates carried Labour's banner in as many constituencies as possible. They were so successful that the majority of Labour MPs elected in 1922 were ILP members. John believed this meant that the Parliamentary Labour Party would be dominated, not by conservative trade union officials as before, but by revolutionary socialists.

That night John was sure that they were going to change the world, and that he had better get into Parliament quickly, or he would be too late. Britain would be a socialist society before he had time to play a real part in the transformation.

The ILP triumph was completed a few days later when it secured the election of ILP leader Ramsay MacDonald as Labour leader instead of the trade union nominee J. R. Clynes. MacDonald had been born 56 years earlier in Lossiemouth, the illegitimate son of a farm worker, and John believed in him, writing:

> From the calling of the Conference to form Soviets in 1917 until his own election as Leader of the Opposition in 1922, Ramsay MacDonald, unreported in the press, travelled like a revolutionary flame from end to end of the country. Even in East London, where the hold of the ILP had never been strong, I could pack halls for MacDonald ... but the so-called moderate leaders could only get either empty halls or crowds of shouting or indignant hecklers.

He was even party to the frenzied attempts by MacDonald's friends to cheer him up (MacDonald was a naturally gloomy man.) On one occasion John and some others dragged him out to see Harry Lauder in the West End. They arranged to meet at the 1917 Club, where MacDonald arrived with a lady whom he introduced as a Polish countess. He whispered at dinner that he had only enough money to pay for his own ticket. John, who was always careless with loose money, found the exact sum required in the lining of his jacket, and slipped it quietly to his leader. MacDonald brooded during the performance but said at the end that Lauder was just like any other Scotsman.

Theatres were one diversion in a frantically busy political life. There was the 1917 Club during the week, and weekends at country houses owned by wealthy ILP supporters. John's social life revolved round the ILP. His friends were politicians like Attlee and Ernest Hunter, then a key ILP figure and MacDonald confidant; left-wing writers such as the novelist Mary Agnes Hamilton, who modelled two of her political agitators in her novel *Follow My Leader* on John and Ernest Hunter (but the main one on Ramsay MacDonald); and left-wing actors and actresses, including Elsa Lanchester. Each weekend saw either a party or a conference. There were whole weeks spent in the frenzied atmosphere of by-elections. The draper's assistant and lance corporal, still well under 30, had come a long way in four years.

CHAPTER THREE

A GLIMPSE OF THE GLITTERING PRIZES

In 1916 Lance Corporal Jack William Beckett, aged 21, had been discharged from the army, sick from service in India's climate. After months in hospital, he emerged with a full set of false teeth and a heart complaint which was expected to prohibit strenuous activity and bring him to an early grave. The physical weakness may have been matched by a sense of inferiority. He was painfully aware that he had sunk from the precarious lower middle class into which he was born to the dreadfully impecunious working class. He knew that his loud voice and vulgar accent told that class-conscious world everything it needed to know about him.

He was penniless. His father was a bankrupt. He had little education. He had an incoherent rage against a society which condemned him and his friends to poverty and death in war, and allowed rich men to profit from their suffering.

Eight years later, in November 1924, John Warburton Beckett, having just celebrated his thirtieth birthday, was Labour's youngest Member of Parliament, after running probably the most professional and energetic of any parliamentary campaign in that election year.

He was already known as one of Labour's most formidable campaigners for his work in getting Major Attlee into Parliament. In October 1924, despite a massive Conservative true majority in Parliament, he gave Gateshead its first, and until 1945 its only, overall Labour majority. The success was down almost entirely to the young, energetic, charismatic, professional campaigner, who understood journalism, advertising and propaganda as few other Labour figures of the time understood them.

He entered the Palace of Westminster in triumph, to the plaudits of his many glittering friends, who included the rising stars of the Labour Party and some of the biggest theatrical celebrities of the day. He had found a use for his loud voice, holding great audiences with his oratory, and he could captivate women with his handsome face and fluent charm. The rage against the world had been turned into an apparently coherent political philosophy, and one which looked to be on the verge of victory.

He had already embarked upon and abandoned a fine career in advertising, and was confidently expected to have an even more sparkling career in Parliament. Some of the rough edges had been removed from his vowels by regular contact with actors and actresses and with the Old Haileyburian Clem Attlee and the Old Etonian Hugh Dalton. He now had money, and after his election entertained his splendid friends lavishly to dinners at the House of Commons and at restaurants, or (if they felt like slumming it a little) at the now declining 1917 Club.

He must have felt that he had a magic touch, that he had put behind him forever any doubts or uncertainties about his own judgement or ability. The young man who had to count his pennies was gone. And if he could arrive in such style, how could anything ever go wrong?

I am sure that, like many another young politician, early in 1925 he saw himself as a future Prime Minister. In his case, no one at the time would have called the dream absurd.

It was in the three years before he became an MP, that the transition was completed. Two men were responsible for its completion. The first was Clement Attlee.

Soon after John and Helen had moved into Attlee's big house in Limehouse, Helen gave birth to a daughter, whom they called Lesley. After Attlee's election to Parliament in 1922, John, Helen and Lesley stayed in the house in Limehouse, though Attlee himself moved with his new wife to a new home in suburban Woodford. John acted as Attlee's private secretary; but the sense of being settled had departed with the older man. Attlee surely never knew how those long, comfortable conversations as they smoked their pipes in the evenings in Limehouse impressed themselves on his younger and less educated companion.

They must have made an odd pair. John was brash, noisy and brimming with confidence and superficial worldly knowledge. Attlee was quiet, diffident and shy. But Attlee possessed an absolute inner certainty. John must have sensed it even as he twitted his friend for his sexual naïvety.

Subconsciously, John was taking notes. In the mid-1990s, I wrote a biography of Attlee. It was a strange experience to become slowly familiar with Attlee's habits of thought, his prejudices, his general approach to life – and to remember my father saying the words, and know for the first time where he had learned them. What Attlee told him stuck, which is one reason why he was such a mass of contradictions, because Attlee's prescriptions were not natural to him.

Clem Attlee ran his life with care and forethought. If he had to leave a job, or abandon a belief, he always made sure that he left a good feeling behind him. When he disowned the religion he had been brought up with, he did it with infinite care and tact so that his family would not be offended. When he found that Toynbee Hall was not all he had hoped for, he gave up his job there so graciously that no one ever took offence, and he was ever afterwards welcome there. That was how he lived, and how, I am sure, he told John that a man ought to live; and John was still solemnly trying to teach his children that lesson 30 years later. Always leave places cleanly, he said. Never leave a mess on the doorstep as you go. Make sure you leave a good reputation behind. Yet no one could have failed to follow this sensible advice so consistently and spectacularly as he did.

John said often, with a perfectly straight face, that he disapproved of inflammatory language, especially for unremarkable policies. He preferred to couch his radical policies in quiet and reasonable-sounding words. But his speeches were always the most extreme and the most inflammatory of any of his colleagues, as contemporaries like Fenner Brockway have testified. He could hardly ask for buttered toast in the morning without sending the shivers up someone's spine. Yet what he said was true – about Clem Attlee. Attlee could make a call for the tumbrels sound like the London telephone directory. It was the foundation of his political success.

It must have been Attlee who taught him that, to carry through revolutionary ideas, your behaviour has to be disarmingly normal. Attlee's was. John thought his ought to be, but never managed to make it so.

He even absorbed Attlee's devotion to Oxford University. For the rest of his life John cheered on the Oxford crew in the boat race every year. James Callaghan wrote in his autobiography that Attlee, as Prime Minister, once asked for someone's background, and when given it, said: 'Thought so. Cambridge man. All statistics. No sense of history.' For the first time, I knew where my father had learned what he thought was the real difference between these two great universities, neither of which he knew anything at all about.

The second great influence, completing the transition into the apparently utterly self-possessed MP of 1925, was another Oxford man, and an old Etonian as well, the great actor-manager Arthur Bourchier. Bourchier, from an old and wealthy family, founded the Oxford University Dramatic Society (OUDS) in 1882 while still an undergraduate at Christ Church. He owned the Strand Theatre and a large touring theatre business, and he transformed both John's outlook on life and his financial position.

The two may have met in the 1917 Club, but it is more likely that Bourchier was looking for a publicist for his theatre, as well as for a political mentor because he was becoming converted to Labour politics, and someone recommended John for both roles. He possessed family wealth and a huge income, yet, wrote John:

> He carried a load of debt big enough to overburden a small nation, and lived in the princeliest style. The fact that he was solvent at all he owed to his remarkable talents and to his two devoted managers.
>
> He never handled money, except for a payment of £5 a week which he called his 'wad' and which had to be paid to him every Friday. This money he hoarded closely. His credit was good in the restricted circle in which he moved, and either the box office or his friends were called upon to pay taxi fares and other such outgoings. It was almost impossible to get a coin from him, yet he would part with large cheques.

John was impressed by Bourchier's vast frame, his loud and imperious voice, and by the fact that when Bourchier walked into the Harcourt Room to dine, everyone turned to look at him, even if the other tables were full of cabinet ministers. He was impressed by the actor manager's frequent visits to Paris: travelling by the Golden Arrow, staying at the best hotels, entertaining lavishly, and afterwards marvelling that one could do so well in Paris on the £22 he had spent in cash, while for months afterwards his managers uncomplainingly paid a series of huge bills.

John travelled a great deal with Bourchier, who told him: 'If you must travel, you should travel like a prince, my boy.' Bourchier's homilies, like Attlee's, were never forgotten. It was probably Bourchier who taught him that even if you had no money and were in debt up to your eyeballs, it was important to look like a million dollars. 'No one ever lends you money if you look as though you need it,' my father used to tell me. And I remember him saying often, to people who obviously thought it was his own idea, that any budding playwright could make a fortune in any age by putting the story of Cinderella in a modern setting.

Bourchier's productions were probably my father's introduction to Shakespeare, and spoiled everyone else's for him, for no one could live up to his friend. Other productions of *Othello* always seemed tame and stagey to him. Bourchier's Iago, he said, 'was no smiling villain, but a garrulous boaster whose lie to Othello was the result of vanity and stupidity'.

John recalled how Bourchier would introduce himself to every new producer by saying: 'Now, my bloody boy, I've got seven bloody tricks, let me do those and I'll do everything else you say.' He remembered with awe the great man as director, impressing on young actors the need for stage technique. One of his favourite stories was of Bourchier telling a young actress to bring up a huge stepladder which was standing in the wings. She struggled on stage with it, and was told to climb it. When she was perched precariously on the top, he told her to look around and tell him what she saw. She stammered the names of a few stage props, until the terrible voice from the darkness roared out: 'Can't you see the door handle which you never turn?' Like many inexperienced actors, she had neglected to treat the set door as though it were a real door.

Bourchier was almost the last of the great actor managers, who could take with him on a well-arranged provincial tour as expensive a company and production as he could use in the West End. Sometimes criticised by fellow-professionals for not working hard enough at his parts, he was famous for 'corpsing' his fellow actors – making them laugh out of character. One evening, bored by the same old play, he made the whole company play it in broken English.

Bourchier, on John's urging, joined the ILP, and so did Bourchier's wife, a glamorous actress many years younger than him, and a very few years older than John, called Kyrle Bellew. She was to have an even more dramatic effect on John's life than Bourchier himself.

Bourchier placed the Strand Theatre at the disposal of the ILP on Sunday evenings, and John organised there some of the most influential left- wing political meetings of the time. The two also worked together to found the Actors Association, the first actors' trade union.

Early in 1923 John was taken to lunch at the 1917 Club by one of his many powerful patrons in the ILP establishment, the MP for Central Newcastle, a former Liberal and now Labour front bench politician, Sir Charles Trevelyan. Trevelyan had heard a great deal about John, liked what he heard, and made him a proposal. Would John like to fight North Newcastle at the next general election? The seat was not winnable, but a young candidate with energy and gifts as a campaigner might take the heat off the city's two winnable seats.

The two men travelled north that very afternoon. The next day John was unanimously adopted as a candidate in a city he had never visited before in his life.

Matters came to a head earlier than expected. After only a year in office, Prime Minister Stanley Baldwin, who had replaced a sick Bonar Law, took everyone by surprise by calling a general election on 6 December 1923. He wanted, he said, to secure a mandate for reversing his free trade policy and bringing in protection in order to reduce unemployment. Within a few weeks of being selected, John was fighting the seat.

His brash and brilliant campaign boosted his confidence enormously. But Trevelyan's scheme went disastrously wrong. The press concentrated their attention on John, partly to avoid giving any publicity to the two Labour candidates with a chance of winning, Trevelyan himself and Arthur Henderson. 'I was 29 years old,' he wrote later, 'filled with fanaticism, fire and crude dynamics. I seemed to have the gift of tongues, and after my first few meetings was addressing larger audiences than any two of the other candidates in the city put together.'

Arthur Henderson had written Labour's constitution and set up its organisation after the war. He it was who, for the first time, had ensured that the Labour Party could enrol individual members. Henderson was, in a real sense, the creator of the modern Labour Party. This was not a Party for which John had any respect or liking at all. He took pride in the fact that he never, ever, joined the Labour Party, which he considered a dreary and uninspired machine. He was only a member by virtue of his membership of the ILP.

Henderson was later to be Foreign Secretary and Labour leader. But he was not a good campaigner. Considered by those who knew him to be a man of ability and integrity, he was ponderous, pompous and dull in public.

He and John addressed a joint eve-of-poll rally. John arrived very late. He had spoken at four exciting meetings and been carried shoulder high through a cheering crowd. He was tired, excited and above himself. The hall, where Henderson had just completed a worthy speech, seemed quiet and drab to him after the excitement of the street. So he worked himself up into a wild revolutionary speech which, he wrote contritely many years afterwards, 'could not have been anything but extremely embarrassing to Mr Henderson'. And then, turning to the stiff, disapproving figure seated beside him, he launched an impassioned appeal to 'march forward led by this great revolutionary who sits here with us tonight'. He meant it mischievously, but underestimated his audience. Instead of being carried away, a large section of it burst into mocking laughter.

Like a man who has behaved badly when drunk, John was filled with self-loathing the next day. He never quite forgot how ashamed he had felt. Fifteen years later, in 1938, a fascist and an outcast from the Party he had served, he could still write: 'It says much for Mr Henderson's fairness of mind that when, in after days, he and I had much to do with one another, I invariably received courtesy and justice.' What John did not do was to learn from his experiences.

Henderson's temper was not improved by the election result on 6 December. John polled well in a hopeless seat. Henderson lost a winnable one which he had held previously, and blamed John for the loss.

Soon after the election, when MacDonald set about forming Labour's first government, the fact that his most senior lieutenant had no seat in Parliament caused a good deal of embarrassment, and Henderson had rapidly to be found a seat at a by-election so that he could become Home Secretary. The Labour Party has always been unforgiving, and that speech may have marked John's card among his Party's power-brokers even before he became an MP.

Yet it did him nothing but good among local activists. Neighbouring Gateshead was held by the Liberals, and the Labour Party there believed they could win next time, so long as they had a sufficiently exciting and energetic candidate. John looked just right to them, and he fought for and won their nomination, to contest the next election, when ever that might be.

Ten months after the formation of the minority Labour government, it fell. John's chance had come.

The 1924 election was precipitated by the Campbell case. A communist, John Ross Campbell, was arrested for distributing a leaflet to soldiers calling on them to 'let it be known that, neither in the class war nor in a military war, will you turn your guns on your fellow workers'. The decision to prosecute Campbell was reversed by the cabinet because of its great unpopularity in the Party. The Conservatives seized the chance to level the charge that Labour was soft on communism. The Liberals offered a face-saving formula: a select committee to look into the whole affair. MacDonald, surprisingly, turned down this chance to save his government. It was rumoured that he feared an inquiry might show he had a more direct part in the affair than he admitted.

Gateshead's sitting Liberal MP at that time was a middle-aged, slightly pompous politician, whom John found it easy to score off. On a tiny sum of money, with a devoted band of supporters, he was justifiably proud of sending to every elector an address, a four-page election newspaper which John, of course, edited himself, and a polling card.

He and the Conservative candidate agreed to stage a debate in the Town Hall, and when the Liberal challenged both of them to debate, they replied that the issue was between a Conservative government and a Labour government, so could not concern the Liberal.

Meetings such as this, in a northern constituency in 1924, could make or break a campaign. It made John's campaign. The hall was packed, and the police estimated that 15,000 people gathered in the square outside the Town Hall. After it, the Labour contingent bore their candidate home in triumph.

He loved the public platform, the applause, the feeling that he could move audiences. Just how good he was we cannot know for certain. He himself always thought he was magical, but not everyone agreed. Mrs Bertha Elliott was a child at the time, the daughter of a prominent member of the Gateshead Labour Party. She wrote to me:

> He was flamboyant, had very black hair (long in the style of James Maxton) and he kept flinging his head back. He also was very rest-less when on a public platform, but he did not stride about. He always sat dangerously on the corner of the chairman's table, with his hand in his left trouser pocket, and he wriggled about so much I remember my mother saying that he got on her nerves and his speech was spoiled for her because she was afraid he would fall off.

Gateshead was one of the poorest constituencies in Britain, with a third of the men either unemployed or under-employed. The poor had to be mobilised; but it was not easy. The women in the poorest wards would not come out to vote because they were ashamed of their clothes. Many other women could not leave young children in order to go and vote. The men in work got home tired and dirty, and did not care to go anywhere until they had washed and eaten – by which time the polls had closed.

So John detailed helpers to wait outside as the shift finished, and marshal the men straight to the polls. He organised street processions to the polling stations led by some of the Irish women councillors, so that 'the women's rags then became the banners of the people's army, and they were not ashamed when there were many of them together to flaunt their poverty'.

Four days before polling day came another communist scare which ended any hope of a Labour victory nationally. The *Daily Mail* printed what purported to be a letter from Grigory Zinoviev, general secretary of the Comintern, calling on the British Communist Party to paralyse the army and navy by forming cells inside them. 'And Mr MacDonald would lend Russia our money!' screamed the *Mail* headline. (The paper also pointed out darkly the sinister fact that Zinoviev's real name was Apfelbaum. Anti-Semitism in the 1920s was not confined to the left.) MacDonald, rather foolishly, confirmed that the letter was genuine. We now know that it was a forgery.

John's friend Ernest Hunter was responsible for MacDonald's campaign, so Gateshead was favoured with a visit from the leader. It was not a success. MacDonald made a speech devoted, John said afterwards, mostly to his own personal grievances. The next day, just before he departed, MacDonald disappointed a huge crowd waiting for him on a big open space by leaving before anyone had realised he was there.

John's efforts were rewarded, however, in this Liberal-held seat, with a majority of 10,000 over the Conservative, and 500 over Conservative and Liberal combined. Never again, until 1945, did Gateshead return a clear Labour majority over all other parties; and in 1945, the Gateshead majority followed a winning trend for Labour. In the 1924 election, Gateshead was one of the few successes in an election at which many of the gains of the 1922 and 1923 elections were lost.

John was proud of it all his life, and he had a right to be. Back in London the next day, he walked proudly into the 1917 Club, where he was welcomed like a conquering hero, and sat in triumph with some of his friends, and a fat man whom Ernest Hunter introduced as Colonel Harry Day, a wealthy variety agent who had won Southwark in South London for Labour. John wrote:

MacDonald arrived a few minutes later and at once engaged Day in animated conversation. I have rarely seen him so anxious to please. He had not greeted me; and someone reminded him that I had just returned from my constituency. He turned briefly in my direction. 'Oh, yes, Beckett,' he said, 'weren't you fighting somewhere? How did you get on?' Stifling the thought that the leader of the Party should know something of the very few victories gained under his leadership, I could not resist thanking him for the warmth with which he had recommended my candidature to the people of Gateshead a week before. He smiled coldly, and returned to an animated discussion of some antique furniture he had seen, but could not afford, with which he regaled Mr Day's wealthy and receptive ear.

Although John's fragile self-esteem plays a part in the way he tells the story, too many similar MacDonald stories are told for us to doubt this one. And John was not alone in his interpretation of the relationship between MacDonald and Day. Seven years later, on 25 August 1931, Hugh Dalton confided to his diary: 'There was for some months after the (1929 Labour) government came in a standing order for a bottle of champagne, with three glasses, to be sent each night to JRM's room. The order was in the name of Harry Day, and he is still without a job!'

To Dalton it was a joke with a serious edge. To John it was one of those things which clouded his judgement with so much anger that he could not see. Dalton did not add, but John did, that Day's 'original name was not Day'.

But if his leader failed to notice the hero, enough people did to make his return to London a thoroughly happy experience, including his old friend Attlee who wrote him a graceful and flattering letter. And something else went swiftly right for him. Most Labour MPs were quite hard up, and John had a wife and child. Parliament had always been considered a place for wealthy men who did not need paying, and the parliamentary salary was only £400 a year.

For John, a few newspaper articles on how it felt to be elected eased the immediate financial pressure. But very soon after he became an MP, some real money came his way. With Bourchier's guidance and advice, and probably Bourchier's money (for he had none of his own), John invested heavily in touring companies and West End theatre, and quite quickly made himself far richer than the rangy, toothless Jack Beckett of 1916 could ever have dreamed of being.

He moved out of Attlee's rooms in Norway House into a splendid detached family home at 48 Anson Road, Cricklewood. Throughout his time in Parliament, John was really quite well off, living in considerable style and able to entertain lavishly. Few of his Labour colleagues could do that. He must have seemed, in the second half of the 1920s, like a young man with a golden touch. He had not yet learned how quickly and suddenly money can evaporate.

Altogether, John was very happy indeed when he first entered Parliament. He loved the attention bestowed on the youngest MP in his Party, the glittering audiences anxious to hear his views and to pay them flattering attention. Life was pleasant and exciting for a young man on the verge of what looked like a luminous political career.

He took care to learn the rules and procedures of the House, discovering to his surprise that quite soon he knew them a great deal better than some MPs of long standing, who relied on the whips for the smallest things.

He was introduced informally to the Prince of Wales by a young Conservative MP, and decided on the spot that the monarchy was not such a bad thing after all, and that this 'earnest and intelligent young man', once he became King Edward VIII, would change the face of the nation, and make everything much better. The huge intellectual leap required for a democratic socialist to believe that the nation's hopes of improvement could rest on a hereditary king does not seem to have bothered him, and little more than a decade was to pass before he was running a fascist campaign to stop the wicked old men who ran the country from forcing the brave young hero king to abdicate. He wrote a weekly Westminster Letter for the *Bradford Pioneer*, the ILP's newspaper, based in the town where the Party had been formed and had its splendid headquarters. It was a prestigious task within the ILP and remarkable that it should go to so young an MP. Moreover, it gave him a sort of power over the Party greats. When one of his early columns praised a speech by Ramsay MacDonald, his leader approached him the next day, for the first time since he had entered Parliament, to say how much he appreciated John's political and journalistic work. But a few weeks later John wrote that railwaymen's leader Jimmy Thomas's buffoonery had made him sick. MacDonald complained bitterly, and Thomas stormed up to him in a fury to tell him that he would ensure that the railwaymen drove John out of Gateshead before the next election. John replied that the fact that he was there at all showed that Gateshead's railwaymen had higher standards than those of their leader.

It seemed to John as though he could do anything. If he could so easily provoke the famous Jimmy Thomas to incoherent threats, he must surely have arrived. It was a wonderful feeling. It may have lasted as much as eight weeks. Then he learned the bitter truth about the powerlessness of a back-bench MP, and his wonderful new world was in ruins all about him. I think he went at once from the pinnacle of triumph to the depth of despair.

It was his old friend Clem Attlee who inadvertently burst John's bubble, and, though neither of them had any idea of it at the time, provided the first staging post on the road to fascism.

During the short-lived Labour government, Attlee had been Under Secretary of State for War, and had come across a scandal which he wanted to see exposed. 'It's the dirtiest business of the whole war,' Attlee said to John. While he was in the government, Attlee simply stored it up in his huge memory. After the general election, when Labour was again in opposition, he handed over the facts as he knew them to John. Attlee was never to be identified as the source of the story. He knew that John had a talent for publicity, and would feel, as Attlee did, that it was the sort of affair that made a mockery of the deaths of his wartime comrades.

The story was this. During the war the Germans discovered a new method of extracting nitrogen from the air, which was much cheaper than the British method. Nitrogen was vital in the manufacture of explosives, and important in peacetime for the production of fertiliser. The armistice terms gave the Allies the right to investigate German secrets, and a commission of three army officers went to Cologne for several months to investigate this one.

But Attlee could not find a copy of their report in the War Office; nor could anyone tell him where it was; nor was there any trace of the three officers who compiled it.

John and Attlee pieced the rest of the story together between them. The British factory making fertiliser, at Billingham-on-Tees, had been sold at a knockdown price to Sir Alfred Mond in 1920, when Sir Alfred was a member of the government. Sir Alfred had set up a company called Brunner, Mond, to exploit the new method of extracting nitrogen. There, at Billingham-on-Tees, Sir Alfred's company was making a fortune because it had a monopoly of this German secret. The senior officer on the commission was a director of this company, and the other two officers were employed by it. The company was using its monopoly of the secret to keep the price of fertiliser artificially high.

Here if anywhere was the 'hard-faced man who has done well out of the war'. Here was the corrupt wartime profiteer whom Attlee and John hated so much. In his innocence, John seems to have believed that he had only to make these facts known, and Sir Alfred would be ruined.

He started in March 1925, with the help of two other young MPs, Neil Maclean and Hugh Dalton, just three months into his parliamentary career, by asking questions in the House about the sale of the Billingham factory. On 1 April he used the mechanism of raising the question on the adjournment. Maclean and Dalton rustled up the 40 MPs he needed for a quorum. He wrote a personal note to Sir Alfred informing him that he would mention him in his speech, and to government whips explaining what questions he would ask.

When the great day arrived, however, Sir Alfred did not attend the debate, and the Under Secretary for War said he knew nothing about it: it was a Treasury matter, and no Treasury spokesman was present. There had, of course, been plenty of time and notice for the Treasury to provide a spokesman. John was left empty handed. As the House rose, he looked up despairingly at the press gallery. They had all gone home, having heard nothing. It had all been completely useless.

The next month Mond's firm was given £2 million worth of government credits, and John found he was not permitted to raise any questions about this. I think he was tormented by dreams of Sir Alfred laughing at him. He turned to the press. He was one of Labour's most prolific political journalists, writing frequently for such papers as the left-wing *Daily Herald* and the virulently right- wing and pro-war *John Bull*, the paper which during the war had 'exposed' the fact that Ramsay MacDonald was born illegitimate. These papers had been delighted to accept his articles on how it felt to be a new MP, but they all turned down his article on Sir Alfred Mond and the fertiliser.

Eventually he managed to place it in Lansbury's *Labour Weekly*. John and the editor, Raymond Postgate, decided to do everything they could to goad Mond into suing. Postgate gave it a splendid spread and accompanied it with a huge cartoon. John put all his energetic invective into the story:

> The Mond company has secured a monopoly of the way of turning the air we breathe into profit ... Lieut. Colonel Pollitt, who was the Chairman of the Commission, is now a director of Brunner Mond's new company, and this generous firm have also patriotically found well paid employment for every other member of the Commission ... The factory at Billingham which had cost the country £1,100,000

was sold to Messrs Brunner Mond for the paltry sum of £450,000 by a government of which Sir Alfred Mond was himself a member ... In addition they have the valuable secret obtained for the State from Germany, which has not cost them a penny ... To suborn State servants is a grave crime ...

I do not, personally, care tuppence about our being prepared for the next war. I wish nobody at all had any explosives more dangerous than Chinese crackers. But ... the gentlemen who are now steadily preparing the next war handed over the national supply of explosives to a private firm. And if the present government get the war they are preparing, they will have to go cap in hand to Sir Alfred and pay what he asks. And capitalists know patriotism is not enough. They like large profits mixed with it.

Big profits have been made by responsible public men out of a deal in which they secretly sold government property to themselves and their friends. And this is hushed up on the plea of the public interest!

John sent a copy of the article to Sir Alfred, with an accompanying note saying he wanted to ensure that it did not appear without Sir Alfred seeing it. Sir Alfred returned a friendly note, thanking him for sending the article, which, he said, he had read with the greatest interest.

And that was that. Except, perhaps, for one small aspect to the whole affair, which is entirely irrelevant to it, but which I am sure that neither John nor his fellow campaigner Hugh Dalton thought was irrelevant. Two years earlier, at the 1923 general election, Dalton had unsuccessfully contested Cardiff East for Labour. His biographer Ben Pimlott records: 'The Liberal MP for the neighbouring Swansea constituency was a Jewish manufacturer, Sir Alfred Mond. At one meeting Dalton told his audience that his own policy was to carry out the old injunction "feed my lambs". Encouraged by applause, he added: "Mond, of course, doesn't get beyond the Old Testament." '

John himself never referred to Mond's Jewishness, so far as I know. But later in his life, and perhaps at the time, he certainly knew a man called H. H. Beamish. Beamish, the brother of the future Conservative MP Tufton Beamish, ran *The Britons*, a propotype fascist publication, and in 1919 he had published *The Protocols of the Learned Elders of Zion*, the forgery which many people in the 1920s believed to prove the existence of a Jewish conspiracy aimed at world domination. In later years, for a while, John believed in the *Protocols*. I have no means of knowing whether he believed in them in 1925, but I suspect not.

In 1919 Mond had sued Beamish for writing that, as a Jew, his loyalties during the war were suspect, as evidenced by the fact that he had allotted shares in his companies to Germans. Beamish had used the courtroom publicity to claim that Jews were a separate race whose loyalty could not be trusted: 'A man can't be both English and Jew.' It was an early and virulent form of what became known in the 1980s as Norman Tebbitt's cricket test.

Mond was awarded £5,000 damages and Beamish travelled to South Africa to avoid paying. There he retrieved his fortunes and produced a book called *The Jews' Who's Who*, which seems to have been quite as unpleasant a document as it sounds. He died in 1948, leaving his money to fund the post-Second World War British Nazis, led by Arnold Leese, and then by Colin Jordan, who eventually beat a path to my father's door to seek guidance from the old master.

John and Hugh Dalton did not attack Mond because he was a Jew. They attacked him because he was greedy and corrupt, and his greed and corruption took a form which they found especially offensive. Dalton's whole life was overshadowed by the First World War, even more than John's. His closest friends, including the poet Rupert Brooke, had been killed. 'People have sometimes asked, since then,' he wrote in his autobiography, 'why I had so few men friends of my own age. The answer is the war. Before that I was very rich in friendships.' In 1925 one of those few friends was John Beckett. They both believed passionately that a man who could corruptly make a fortune over the blood of their dead wartime comrades was a man who ought to be pilloried and hounded from public life.

In 1925, nonetheless, there may have been a part of both John and Hugh Dalton which saw a connection between the fact that Mond was corrupt and the fact that he was a Jew. As they both grew older, Dalton must have started to see that this was dangerous and wicked, until by 1945 he was considered the firmest Zionist in the Attlee cabinet. For John, the supposed connection turned into an obsession that helped to destroy him.

John was enraged by his own impotence. It was as though the cup from which he had started so happily to drink when he entered the House had turned out to contain the bitterest poison. From believing he could do everything, he was within six months plunged into the bleakest despair and believed he could do nothing. All the procedures of the House of

Commons seemed designed to ensure that it should never become anything more than a gentleman's club.

To add to his misery, this practised and accomplished orator blew his big chance to make a parliamentary name for himself. His old patron, Sir Charles Trevelyan, arranged for John to represent the Party in an important and contentious debate on a motion to place foreign affairs under parliamentary control. He knew nothing about the subject. He was briefed heavily by every research organisation and lobby group there was, and had not yet acquired the skill to abandon what he did not need. Trevelyan, Clem Attlee and Hugh Dalton all impressed on him that this was his big chance to secure for himself a glittering parliamentary future, and that he was lucky and very favoured to get it. When the big night arrived he was in a pitiful condition. 'The House roasted me, and the Speaker called me to order for irrelevance several times. They were both right.'

The House, which he had entered with such pride just three months earlier, now suddenly seemed like a prison. He resented being seen as lobby fodder. He despised the House's antiquated formalities. He found the chamber where MPs debated miserable, stuffy and unhealthy, with its artificial light and its lack of ventilation, and the speeches made there unbelievably pointless and tedious. (MPs now work in rather more comfortable surroundings because the chamber of the House of Commons was bombed in the Second World War.)

The only alternatives, the tea room or the library or the bars, made him even more miserable. 'I am not a clubable type of man,' he wrote rather stiffly, 'and the library conversations were almost worse than the debates. The main subjects were political gossip, wearisome anecdotage, or, endlessly and tediously, the kind of "funny" story associated with barrack rooms.' Which is an odd thing for him to write; for John had a remarkable talent for embroidering anecdotes; he enjoyed political gossip; and he had a wonderfully funny store of the most scabrous stories imaginable, which he told with enormous zest and flair. 'There was little else to do,' he wrote miserably, 'except walk like caged lions up and down the length of the terrace.'

Here was a man of just 30, the youngest MP of his Party, tipped by the press for a brilliant parliamentary career, walking on the terrace of the House of Commons with its wonderful views over the river, rubbing shoulders with the most famous men of his day, the envy of everyone he had ever known, who felt simply caged up and utterly alienated from the place.

He grew quickly to despise most of his fellow Labour MPs. The safest Labour seats, which had survived the 1924 electoral setback, were generally in the pockets of the unions, and given to elderly trade union officials as a kind of retirement present.

The unions have always tended to see the Parliamentary Labour Party as a sort of junior partner. It is an instinct which persists to this day. MPs have their uses, but they do not do the real work of the Labour movement: that's done in trade union offices. Being an MP is seen as a consolation prize for a long-standing union official who has never quite climbed to the top of the tree and is no longer up to the arduous work of union organisation.

'These cohorts of aged men,' John raged, 'putting on physical and mental flesh daily as they sucked their pipes round the map room in the Library, which became, by ancient lore, their refuge from the cares of the world.' Many of them, 'through a hard youth in the pits and a too easy middle age in a trade union office', were prematurely aged. John had no patience with them.

Not so his friend Hugh Dalton, who, John wrote, 'tolerated fools gladly, spending hours in the library and smoking rooms, listening with an air of cordiality and interest to the dreariest anecdotage'. John was the first of many to notice the foundations upon which Dalton built a career which peaked in 1945 when he became Chancellor of the Exchequer. But John, having no talent for flattery himself, never saw what more perceptive observers saw: that Dalton was not very good at it. Dalton became known as 'the man who slaps you on the back and calls you by someone else's Christian name'. 'Morning, Tom,' he called to an aged trade union MP in 1945, and then confided to a much younger politician, Roy Jenkins, 'You'll never get anywhere in the Labour Party until you learn to call that man Tom.' Jenkins pointed out that the man's name was Bill.

Dalton cultivated obscure trade unionists who had block votes at their disposal, offering his impressive contacts, sophisticated knowledge and extensive intelligence in return for their influence inside the Party, laughing a little too loudly at their jokes. Intending to leave them feeling grateful, he often only left them feeling patronised.

John and Hugh Dalton talked for hours, in the House and at Dalton's Westminster flat, John raging against the way things were, Dalton listening with flattering attentiveness. With his eye for success, he must have seen that John would either rise to the top or burn himself and his boats with the heat of his passion. 'Had I listened to Dalton's good advice,' wrote John, 'and to Attlee's, my career would probably have been very much more distinguished in the parliamentary sense.'

Instead he listened to Ellen Wilkinson, the young recently elected MP for Middlesbrough, who was to become Education Minister in 1945. She was a tiny bundle of energetic idealism, one of a group of intellectuals who had recently left the newly formed Communist Party. Their friendship began over a weekend spent in her constituency a few months after the election. It was supposed to be a weekend of open-air meetings, but it rained continuously, and they hardly left their small commercial hotel, deserted except for themselves.

She considered herself well to the left of John and his friends Dalton and Attlee, and at first told John he was 'one of MacDonald's good little careerists'. But they were firm friends by the end of the weekend. 'Our friendship,' noted John caustically, 'endured until I had become the Parliamentary Whip of the extreme left and was almost entirely severed from the Labour Party, while Ellen was a Parliamentary Private Secretary attached to the Labour government and supporting its most reactionary measures in the division lobby.' Friends they certainly were; lovers they may well have been. John was fast acquiring a reputation for sexual profligacy. The discovery that he was attractive to women, like the discovery that he could move great audiences with his oratory, rather went to his head. His relationship with Ellen Wilkinson was certainly different from that with his other Labour Party friends. Ten years later, when he was no longer able even to talk to them, John wrote of other old Labour colleagues, and they wrote of him, with a kind of affectionate sadness. But he and Ellen Wilkinson wrote of each other with a sharp sense of personal betrayal.

In the 1930s Ellen Wilkinson embarked on the great love affair of her life, with Herbert Morrison. John never spoke of it, but I am sure that it was a thought he found almost unbearable. I believe that the blackest moments in his wartime prison cell after 1940 were when he contemplated the nocturnal activities of the man whose diktat kept him locked up.

She, footloose, fancy-free and sharing to the full the sense of liberation which radical young women had in the 1920s, was in a position to form a personal as well as political partnership with a young, good-looking fellow Labour MP. John seems to have lived and travelled as though he, too, were footloose and fancy-free; but of course, he was not. In his Cricklewood house, he had a wife and daughter. It seems quite likely that, in her husband's first year as an MP, Helen was starting to feel more than a little neglected.

Yet that was not why she left him. Nor was it sexual jealousy which caused her, one day in John's first two years in Parliament, to pick up her child and walk out of his house, never to return, leaving not even a note to tell her husband where she had gone.

It was simply that she watched him spending what seemed like huge sums of money in entertaining, at the House of Commons and in expensive restaurants. She knew that the money was coming from shaky theatrical ventures; and she was a working-class girl who had been brought up to be careful about money.

John was still sure, however, that nothing could touch him. He was driving his life like the powerful racing cars and motor bikes which he soon started driving on weekends at Brooklands. Helen could not see the immovable concrete obstacles into which it could so easily crash, but she knew they were there. Her warnings may have been too vague for him to understand, or perhaps he understood and thought them foolish. So she left him and took her daughter to live with her mother. John woke up one morning to an empty house. It disturbed him, and upset him, but not enough.

Ellen Wilkinson introduced him into a circle which he had not known before, and which was more radical than that of his London ILP friends Attlee and Dalton. Her friends were communists and former communists, and to John's taste far too much like the Clifford Allen circle which he had grown to dislike so fiercely. 'One end of Bloomsbury is very like another,' he mused. But they, like him, were impatient with the Labour leadership and not afraid to say so.

Every fortnight he left Westminster for a speaking tour in the north-east, often with Ellen Wilkinson. There he recharged his batteries, rekindled his idealism, and remembered his despair. He was a favourite speaker not only in Gateshead and Newcastle, but throughout Durham:

Each time I spoke in Gateshead I saw huge audiences of expectant and suffering faces; my own friends who had walked in broken shoes and thin coats through the cold and rain of the election period were unable to find sufficient food and comfort for their families. During the war they had managed to accumulate the necessities of life and a few small luxuries. For the first time they had known what it was to have just that little margin which they could use for pleasure and comfort. From 1918 to 1923 this was steadily stripped from them until by 1924 they had sold or pawned the purchases of the war years and were in a worse condition than that they had first known. I felt intensely my powerlessness to help.

As for his fellow Labour MPs, 'These smug, comfortable men on the benches beside me, had promised to dedicate their lives to the underdog; yet lived handsomely on pennies extracted from hungry men.' One day in September 1926, his hosts asked him to sign a visitor's book and, in his huge, flamboyant handwriting he left an impromptu verse:

'Oh better far to live and die
Under the brave red flag we fly
Than play a mean and greedy part
With a Tory head and a pirate heart.'

It was, of course, his adaptation of the pirate king's song from *The Pirates of Penzance*, and the song ran through his tuneless head all his life:

'Oh better far to live and die
Under the brave black flag I fly
Than play a sanctimonious part
With a pirate head and a pirate heart.'

When not speaking with Ellen Wilkinson, he was touring the Durham coal-fields with miners' leader Arthur Cook, and he, too, though in a very different way, helped lead John into parliamentary rebellion. Cook was the most extraordinary orator. According to John:

By every accepted rule he was a poor speaker. His appearance was feeble, his voice high, thin and harsh, and he had no ability what-ever to build logical arguments or even construct sentences flowing into a coherent whole. Yet for well over an hour, coatless, with his shirt sleeves rolled up, he would passionately declaim slogans expressing in a nutshell the views he desired his audiences to take.

They spoke together at the 1925 Durham Labour Women's Gala. John spoke first. He was a favourite with Durham audiences. The fire and fury,

59

the noise and the passion, and the belief that this clever young man would one day be in a position to do the things he talked about, drew them to him, and they cheered him. But then Cook rose, and his reception took the roof off.

Everyone knew that the mine-owners were going to demand longer hours for less pay, and that Cook was going to refuse. Everyone knew that, short of a miracle, there was going to be a strike, the most bitterly fought strike in British history. The miners in that audience knew that they would soon be watching their families slowly starving.

Cook had won from the Trades Union Congress a promise that they would back the miners with a general strike. The harsh fact was, though, that the government was prepared for such an event, and the TUC was not. The government had staved off the strike the previous year with a subsidy to the mine-owners to enable them to avoid wage cuts. That bought twelve months, which the government had used to make sure essential services could be kept running during a general strike. The TUC had not prepared systems to make sure that it was run smoothly and effectively; its main concern was to try to ensure that the strike never happened at all.

The general strike was called on 1 May 1926, and John threw himself wholeheartedly into it. At least, he tried to. The moment the strike was announced, he went home and fetched his small two- seater car, intending to travel to Gateshead at once, carrying messages and addressing meetings along the way. But first he had to get the messages and an itinerary from TUC headquarters in Ecclestone Square.

He found the headquarters in confusion, and it was impossible to see anyone with authority, or obtain information or permission to do anything. 'I found eventually,' he wrote, 'that the Council was split up into a number of committees which were sitting behind closed doors, and that nobody could do anything until they broke up. Although a large staff of very capable men and women existed, none of these had any instructions, or power to act.'

He caught two left-wing General Council members, Alonzo Swales and Fred Purcell, as they came out for some air. Over the third pint, they started to confirm his fears. They told him that the Council had no idea what to do, and was terrified that the strike call would be ignored. Ernest Bevin of the TGWU had been given overall control.

Someone mentioned that there was work to be done in the transport department. There, a harassed official had been told to have cars waiting for all Council members. John hung about with the other chauffeurs assembled until 1.30 a.m., and then was told to drive Ben Tillett home. It was a strange journey, and fed all his worst suspicions and forebodings:

> He gave me first an address in Brook Street. I drove him to a large house, and waited outside nearly an hour. Tillett came out in excellent spirits, and on the journey home gave me a somewhat incoherent account of the rich man he had been and was going to be again. He did not like my little car, and compared it most unfavourably with a Rolls Royce which he had or was going to have, I was unable to make out which. I tried to get some information upon the progress of the strike, but all he would tell me was not to worry, because Thomas was going to see Abe Bailey, 'and he's a darned good chap, and a pal of Samuel's'. I reached home about three o'clock, wondering what use this wealthy oriental influence was to the working class.

They still had no work to offer him the next morning, so he went to Hyde Park and used some of his furious pent-up energy giving an anti-strike speaker the hardest time of his life. He wriggled through the crowd, climbed on the platform, and drowned out the speaker with his statement that he would spend ten minutes outlining the real truth. Seeing that only physical violence would stop him, the meeting's sponsors let him go on. At the end of his ten minutes the crowd kept him answering questions for another hour until the sponsors of the meeting managed to get it closed; then a section of the crowd dragged him to a platform hung about with a red flag, and he gave his speech all over again. It was, though he does not mention the point when he tells the story, probably his first speech from a communist platform.

That lifted his spirits a little, and next day he managed to see Arthur Greenwood, then head of the Labour Party's research department and later the Party's deputy leader. 'Greenwood was a good fellow, and had he ever been able to discover of what part of the work he had been given charge, he would undoubtedly have made a great success of it.'

Greenwood handed over what he assured John were vital and confidential messages to strike organisers, mapped out his route, and promised to telephone ahead at all the places he was to visit on his journey north, advising them to organise a meeting for him to address.

John's first stop was Biggleswade. There, he handed over his top-secret envelope to the secretary of the strike committee, who opened it with due solemnity. In it he found the strike instructions sent by post several days previously, a few Labour Party propaganda leaflets, and a sample copy of a pamphlet on agricultural policy.

That, incidentally, is still the way the Labour Party reacts to crisis. Nearly 60 years later I myself sat despairingly in the Labour Party press office as the 1983 general election campaign sunk deeper into the mire, and watched as huge bundles of paper were despatched daily to agents in every constituency in the country. One day I looked into one of the parcels. The first document I found was an impenetrable analysis of the political situation in Pakistan. 'They talk of nothing else in Scunthorpe,' remarked Gerald Kaufman, who also saw the parcel.

But Yorkshire, Durham and Tyneside lifted John's volatile spirits again. The TUC pennant on the front of his car ensured that he was cheered everywhere he want. In Gateshead the road was blocked solid with people waiting to hear him for several hundred yards before the Labour Party headquarters, and on the common land opposite he reckoned there were another 20,000 people.

He spent a couple of days there and then began his drive back to London. As he was entering Barnet in Hertfordshire, he saw posters declaring the strike at an end. 'With no attempt at bargaining, with a complete disregard for the loyal hundreds of thousands who had answered their call, the TUC leaders had surrendered unconditionally,' he wrote.

CHAPTER FOUR

A COMPLICATED LIFE

May 1926 was the month when the generation of 1918 realised that they would have to learn to live without the dreams that had made their wartime nightmares bearable. For John, managing the despair was made even harder by the complexity of his life. He was effectively living three lives.

There was the increasingly accomplished young parliamentarian, close to Labour's rising stars such as Dalton and Attlee, spending weekends at the country houses of wealthy political heavyweights like Charles Trevelyan, and getting to know everyone who mattered, from Neville Chamberlain to David Lloyd George: the young MP with a great future before him.

There was the London socialite, seen constantly with leading actors, holding glittering theatrical dinners at the House of Commons and in the best restaurants, and carrying on a very public affair with one of the most glamorous actresses of the day.

And there was the increasingly bitter militant from a mining constituency, despairing and angry as he saw the suffering of his constituents, moving leftward at breakneck speed and, in 1926, briefly very close to the Communist Party.

The young parliamentarian enjoyed rubbing shoulders with the powerful, while the young militant stared with horror at their feet of clay.

The young parliamentarian seemed able and willing to play the parliamentary game. He persuaded health minister Neville Chamberlain to give a big loan to the Gateshead Board of Guardians, because they had hundreds of starving families to feed and could not begin to do so from the rates of a poverty-stricken borough. He had a grasp of cynical political realities, writing later that this loan 'was a tremendous fillip to the Labour cause in the town, and (Chamberlain) was far too shrewd a man not to have known it, but he was also too just a man to withhold help in order to make Party capital'. He played the same civilised parliamentary game with Home Secretary Sir William Joynson Hicks, presenting a petition for a reprieve for a Gateshead woman sentenced to death for murder. Joynson Hicks sent for him. 'I'm reprieving that woman of yours. The news will be out tonight. I thought you would like to be the first to send it.' John telegraphed the information to the people responsible for the campaign, and received credit which he happily admitted was quite undeserved.

The father of the House, T. P. O'Connor, sought him out in the library. 'So you're the young man with a ten thousand majority. Well, anyone can get a ten thousand majority, but I'll tell you how to keep it. Never do anything. Never, never do anything. Directly you do something you'll upset someone and if you do enough you'll upset everybody. Look at me. I never do anything and I keep my seat, not like Winston and the other busy-bodies who rush round upsetting people and are in and out like Jacks in boxes.'

John laughed his loud, cracked laugh, no doubt, but really he did not know what to think. The accomplished parliamentarian admired the old man's languid cynicism. The militant in a hurry was disgusted by it.

The militant despised the witty cross-talk in the House between Chancellor of the Exchequer Winston Churchill and Labour's Philip Snowden when 'the real struggle was talking place outside Parliament'. But the parliamentarian enjoyed the exchanges, and his memoirs offer that rare and precious thing, a new Churchill story.

Churchill, he says, listened for more than an hour to a storm of angry invective from Snowden, an acid, bitter man who always appeared to loathe his fellow human beings. Then Churchill rose and congratulated Snowden. He had, he said, watched Snowden's brilliant political career with great sympathy, and had noticed that his natural kindliness and charm had been a handicap, making his life one long contest between his amiability and the cultivation of sufficient acidity. 'It is with great pleasure that I notice that the Right Honourable Gentleman has at last won this long struggle against his better self.'

The parliamentarian still had lines open to Ramsay MacDonald, and even seems to have made a half-hearted attempt to justify the Labour leadership's role during the general strike. But the militant had already identified the Labour leader to whom he would transfer his disappointed loyalty.

John Wheatley had been housing minister during the short-lived Labour government. He was the only left-winger included in that cabinet, and was probably the government's only real success. He had instituted a big programme of council house building, and John had watched him perform in Parliament, later writing:

Intimates of MacDonald had told me much of an unpleasing nature regarding [Wheatley]. The worst allegation was that he considered himself a better man than MacDonald. Later I knew him well, and it was certainly true that he considered himself, and most of his friends, to be far better men than MacDonald. While I listened to his speech, full of that challenge we longed for and received from no other cabinet minister, I made up my mind that ... here was a leader of whom I should feel proud.

Wheatley and Jimmy Maxton led the small group of Glasgow MPs called the Clydesiders, who during the 1924–9 parliament established themselves as the shock troops of the left.

In his Gateshead constituency the militant felt despair. After the general strike his public meetings were 'crowded but indescribably dejected and I had no message to cheer them. I had lost faith in the triumphant campaign launched by MacDonald and enthusiastically taken up by the bulk of the Party, to point out that, as industrial action had failed, the thing to do was to return a Labour majority at the next election. I no longer believed that poor people could benefit by spending their few spare coppers and tired evenings working for men who had led them so disastrously in the industrial field.' Loss of faith that democratic politics could change things was another staging post on the way to fascism.

Back in London he found some comforts. His old friend Arthur Bourchier was nearly 60, while Bourchier's wife, Kyrle Bellew, was still a young and stunningly beautiful woman, just five years older than John. John and Kyrle were conducting an affair that was known to everyone in their joint circles, which meant both the political and theatrical establishment.

It was not reported in newspapers, as it would be today. This was partly because Bourchier himself knew of it, and apparently had no objection. Newspapers which might have been tempted to write about it saw reports of dinners at the House of Commons given by John Beckett MP and attended by Arthur Bourchier, and concluded that Bourchier could hardly be a wronged husband, if he publicly appeared at dinners given by the man who was supposed to have wronged him.

In the wake of the general strike, the militant in John moved close to the Communist Party. He was not alone. The CP's membership doubled in the twelve months after the strike, because communists alone helped those miners whom the strike left jobless.

The victorious mine-owners were able to pick and choose whom they took back, and the most prominent strikers were left, with their families, to starve. Neither the Labour Party nor the unions seemed able or willing to help them. But the CP was. Money from the Soviet Union was brought in by Comintern agents and distributed by the Party. John himself obtained money for his hungry constituents from the CP and from a Soviet front organisation, the International Class War Prisoners Aid Society.

Nationally, at least £270,000 of Soviet money went into the mining communities. Locally, 'in my own Gateshead mining villages at Low Fell and Wreckenton I watched the slow disintegration, through hardship and hunger, of a fine and courageous community, and had the devil offered the help withheld by their fellow countrymen, I would have been grateful. Had the CP possessed the smallest ability or tactical common sense, it could have reaped a great harvest.'

John himself would probably have been part of that harvest. In 1926, despite his subsequent denials, I am sure he could easily have joined the CP. But the CP turned on him and his friends, and even on A. J. Cook, forfeiting not only its ILP sympathisers but all its support in the mining communities. John probably never knew why. The reason, we now know, was that Moscow had imposed on it a fiercely sectarian policy called Class Against Class, according to which the bitterest abuse had to be reserved for non-communist socialists.

Ellen Wilkinson, a former communist and still close to the CP, invited John to her flat for parties at which he met leading communists like Tommy Jackson, who told a rally around that time that they would take the Labour Party by the hand 'as a preliminary to taking them by the throat'.

Wilkinson also asked him to undertake a mission abroad on behalf of Red Aid, and he agreed, out of gratitude for its aid to the miners. In 1926 Marshal Pilsudski led a military coup in Poland, and was treating left-wingers and racial minorities with great brutality. John agreed to lead a fact-finding delegation of three, with his friend Arthur Shepherd, MP for Darlington, and Winifred Horrabin as secretary.

He spent a month in Poland, playing cloak-and-dagger games with government spies and drinking huge quantities of vodka with revolution-aries of all types. He took to the Polish communists: 'A persecuted party is always good as far as its personnel is concerned. These men were hunted like rats and only the utmost courage and sturdy fanaticism could keep them in the ranks.' But he could not quite shake off a certain admiration for the brutal old marshal who had replaced a chaotic democracy with what seemed to John to be a relatively efficient and pragmatic dictatorship.

The government gave them access to the prisons. There the delegation found evidence that there was a great deal of torture when men first went inside, to get them to betray the names of their comrades.

But what shocked him most was the condition of Polish miners, working ten hours a day for a miserable wage – and the fact that the pits were owned by two combines, both controlled by British companies. 'It was unpleasant to realise that our hungry unemployed miners in Durham had lost their employment in order that "British" financiers could profit by the callous sweating and exploitation of Polish labour.' The inverted commas around the word British tell their own story.

Poland added to his stock of anecdotes. At one small town, where they were to observe a trial the next day, the owner of the town's only inn showed them to a large room with a stove on one wall and a single huge bed. It was desperately cold and they had travelled all day and all night in a crowded third-class carriage, sitting on bare boards and watching with growing nausea as all the other occupants ate raw herrings with their fingers.

So the two Polish interpreters settled down on the floor beside the stove, and the parliamentary delegation, fully clothed, made itself as comfortable as possible on the huge bed and fell into a deep sleep:

> Early in the morning I awoke intensely hot, and found myself almost smothered by the large form of mine host. I wriggled out and surveyed my companions. On the other side of the bed was the Member for Darlington with our large hostess sleeping coyly beside him. In the middle Winifred could hardly be seen beneath the two daughters of the house. We found that this was the family bed which guests were allowed to share.

When they arrived at the trial, they wished they had stayed away. In the courtroom, the dozen or so prisoners greeted the delegation with communist slogans. 'These prisoners were not communists,' he wrote, 'but simply ill-treated and half-starved peasants who blamed their foreign masters for their ills.' They had, he discovered, been told that the delegation would be so pleased by the slogans that it would order their release. The trial was a farce and all the prisoners received long sentences.

A visit to Posen on the return journey marked another staging post on the road to fascism. Posen had been a German city until the Versailles treaty. Now it was Polish. What John saw was this:

> A highly civilised and efficient German municipality has been obliged to revert to a primitive and corrupt system of local government. Heartbreaking as it must have been for the citizens of Alsace and Lorraine to leave German municipal methods for those of France, their lot was easier than that of the Germans in Posen. Every evidence existed that the Poles were deliberately trying to suppress German language and culture, and were smashing the German trade union machine and battering down the standards of life.

Wages were pitifully low, and ownership of industry was shared between Paris and London. 'The despairing engineers of Tyneside had fought and defeated Germany in order that British and French financiers should be able to force German workers to undercut them in the world's markets.'

All three John Becketts were still much in evidence as 1927 opened, but only two of them celebrated Christmas that year. The young parliamentarian had all but disappeared. He seems to have decided finally, quite early that year, that the House of Commons was not for him.

Ever since he was at school, he had wanted to be a lawyer. Probably it was what his mother wanted most for him, for it seems likely that she was rather a wise woman, and could see that no good was going to come from mixing John and politics. But, having left school at fourteen, he did not have the necessary educational qualifications to read for the bar.

Sir Patrick Hastings, the Labour Attorney General who had been at the centre of the Campbell affair in 1924, agreed to try to obtain for him an exemption from the preliminary examination, on the grounds of his war service and his public service.

But John was not going to leave the House of Commons without showing what he thought of the place. He started the year by making a radical, and unwelcome, proposal to his parliamentary colleagues about how they might stifle Stanley Baldwin's trade union bill.

Like similar laws passed under the Thatcher government six decades later, its purpose was to take advantage of the fact that the trade union enemy was defeated and helpless, and to ensure that it stayed that way by virtually outlawing the strike, the only real weapon the unions possessed.

The bill was also designed to cripple Labour Party funds by making trade union members 'opt in' to the political fund instead of 'opting out'. Typically, John told everyone that he was rather in favour of the second part, because working men should not be dragooned into contributing money to keep politicians in unaccustomed luxury. This stance did not endear him to fellow Labour MPs.

Still, the bill had to be stopped if possible, even if he could not agree with his colleagues about the reasons why. So he proposed that it should be stopped by filibustering.

Start with one MP making a strong protest in unparliamentary language, and refusing to apologise. With ingenuity, determination and an endless supply of points of order, that member's suspension could be made to last for over half an hour. There were 156 Labour MPs, and suspending them all would take ten days. Once they were all excluded, he believed Parliament would be seen to be a Conservative rump outfit, and would lose all authority. By now, the argument that if successful the tactic would destroy parliamentary government was something that John counted, if at all, in its favour.

He had, of course, a better chance of flying to the moon than of persuading the Parliamentary Labour Party to adopt the plan. Yet direct action in Parliament increasingly seemed to John all that was left. After one of his unrestrained attacks on Prime Minister Stanley Baldwin (for whom he had conceived a special loathing), one of the stupider Conservatives, Luton MP Terence O'Connor, crossed the floor and asked him to 'come outside and take a damned good hiding'. John said he would follow the man after the vote, and this led to a farcical scene.

They somehow missed their assignation, and both, like schoolboys meeting to fight at the school gates, claimed that the other had chickened out. John insisted that he scoured the corridors and was told that Sir Terence had left, while Sir Terence told a Luton audience that weekend that he had taught John a lesson he would not forget – 'the proper way to deal with cowardly socialists'.

The ILP's Luton branch sent John a newspaper report of the meeting at which this was said, and John sent a letter to the Luton papers announcing that he would speak in the town and repeat what he had said in Parliament, so that Mr O'Connor could attend and attempt to take retribution. The idea that two Members of Parliament would stand in the middle of Luton market square and slug it out, surrounded presumably by their various cheering supporters, seems rather to have appealed to him.

John was very proud of that Luton meeting. The hall, and an overflow hall, were both full to capacity, the streets were packed, a third overflow meeting was held in the market place, and there was apparently no sign of Mr O'Connor, who at the next election found a safer seat and finished his career as Solicitor General.

A month later, in May, Stanley Baldwin told the House of Commons that some of the trade unions were controlled by the Communist Party, and John rose on a point of order to ask the Prime Minister to admit that he had lied. The Speaker, as he was bound to do, ordered him to withdraw, and John offered to do so 'if the Prime Minister will withdraw the lie he told'. The House voted for a week's suspension by 321 votes to 88. It was the first of several suspensions.

Oddly, he hated it. From the moment he called Baldwin a liar, 'I was conscious of a concentrated disapproval and dislike almost physical in its strength. The sense of isolation is acutely painful.' It was some compensation that the newspapers printed all the unkind things he wished to say about Baldwin, and attendance at his meetings rose steeply.

The consequence that mattered, however, was something that he could not see clearly at the time. Paradoxically, it nailed him to politics forever, so that in future, on the many occasions when he wished he could leave politics and take up an honest trade, the road was barred.

It killed his dream of becoming a barrister. Sir Patrick Hastings told him that it had prejudiced the benchers against John, and there was now no chance of his getting the exemption he sought to read for the bar. His most cherished career was closed to him.

Most people only have the chance to make their careers once. John was 33, and had already thrown away three careers, in advertising, politics and the law.

In the autumn of 1927 he travelled to South Africa to join Arthur Bourchier on a tour in which John had a financial interest. The trip changed everything, for two reasons. One reason was personal, and we will come to that in a moment. The other he anticipated when talking to a South African Labour MP on the three-week boat trip: 'I sensed that the result of this trip would make me extremely unpopular with the anti-impe-rialist section of the ILP. Trips abroad contributed largely to my downfall in the Labour Party. Had I not seen for myself, I might have been content to echo the shibboleths of the anti-imperialists.'

Men like Fenner Brockway on the Labour left were as committed to equality for foreigners as for the British, for black as well as white people. John's passion for justice did not, in the end, extend beyond these shores.

He had been a very active anti-imperialist before his visit to South Africa, though it was not a side of his work that he ever chose to reveal in later years. As late as February 1927 he had been in Brussels for the foundation of the League Against Imperialism, and the following month he was one of the prime movers in the foundation of its British Section. His friend Fenner Brockway became chairman of the section, George Lansbury treasurer, and John joined the executive.

He seems to have had a wonderful time in South Africa, accompanied (probably) by Kyrle for much of the time, and dallying for a month in Natal because of the pleasures of surfing and socialising. There he talked at length with Manilal Gandhi, a son of the Indian leader and himself the spokesman for Natal's Indian population, and with prominent white politicians. These white politicians complained that Indians were undercutting white labour, and John remarked on the fact that outside Durban and Pietermaritzburg, the retail trading establishments were mainly Indian.

To repay Mr Gandhi's hospitality, John invited him to lunch at his hotel, and was told that his guest would not be allowed to enter. He was horrified. But it was not the straightforward anti-racist horror that Brockway would have felt. John wrote: 'If Mr Gandhi, who was an Oxford graduate and a member of the Inns of Temple, desired to travel by tram, he had no recourse but to share a "Jim Crow" with the most primitive South African native.' It does not seem to have occurred to him that the system of dividing the races might itself be the trouble.

He could not accept Gandhi's wish to give the Indians equal status with the whites: 'Although there were a number of educated Indians, the great majority were little more advanced than the South African natives, and in most cases by no means such good physical and moral types.' The blame for the situation, he thought, lay with the greed of early white settlers: 'Had they not supported cheap Asiatic labour, the country would not now be overrun.'

He hired a car and drove through Zululand, seeing 'a great deal of these magnificent people'. Here again, he found it easy to make sweeping racial generalisations on the briefest of acquaintances. He did not agree with those who told him that Zulus were mentally deficient, and thought they could do well if educated; but on the other hand, 'The people seem happy as they are, and I was told that urban life seriously affected their physique.' Once again, he thought the greed of the whites was to blame, for this led them to exploit Zulus in the mines of the Rand, and use them as house-boys and rickshaw runners. 'For me the rickshaw runners constituted the one really repulsive feature of life in Durban. The average life of a runner is less than seven years, and the spectacle of these fine men running like burdened animals is a blot upon South African civilisation.'

A minister drove him to see a scheme designed to give a fresh start in life to 'poor whites' and provide them with the technical knowledge necessary to supervise black, Indian and Chinese labour. John approved whole-heartedly, 'but I wondered whether they could build a white man's country unless white men performed the necessary manual labour. The argument that white men should not have to do hard work in a warm country seemed to me not to carry weight.' White men managed, he noticed cynically, to play strenuous games of golf and tennis there.

He took these views to a rather puzzled Trades Union Congress, and to what was probably an even more puzzled confidential meeting of the Executive of the South African Native Congress. He admired its members individually but ended up certain that the problem should be resolved by setting aside specific native areas, 'rather than in unhappy attempts to mingle the two races, with hardship and grievance to both'. This must deeply have shocked friends such as Brockway and Lansbury when, as I am sure he did, he lectured them on his return about how to solve the problems of race in South Africa. Of course, South Africa did eventually try John's prescription, with disastrous results.

Thus, as he wrote in his baffled way, 'as so often happened in my political life, I found myself out of step with everyone'. It was a talent he had. South African newspapers quickly discovered what London newspapers already knew, that John Beckett was generally good for an outrageous quote. They asked his view on every conceivable issue, including a rather arcane dispute about whether the British or Dutch flag should have primacy, at a time when British South Africans flew Union Jacks from their cars. His reply was to mock 'the love shown for England by flying German-made flags on American made motor cars', and he suggested that orders for Birmingham and Coventry would be more appreciated. Four newspapers carried furious leaders the next morning, all of them comparing him with Rudyard Kipling's Pagett MP. It was one of his own favourite poems:

'Pagett MP was a liar, and a fluent liar therewith –
He spoke of the heat of India as "The Asian solar myth";
Came on a four months' visit to "study the east" in November,
And I got him to sign an agreement vowing to stay till September ...
March came in with the koil. Pagett was cool and gay,
Called me a "bloated brahmin", talked of my "princely pay"
March went out with the roses. "Where is your heat?" said he.
"Coming" said I to Pagett. "Skittles" said Pagett MP ...'

The heat of India, of course, eventually gets to Pagett and he begs to be allowed to go home:

'... And I laughed as a drove from the station, but the mirth dried
    out on my lips
As I thought of the fools like Pagett who write of their "Eastern
    trips",
And the sneers of the travelled idiots who duly misgovern the land,
And I prayed to the Lord to deliver another one into my hand.'

Business beckoned. Arthur Bourchier was to meet John at Johannesburg station. He was not there. Instead, the director was there to tell John that Bourchier was seriously ill. They took him to the theatre for the evening's performance of *Ambrose Applejohn's Adventure*. From the front row of the stalls, he could see that his friend was in a high fever and very ill. In the first act he introduced business and dialogue from the other two acts. The last act became almost farcical, with the bewildered company striving to adapt themselves to the jumbled playing of the leading actor.

As John arrived in his dressing-room after the performance, Bourchier collapsed. He and Bourchier's brother-in-law and manager, Lionel Falck, took him back to the Rand Club where he was staying and went out in search of a doctor. Bourchier died two days later. He had wanted to be cremated. The only cremation facility in Johannesburg was the Indian burial ground. John was one of the four pall bearers:

As I helped to carry the heavy coffin over broken ground to the Indian's sweet-smelling funeral pyre, I wished that I could believe that dead men still lived and could see their own obsequies. The beautiful semi-tropical gardens and reverential white-robed attendants, the primitive yet impressive log structure on which he was to rest, made an unforgettable scene, and one which could have been appreciated by no one more keenly than the unconscious chief actor.

Lionel Falck placed a match to the pyre and the flames shot up as the mourners were ushered away.

* * *

Back in England, the House of Commons seemed drearier and more pointless than ever. John no longer believed that the Labour Party was going to do any better than the old parties, or that radical change could be effected through Parliament. 'There were also,' he writes carefully, 'personal matters which made me feel that I should be happier out of public life.'

This is no doubt a reference to Kyrle's view that, now her husband was dead, there was nothing to stop them marrying, except the inconvenience that John was still married to Helen – not a comfortable position for a rising young politician in 1927.

There was already unhappiness in Gateshead. John was used to the south, where they were more liberal about sexual behaviour and had a less strongly developed sense of the dignity of their representative. His Gateshead activists had taken to Helen, and felt that their MP had treated his wife badly. It did not help matters that he was seen around London with a glamorous actress. And they did not much like the publicity which surrounded his parliamentary scenes. Many were still MacDonald loyalists.

He could probably have hung on to Gateshead – his campaigning skills were still greatly prized there – but there was likely to be opposition. Most politicians would have trimmed a little and fought to keep their constituency. A man as disillusioned with Parliament as John could see little point in the battle.

So early the next year we find him telling the Gateshead Labour Party that he would not be contesting Gateshead at the next election.

He told his Party activists how he was feeling. Their conditions had deteriorated steadily: 'I cannot see any hope of improving things for them, even if, as I think probable, they continue to return me for another five years. As you know, I am a person who likes action. I do not find, at the moment, sufficient outlet and hope in Parliament.'

The work that really needed doing was that of educating Tory areas to vote Labour. 'I have a considerable liking and aptitude for educational and propaganda work, and I believe I can serve the army of labour better in the field than in Parliament. All these things have been long in my mind, and this letter is the result of months of anxious thought and soul-searching.' There are, he told a local newspaper reporter from the *North Mail*, 'at least five to ten years of hard propaganda work to be done in the country before parliamentary socialism becomes a practicability ... I shall devote myself in the new campaign mainly to work in the south of England, which is the great bulwark of toryism.'

So that was it. Back to the life he had so loved as part of the ILP's extended family, the confident brotherhood of men and women who took him to their hearts and his message to their souls, and fed him tea and optimism, as he travelled round the country with the gospel of socialism. Back to the drafty meeting halls where bumbling but good-hearted local chairman forgot their visitor's name, and bleared round the room, and talked too long, and John had to step in to make sure the meeting finished before the pubs closed. Back to where there were no hard-faced Tories who had done well out of the war, no smooth-faced Labour politicians on the make, where the air was pure and honest,

> 'Where the wine is on the rafter
> And the beer is in the wood
> And the God that made good laughter
> Has seen that they are good.'

It would never do, of course. The revolutionary optimism of 1920 had gone, never to be seen in the land again until 1945, by which time John had thrown away his right to be a part of it. And John had changed, too, though he was quite capable of hiding from himself the extent of the change. He had become much richer, much better known, and, crucially, his life much more complicated.

He was no longer the young man who could travel as cheaply as possible and bed down at the end of a long day in the front room of an impoverished local activist. He must have half recognised the change in himself, because he told Gateshead he would concentrate on the south of England – which would, of course, enable him to keep in touch with his theatrical interests.

A part of him must have realised that he was kidding himself, for he seems to have been looking everywhere for alternative ways of living. He increased his involvement in the theatre, for the first time, with Kyrle, financing and managing his own West End production. And behind the scenes he was soon making plans to get another parliamentary seat, or even to dowse the fires he had ignited on his Gateshead boats. In later years he claimed that the invitation to seek nomination at Peckham in South London came to him entirely unasked. That's not quite how his friend, the Peckham MP Hugh Dalton, saw it.

Dalton had fallen out badly with his agent and some members of the Peckham Labour Party, and had decided to decamp to a constituency where the local workers were rather less awkward. Some leading Peckham activists approached John, assuring him that if he did not approve of the agent, the agent would have to go. John promised to talk to Dalton, and did so in November 1928. John's account of this conversation was that Dalton pressed him to accept, saying that if he would 'go there and clean it up', he would be doing the Labour Party a service. Dalton's autobiography records that John Beckett was 'a friend of mine at this time, and had great energy and some ability. His later association with Mosley surprised and disappointed me.'

Yet Dalton's diaries cast a curious light on all this. As far back as July he seems to have been rethinking his friendship with the young man from Gateshead who did not seem to mind how many enemies he made. His diary entry for 20 July reads:

> To Liphook to spend the night with the Webbs (Sidney and Beatrice) and walk next morning ... He (Sidney) says he hears that Mrs Bourchier came back from South Africa with Bourchier's ashes and Beckett in the same cabin, and fancies that her wealth may not have been wholly absent from Beckett's mind.

Nor was that all. John's growing friendship with John Wheatley had not passed unnoticed in the household of the influential Webbs. The young and ambitious Dalton seems to have been warned off in no uncertain terms: 'Beatrice thinks John Wheatley is a real Tammanny Hall type – his stock has never been lower.'

By then John already knew of Dalton's troubles in Peckham. Two months earlier both men had been guests for the weekend at the country house of Sir Charles Trevelyan. On a long walk that the three took together, John seems to have listened quietly as Dalton described what was going on and asked Trevelyan to help him find a northern seat.

In November Dalton was adopted in Bishop Auckland. In his diary of 6 November, he wrote:

> Parliament meets. Everyone very congratulatory about Bishop Auckland. MacDonald in good form in his opening speech ... Lunch with John Beckett who is after Peckham. (Good luck to him!) ... Beckett says that MacDonald is now being motored about by Paddy Naismith, a film actress, said to be engaged to Derwent Hall Caine – a little bit of fluff with an elegant car. I saw her hanging around at Birmingham. They motored to and from Wolverhampton. People are wondering where they really slept!

The only serious opposition in Peckham was solicitor Lewis Silkin, a Labour member of the London County Council, friend and ally of Herbert Morrison, future minister in the 1945 government, and the founder of a legal and political dynasty. According to John, they had known each other well, and Silkin harboured a grudge because John, as secretary of the ILP divisional council, 'had been obliged to take certain steps towards him which he had resented'. Unfortunately Silkin has left no papers from which more we might learn more.

On 19 December, Dalton told his diary: 'Beckett endorsed for Peckham! We couldn't, it was felt, be a court of morals, and nothing in this case was really public.' John's account was: 'In spite of the fact that Silkin was a far wealthier man than I, and was strongly supported by Herbert Morrison and the London Labour Party, he received few votes, and I was selected.'

Gateshead's Labour Party had already chosen a successful London barrister, J. B. Melville KC, to replace John. Melville seems to have been John's friend and protégé, so perhaps John still dreamed of being a barrister – or perhaps he was repaying a debt. In any case, the candidature caused no end of trouble. Not only was Melville seen as yet another rich middle-class southerner carpetbagging into Labour's northern heartlands; he also seems to have sailed very close to the wind in the way he gathered support locally, so much so that Labour's National Executive refused to endorse him. Dalton's diary records on 5 November 1928:

National Executive from 10.30. The case of Melville at Gateshead comes up. Robinson threatens, through NUDAW, to circularise trade unions on the incursion of middle class candidates. Quite a sense of class war in the air! We are rather intimidated by this but shouldn't have endorsed M anyway. It is alleged that M offered Forster [the ex-Gateshead secretary, Robinson's chief backer] the refusal of the agency at £350 a year with a five year contract. This greatly shocked constituencies. Agreed that we don't endorse, owing to irregularity, but that Uncle and Morrison see M and try to persuade him to withdraw altogether, and also that they go to Gateshead. A fine mess these lawyers make of their affairs!

'Uncle' was Arthur Henderson, Labour Party secretary, and Herbert Morrison was then chairman.

John probably thought Melville was being victimised for being his friend. In any case, he seems to have taken prompt action in Melville's defence. Just five days after that meeting a local newspaper carried an exclusive and sensational local story. 'I have reliable authority for stating that two highly important developments have occurred in the mystery surrounding the resignation by Mr John Beckett MP of his seat at Gateshead, and the circumstances of the selection of a successor,' the *North Mail*'s labour correspondent reported breathlessly.

It appeared that Beckett might stay on in Gateshead after all. He had been approached by unnamed members of the Gateshead Labour Party. 'I am unable to make public at this stage the details of the terms of the approach, but I understand that they are of a most interesting character.'

Mr Beckett, 'contrary to rumours circulating in the party, has no intention of severing his connection with politics, and I am able to announce that he has received a warm invitation to contest a Labour stronghold in the South country'. This was putting it a little strongly: it was another five weeks before John was endorsed to fight Peckham.

The *North Mail*'s informant must have been John himself. It looks like a warning to the national executive to keep a hold of nurse (in the shape of Melville), for fear of finding something worse (Beckett himself). Ten days later Henderson and Morrison arrived to meet the local Labour Party and explain why they could not endorse Melville. They left without comment, and the only quote the local press could obtain came from an unnamed delegate who said, 'We have no candidate at present. Why not let John

Beckett stand for us again? He says he wants to go to Parliament again, and we are quite willing to send him.'

Melville was re-selected by Gateshead, and this time the national executive made no objection. He became attorney general in Ramsey MacDonald's 1929 government, but died suddenly within a few months. It was his death which led MacDonald to offer the post to a rising young lawyer with, at that time, no seat in Parliament and no political ambitions, named Stafford Cripps, who was to become Chancellor of the Exchequer in 1947.

This game of musical chairs ended in good time for the 1929 general election. Peckham found itself with a candidate who was saying at every opportunity that his support of Labour's leaders was entirely contingent on their carrying out approved Labour policy. His campaign was opened by the Clydesiders' leader Jimmy Maxton, a pretty clear statement of where he now stood in the Labour Party.

Peckham also found itself with a candidate whose turbulent lifestyle during his five years in Parliament provided ample material for whispering campaigns. Naturally the relationship with Kyrle surfaced, but John found, to his delight, that while this would have been deeply damaging in Gateshead, in Peckham it seemed if anything to do him good. Early in the campaign he overheard a conversation between two men on a bus which cheered him up no end. 'That John Beckett, 'e's carrying on with that actress, Kyrle Bellew.' 'Is 'e?' Pause. 'Lucky sod.'

It was rumoured that he had been thrown out of Gateshead by an indignant local Labour Party for his behaviour. But the rumour seems to have done little harm: he turned Dalton's 800 majority into an apparently impregnable 6,000 majority.

CHAPTER FIVE

BURNING BOATS

Did Ramsay MacDonald offer his one-time friend John Beckett a government job after the 1929 election – a last peace offering? John certainly thought he did, though in a rather roundabout way.

While Dalton, Attlee and Ellen Wilkinson waited for the call to MacDonald's Hampstead home hoping for the preferment they had earned, John was approached – on his own account – by 'one of Labour's leading journalists, known to be in the confidence of three of the big five', who 'asked whether I would join the government as Parliamentary Secretary to the Air Ministry'. No, John said, he would not: 'Tell them to find a conjuror to get aeroplanes out of a hat, as Tom Shaw gets jobs.' The job went to Fred Montague, a well-known member of the Magicians' Circle.

MacDonald signalled early what sort of government he was going to run. He dropped the one left-winger, and the one success, of his 1924 government, the housing minister and Clydesiders' leader John Wheatley. In a pre-election list of possible ministerial appointments, Wheatley was pencilled in for the Ministry of Labour. By the time the results were declared, MacDonald had decided that he could afford to keep him out.

Wheatley was quickly becoming John's new hero. He was 60 in 1929, a Catholic born in Ireland whose parents had migrated to Glasgow when he was seven. The oldest child of a family of ten, he followed his father down the mines and worked there for fifteen years. In 1901, aged 32, he became a reporter and then an advertising canvasser for a Catholic newspaper, the *Glasgow Observer*. Five years later he started a printing business, which prospered and made him fairly rich, allowing him in 1923 to found a weekly newspaper, the *Glasgow Evening Standard*, which lasted until 1960.

A grim poverty-stricken childhood, and friendships with socialists like James Connolly (a frequent visitor to the Wheatley household until his execution in 1916) combined to add the socialist faith to his Catholic one. The two faiths coexisted uneasily. The Catholic Church in Scotland thought socialism was godless and wicked, while Scottish socialists saw Catholics as reactionaries whose aim was to keep the workers in their place by telling them that all would be put right in the next world. One Catholic priest persuaded his indignant parishioners to go to Wheatley's home and burn him in effigy in front of it; and in 1909 Wheatley had a public debate with Hilaire Belloc on whether Catholicism and socialism were compatible.

Well before the First World War, he and James Maxton had become, as they were to remain until 1930, the joint leaders of the Independent Labour Party in Scotland. He was the architect of Labour's extraordinary success in western Scotland in the 1922 general election which saw ten new Labour MPs, including Wheatley and Maxton themselves, elected to Parliament. As their train left St Enoch's station for Westminster, they were given an almost religious farewell. 'It is important,' writes Sheridan Gilley in the *Dictionary of Labour Biography*, 'to understand the almost apocalyptic expectations of the Glasgow poor in order to judge Wheatley's acute frustrations with Westminster politics, and the increasing disillusionment and embitterment of his Clydeside radical colleagues.'

That year they supported MacDonald for Labour leader because he was seen as the ILP left-winger, although Arthur Henderson warned them prophetically that it would not be long before 'you Clydeside men' started to regret the choice.

It was not just Wheatley's Catholicism which marked him out from his Clydeside colleagues. It was also his distaste for the internationalism of the Labour movement. He, like John Beckett and unlike all their ILP friends, thought that a British socialist had done his duty when he had seen British workers all right.

In the House of Commons, Wheatley's great strength was his close reasoning and mastery of detail. He was not a flamboyant orator like Maxton, but he could hold the House in his spell in a way that Maxton could never do. He was a politician of immense personal power.

If any of the Clydesiders were to have office when Labour first came to power in 1924, it had to be Wheatley, and he was given the job that the former Glasgow slum-dweller wanted most, that of Minister of Housing and Health. His Housing Act was the government's main, if not its only, achievement. It provided for a steadily expanding investment in public housing at modest rents.

After the Labour government fell, it was Wheatley who ensured that the ILP would in future be the vehicle for left-wing opposition to MacDonald. But between 1927 and 1929, Maxton was forced to make the running. Wheatley's health had become poor, and his attention distracted by attacks from the Conservative candidate in his Glasgow Shettleston constituency, who targeted his Catholicism as well as his socialism, and whom he unsuccessfully sued for libel.

Wheatley was short, dumpy, unprepossessing and calculating, peering myopically through thick round spectacles. Maxton was the opposite in every way: painfully thin, handsome and romantic in a raddled sort of way, with long, flowing black hair. An eloquent, romantic former schoolteacher whose spellbinding oratory was legendary, he lived on his nerves and a constant supply of tea and cigarettes.

It was Wheatley, not Maxton, whom MacDonald really feared. Wheatley had one of the finest political brains of his generation. Maxton, though nominally the leader of the ILP, understood as well as anyone the reality of their relationship. 'I am asking you because you are my leader,' Wheatley once said to Maxton. 'Aye, John, I am your leader,' replied Maxton. 'And you will discover that I am the cutest leader you ever led.' Maxton was containable – and when Wheatley had gone, Maxton was contained. Wheatley was not containable.

John Beckett, who knew an instinctively powerful politician when he saw one, wrote in 1938 that he had only known three great men in his time in the House: Winston Churchill, David Lloyd George and John Wheatley. Fifty years later, in 1980, I told the then very old Fenner Brockway that Wheatley had been John's political hero. He was visibly surprised. 'That shows his judgement was better than I thought. I'd have thought he would be more attracted by the romanticism of Maxton.'

Another Labour politician recognised Wheatley's special qualities at that time. Sir Oswald Mosley, just entering MacDonald's government with a brief to conquer unemployment, said Wheatley was the British Lenin. Wheatley never lived to see the direction his admirers Beckett and Mosley took. If he had lived, at least one of them would probably not have taken it.

Very quickly – within a few days of Parliament reassembling in June 1929 – the battle lines were drawn up. The events of those few days shaped the Labour Party for many years to come, and decided the fate of many a young and promising politician, John Beckett and Fenner Brockway among them.

MacDonald's decision to exclude Wheatley from the government was greeted by the *Daily Express*, correctly, as a declaration of war on the left. When the Parliamentary Labour Party met, Wheatley said, prophetically, that the country was entering one of its periodic slumps, and cuts in the standard of living were inevitable. The Labour Party, without an overall parliamentary majority, could only apply capitalist measures and administer those cuts. So it should wait to form a government until it had an overall majority.

Fenner Brockway wrote after that meeting: 'There are few men who can speak so impersonally as Wheatley. His thick-set body did not move, one could not see his eyes behind the thick pebble glasses. Nevertheless he gripped; there was a quality of strength and certainty in his voice and his reasoning was remorseless.' John agreed: 'Wheatley was the most effective debater I heard in the House during eight years' membership. Maxton's courage, loyalty and personal charm made an excellent foil to Wheatley's somewhat hard and unemotional exterior.'

When the ILP group met, a few days later, Maxton, as chairman, ruled that the group should consist only of MPs who accepted ILP policy. He was saying, in effect, that they must put ILP policy before the policy of the government, and vote against the government if the two conflicted, as they inevitably would. This ruling reduced the ILP from 100 or so MPs to a hard core of just nineteen. Fenner Brockway wrote in his autobiography:

> We acted closely together, appointing John Beckett as secretary. He ... was an aggressive young rebel, but without basic socialist philosophy. I had spoken at one of his election meetings in a crowded music hall. My speech was heard with indifference; then Beckett spoke with unrelieved denunciation of the rich and much abuse of his Tory opponent. The audience loved it.

Years later Brockway wrote to historian Colin Holmes:

> Beckett was young, enthusiastic, dynamic, a a tremendous worker. By his energy, spectacular methods and ability to win people by his 'rabble-rousing' oratory at street corners, he built up a huge following at Peckham ... There was no policy in his speeches, just punch and hit. A boxer.

Fred Brooks, one of Labour's activists in Peckham, bears out Brockway's estimate of the effect of John's oratory. 'I heard him speak many times,' Brooks wrote to me. 'He had a great personality and could hold a big crowd under almost any circumstances. I once saw him speaking on the corner of Finsbury Circus and it was during the lunch hour. I reckon a good many went without their lunch that day!'

Wheatley worked out policies, Maxton articulated them, Beckett worked out the parliamentary tactics. In the debate on the King's Speech, Maxton put the demands of the left. 'I am going to promise the cabinet active hearty support and work on one condition and one condition only, that they will arrange the affairs of this country that no unemployed man, his wife or child, shall have any dread of starvation or insult.'

It soon became clear that this modest demand would not be met, and by midsummer Maxton was asking the House of Commons: 'Has any human being benefited by the fact that there has been a Labour Government in office?' In October he said: 'It would be foolish to expect the government to deliver socialism but ... the government had it in their power to stop starvation.'

John made a close study of parliamentary rules and procedure. With the Liberals and the Conservatives supporting most of the government's measures, he saw himself, and was seen by the ILP group, as the chief whip of the only real opposition party. It was he who knitted the nineteen MPs together into an effective force, known before long as the 'parliamentary suicide club'.

Immersed in the technicalities of organising opposition, John for a time forgot his despair. For the first year or so of the new Parliament he enjoyed himself enormously, knowing the group depended on his organisation, his flair for publicity, his grasp of procedure, and his recklessness; and trusting Wheatley for the grand strategy.

It seems genuinely to have come as a surprise to him that the government, with all its powers of patronage, was able to keep most of its MPs trundling obediently into the government lobby. He could find excuses for some of them, but for one in particular, there were no words too bitter:

My revolutionary mentor Ellen Wilkinson sat demurely on the bench of repentance in the second row, reserved for parliamentary private secretaries who may be seen but not heard. Just after the election Ellen had telephoned me urging me to meet her as soon as possible. She sounded tearful and deeply distressed, and I found her in a state of the most abject depression. At tea she wept, and told me that enquiries had elicited the fact that she was not to be given a post in the new government.

I … said that surely after her strong opposition to MacDonald and his friends, she could not have thought that she had any chance whatever of being selected, adding that I could not understand her desire to be a member of the kind of ministry we knew would be formed. Sobbing afresh, she said that she had not dreamed her sincere opposition to certain proposals would be punished so severely; that it was an insult that men of the poor calibre of Mr Y and Mr N should be included and she left out. Her last words to me as I drove her home were: 'You'll see, if this is what being a rebel does, I'll show them something different in future.'

This account is, of course, not corroborated by any other source, and particularly not in the only biography of Ellen Wilkinson. I think it is probably substantially true, though, like many of John's stories, perhaps a little embroidered. But if it is true, there is a certain vindictiveness about the way John recounts this private conversation for publication, when he discreetly hid the names of other parliamentary colleagues. He tells us, for example, about an unnamed Durham miners' MP who had for years been an outspoken supporter of the Minority Movement, the communist front organisation in the trade unions:

I approached this man to ask him to vote for 5/- a week for the unemployed man's child instead of 2/-. He refused. I reminded him of his past activities and said: 'What about the revolution now?' 'Och,' he replied. 'Brother … can look after that in Durham. I've got economic security for the first time in my life and I'm not going to lose it.'

Of course, unlike his Durham friend and many other Labour MPs, John had a source of income outside Parliament. He had his theatrical interests, and was, by comparison with many Labour MPs, quite well off. When MPs were told that the unions would not give rebels financial help in their parliamentary campaigns, and that the Party would withdraw recognition from them and extinguish their parliamentary careers, it was a serious matter – as John recognised – for men 'who had been absent from their trades for many years, had no other means of existence, and had wives and families to support'. He was not in that position. He was sending his estranged wife enough money to enable her to send their daughter Lesley to a private school.

The first battle was over the government's refusal to raise unemployment benefit to the amounts promised in the manifesto. The ILP managed to get nearly 40 Labour MPs into the division lobbies, and another 50 abstentions, so that in order to get its Unemployment Insurance Financial Resolution through the House, the government relied heavily on the Conservative and Liberal parties.

The ILP decided, as a deliberate act of policy, to smoke out their colleagues. Many MPs liked to appear as good party men at Westminster, and rebels in their constituency. One way – still used, though made harder by the speed of modern communications – was to move an amendment to a government proposal, and then, when you got a kindly but unhelpful reply, rise and say that in view of the Minister's sympathy, the motion would be withdrawn.

John pointed out to his ILP colleagues that, to withdraw a motion in this way, you had to have the permission of the House. Of course normally it was a formality and, no one ever opposed a member who wished to withdraw. But they did now. The ILP refused to allow such motions to be withdrawn without a division, placing their Labour colleagues in the position where they either had to face the serious consequences of defying the whips, or vote against their own motion.

John was very pleased with this tactic. 'We forced them to vote against the rates of benefit which they had loudly abused a Conservative government for refusing; against compensation for miners whose pits were closed; and against a dozen other things, in the purely vocal clamour for which they had spent their political lives.' It did not, however, improve the temper of his fellow Labour MPs, among whom he was rapidly becoming hate figure number one.

'He loved it,' Fenner Brockway wrote to Colin Holmes. 'We continually had to restrain him from going to extremes in action and language ... He was contemptuous of the Labour majority. Couldn't find a word sufficiently bad to say of them.'

The Prime Minister himself decided to try to reason with him. John had placed a question on the order paper asking how many commissions and committees had been set up by the government, and how many of the chairmen and members were opposed to Labour policy.

First the whip asked him to withdraw the question. Then MacDonald's PPS asked. Finally, John was asked to see MacDonald. In the Prime Minister's room in the House of Commons, MacDonald talked of their 'long friendship' and asked him to abandon 'embarrassing and disruptive activities'. John said he would withdraw the question if he could have an assurance that no other committees would be set up without a Labour party or neutral chairman. Unsurprisingly, MacDonald was furious. It was the last of John's boats, and he had casually thrown a match on to it.

Old friends were wary of him now, and he was unsparing with them. 'Attlee, Greenwood, Morrison, Dalton and the rest failed,' he wrote, 'not because a brutal opposition majority was too much for them, but because of their own inability and time-serving subservience to leaders who, when they were no longer in office, they could not sufficiently abuse.'

Dalton's references to John in his diary become positively acid. One of them, in August 1930, reads: 'Frank Owen to dinner. Ruth (Dalton's wife) dislikes him as vulgar, untrustworthy and careerist. She thinks he is the same type as John Beckett.'

But John was right to point out that the government's failure was not due to Labour's lack of an outright majority. Theoretically, the Conservatives and Liberals could combine and muster 320 votes, enough to vote out the Labour government with 287. The reality, though, was that nothing of the kind was going to happen. The Liberals had been wounded by their poor showing in the election and their relegation to the status of third party, and did not want to precipitate an early election. In any case they had produced a programme to deal with unemployment which involved public works on a huge scale, so they could hardly have opposed radical measures on unemployment if MacDonald had been inclined to introduce them.

Conservative leader Stanley Baldwin studiously avoided criticising the government too much, to the evident irritation of many Conservatives, and he was severely weakened by internal divisions. At by-elections the government had the benefit of a divided and ineffective opposition, because the press lords put up Empire Free Trade candidates against official Conservatives. The government had the general support of two Irish members, two independents and some of the Liberals, and might even have survived a combined attack by the Conservatives and Liberals, in the unlikely event that such an attack was launched. As Roy Jenkins writes in his biography of Baldwin, 'The MacDonald government, despite its many faults and vicissitudes, was left almost miraculously free from strong and sustained attack by its principal opponent.'

John bought (or, probably, rented) one of a group of splendid old houses in Lincoln's Inn which were pulled down in the 1930s. He possessed a rare panelled room which had survived the great fire of London, and had it carefully restored and redecorated. Within walking distance of Fleet Street, the House of Commons, and the West End, it became a meeting place for journalists and left-wing politicians. Guests regularly included John Wheatley and James Maxton, the miners' leader Arthur Cook, William Mellor, editor of the *Daily Herald*, and Stanley Baldwin's son, the left-wing Labour MP Oliver Baldwin.

He saw a good deal of the left's new rising star, Aneurin Bevan. But John failed to persuade him to throw in his lot with the ILP, although Bevan often voted with them. He put this down to Bevan's weakness: 'He is too honest to see eye to eye with the powers which could give him the political recognition his abilities deserve, and too lazy and comfortable to break away.'

Among Labour MPs, only his own group of rebels, and those close to the rebels, dared to be seen with him. Old friends such as Attlee and Dalton were lost. But like many MPs who are political lepers in their own parties, he started to make friends among the rebels of other parties. They felt something of his impatience with the old leaders such as MacDonald and Baldwin, who belonged to the world before the Great War. New friends included W. E. D. Allen, Ulster Unionist MP and, though John did not know it, an MI5 agent, who was to play a crucial part in his future. Leslie Hore-Belisha became a regular visitor to his flat, and John wrote in 1938: 'It seemed obvious that the heights he could ascend would be restricted only by the extent to which he could mask his enormous personality and intelligence and uproot the social sense he showed in his early political days.' The year after John wrote that, in 1939, his fascist friends targeted Hore-Belisha at the War Office because he was a Jew.

But for the moment, only one of all these men mattered. John Wheatley was John's new leader. Wheatley, with John Beckett at his side, was going to lead the nation to socialism.

Wheatley was respected, but not liked. People thought him cold and calculating. He was the opposite of the career politician whom John had grown to despise. He entirely lacked Hugh Dalton's easy familiarity, and could not pretend to a friendship he did not feel. His eyesight was so bad that he was unable to recognise people unless they hailed him. The way to popularity and success in the parliamentary Labour Party, then as now, was, as John put it, 'by an almost repulsive indulgence in affectionate and usually meaningless camaraderie'. Wheatley 'had everything necessary to a great statesman except the ability to seek friendship or tolerate fools gladly'.

In the twelve months after the 1929 election, Wheatley became a close friend. The left-wing Scottish elder statesman of 60 and the London firebrand of 35 dined together, and planned ILP tactics, every week during the winter of 1929–30, either in John's flat or in a favourite Soho restaurant of Wheatley's. John never, for the rest of his life, talked of this friend with anything other than respect.

'Wheatley's only fanatical belief was that hardship and suffering in Britain should be regarded as criminally wasteful and unnecessary,' he wrote. 'His mind was full of plans for the creation of an effective opposition to the existing palsied leadership.'

To John – and to no one else – Wheatley confided his real view of his friend Maxton, as a good and brave man who could not lead an effective political movement. John persuaded Wheatley that what was needed was a new political party – an organised party, not a loose association. Wheatley took that message back to the sceptical Maxton, and with some difficulty persuaded him.

This strange triangle – Wheatley and John Beckett in London, Wheatley and Jimmy Maxton in Glasgow – decided that the ILP was to be transformed into a new political party, to do all the things they had dreamed of, and to replace the Labour Party. In 1929 John believed firmly that Wheatley, with himself at his side, was going to lead Britain to the new Jerusalem. The exciting times of 1920 had come again.

They planned the new party in detail. They also planned ways in which to asset-strip the Communist Party, bringing its best people over to the ILP – an ambition which has a sad irony to it, because what actually happened in the 1930s was that the Communist Party asset-stripped and destroyed the ILP.

As part of the plan, Wheatley stood for the National Administrative Council (NAC) of the ILP – its ruling body – at the ILP Easter conference. He had left the NAC some years before. During the conference he was taken ill, but returned to London the next week, and dined with John on Tuesday evening.

'He was full of plans for re-organisation,' John recalled, 'and we spent several hours checking over the details of a number of schemes he intended taking to the NAC to put into immediate operation. On Wednesday he returned home, and on Friday we heard of his death.'

That night John travelled to Glasgow for the funeral with fellow London MP W. J. Brown. They were met at the station in the early morning by Jimmy Maxton and David Kirkwood. John joined the funeral procession and later spoke with Maxton at 'Wheatley' meetings in Manchester and Liverpool. But the bottom had fallen out of his life. He had no sense of direction any more:

> We talked of the necessity for carrying on the work that Wheatley had left to our hand, and for a short time that thought did have an inspiring effect upon many, but in our hearts we knew that it could not be done. We were the men with whom Wheatley might have built civilisation in Britain, but without him we could only hope to fight on, whatever the consequences might be.
>
> On Maxton's frail shoulders had fallen the sole burden of leadership, and I saw much of him at that time. I have never associated with a kinder, more impeccably honest, loyal and courageous man. But he is without ambition, has no patience for detail, and a queer philosophy adapted to his inherent laziness which makes him an impossible leader for any movement. He himself denounces leadership, claiming that he has no right to make up people's minds for them. His politics are socialist, but his habits of thought and temperament are completely anarchist.

Wheatley, says Maxton's latest biographer, Gordon Brown, 'was the thinker and strategist, Maxton, sixteen years younger, the popular leader and orator'. As Hugh Dalton smugly confided to his diary: 'The death of Wheatley will make some difference to the left I think. They will be like sheep without a shepherd.'

John was now the most disliked man in Westminster. Everyone loved Maxton, and some of the other Clydesiders, especially George Buchanan, but John made no attempt to hide that his own strategies caused them embarrassment in their constituencies. It was not in his character to hide his cleverness, even if it would only make him enemies. It had been his task, as ILP whip, to confront fellow Labour MPs with their own cowardice, and he had done it not always wisely, but always thoroughly. He did not spare the feelings of those he felt had behaved badly. He was 'the least likeable of the ILP Members', according to future Labour minister George Strauss, and Fenner Brockway told me: 'The Labour leadership wanted John out more than they wanted any of the rest of us out, because he denounced them in more violent terms than the rest of us.'

He had gambled everything on Wheatley, and Wheatley was gone. There was no hope, nor any way back that he could see. It was, literally, a matter of fighting on, and damning the consequences. He no longer thought he had anything to lose.

The Labour Party machine was fighting back. It was starting to undermine the ILP members in their constituencies, getting loyal MPs to hector them in the corridors of the House of Commons, and even denying them a hearing inside the chamber. ILP members found it increasingly hard to get replies to supplementary questions and opportunities in debate. Ministers were able deliberately to ignore their questions; backbenchers produced inspired interruptions to get ministers off the hook when ILP members tried to press their point; and the Speaker generally made sure that John did not catch his eye, so much so that at one point an orthodox Labour MP, John's former friend Seymour Cocks, rose to ask whether 'it is in order for anyone else to be heard except the Member for Peckham'.

While Wheatley lived, it was all bearable. John believed that one day, under Wheatley's leadership, they would triumph. Suddenly, there was nothing left in the world except gestures. Wheatley died on 12 May 1930. By the end of July, John had seized the Mace of the House of Commons – the first person to touch it since Oliver Cromwell – and made for the gentleman's lavatory; and he had married Kyrle Bellew in a sudden and widely publicised ceremony in Gretna Green just three days after his divorce from Helen became absolute. It was like pouring petrol over a political career and putting a match to it.

He contrived to have the most sensational marriage of the year, and it helped make him, for a while, one of the best known politicians in Britain. He later told me how it happened.

He and Kyrle had always intended to marry as soon as his divorce from Helen became absolute. The two of them were driving to Glasgow with Jimmy Maxton and George Buchanan (presumably on one of the many trips they made to ensure that John Wheatley's parliamentary seat fell into the right hands.)

At Gretna Green, they stopped for coffee, or so John thought. But as he got out of the car he found Kyrle at his side and the pavement full of photographers. The staff at Gretna Green were expecting them. Kyrle, Maxton and Buchanan had planned the wedding for that day, as a surprise for John. Maxton and Buchanan were the witnesses, Maxton acting as best man. They must have thought it would please John. It probably did. It also helped to finish him, and surely old political hands like Maxton and Buchanan must have predicted that too.

Then, on 17 July, came the Mace episode, which earned him instant fame and a permanent footnote in history. The mace is an important parliamentary symbol. The Serjeant at Arms solemnly bears it in to the Commons before each sitting, and carries it out afterwards. The actions of the House have no legal validity when it is not there, and to handle it is sacrilege.

One ILP colleague, W. J. Brown, had failed to get any information out of the Home Secretary on the matter of a child of eight who was apparently ordered to be birched by a court. Another, Fenner Brockway, pressed the Prime Minister for an answer on the matter of the imprisonment in India of Gandhi, Nehru and 6,000 Indian Congressmen. Getting no answer, Brockway refused to sit down. He was, inevitably, 'named' by the Speaker, and the Prime Minister moved his suspension from the House.

In the division on Brockway's suspension, only the ILP group supported him. The ILP therefore had to nominate two tellers for the vote, and they put up John and W. J. Brown. As the tellers walked up to the Speaker's table, John told Brown he intended to take the Mace away in protest. Brown wished him luck, and said that he could not himself risk suspension because he had an important meeting with the Chancellor of the Exchequer that afternoon on a matter concerning civil servants, whose trade union he represented.

Brown and Beckett reached the table and Beckett shouted: 'Mr Speaker, these proceedings are a disgrace.' Then he picked up the Mace, and almost fell over. The Serjeant at Arms carried it as though it were very heavy, so John was braced for a considerable burden. The Mace turned out to be no heavier than an umbrella. 'It was as hollow as the proceedings over which it presided,' he wrote afterwards. Recovering his balance, he put it on his shoulder, turned on his heel and walked out of the chamber.

He had rather expected to be relieved of his burden very quickly. In fact, the 30 or so Members at the Bar of the House parted to let him through, and roared their disapproval as he did so. He found himself in the Inner Lobby, wondering what to do with his trophy. He decided to take it to the gents, 'and place its head in one of the magnificent porcelain receptacles' to be found there. But at last, two large attendants arrived, and he was relieved of his burden.

'What in the world was the idea, John?' asked Brockway as the two men were escorted through New Palace Yard by the police. John replied, 'It came to me suddenly – the House is in session only when the Mace is on the table. If I could get away with it, they couldn't suspend you.'

Years later, Brockway told historian Colin Holmes: 'I was a bit annoyed about the Mace, felt he had destroyed the dignity of the protest and its purpose. He revelled in the incident. Chuckled hard as the police sergeant escorted us out.' In his autobiography Brockway says:

I first met Beckett in the years immediately after the war; he was organising the National Union of Ex-Servicemen on a socialist and anti- war basis in opposition to the British Legion, and I was able to help him by introducing a number of subscribers who contributed generously. Despite his subsequent political development, I have a friendly memory of earlier association with Beckett and particularly of the motive which led him to run away with the Mace.

This is a remarkably generous assessment given the rubbish John was talking – just how long could he expect to delay Brockway's suspension?

Of course, John's motives were not that simple, and it is doubtful whether he himself ever quite understood them. He told Brockway part of the truth. There was also despair in the gesture. Then, too, there was probably some truth in the accusation, most pointedly levelled by Ellen Wilkinson, that it was publicity-seeking. She wrote in the *Daily Mail* four years later (on 22 November 1935): 'The time for the P. G. Wodehouse "silly ass" member is surely gone. The man who wants to carry off the Mace or do a tribal dance before the Speaker to call attention to himself will meet with cold contempt from those of us who have been very close to grim reality in the Distressed Areas during the election.' This, as it happens, was the only mention of the Distressed Areas in the article, the rest of it being on such vital matters as the advantages of knowing when to bow to the Speaker.

He told me about it, when I was quite a young child, and I asked, more for something to say than anything else, 'So why did you do it?' He laughed his loud, sudden, cracked laugh and said, 'Sheer bloody bravado.' And that was part of it too.

When I met Brockway in 1981, he took me to the splendid bar near the terrace of the House of Lords and told the barman: 'Give this man a very large whisky. His father and I were thrown out of this place together.' (A lifelong teetotaller, Brockway had discovered the joys of whisky in his eighties.) He told me that John Beckett had been his closest friend throughout the 1929–31 Parliament. 'He left his mark on this place, even if it was more of a streak. He wasn't really a socialist – he was a rebel. I was attracted by the rebel in him.' When I told him my father had left an unpublished autobiography, he was very concerned to know what John had written about him, and offered to write an introduction to it for publication once he had read it. (He never did read it. I checked the references to him and decided against showing it to him – a very stupid decision.) Despite everything that had happened, John's good opinion still mattered to him. Brockway seems always to have been inclined to generosity where John was concerned. He also told Holmes: 'He was loveable in his utter devotion. He might have become a great personal force and it was sad to see him wasted.'

But wasted he certainly was. Only six MPs voted against his suspension, though many more voted against Brockway's. He had provided the Party leadership with an excuse to target him which most of his parliamentary colleagues were prepared to support, and the leadership seized on it. The very next day, Labour Party secretary Arthur Henderson told the Party's national executive that John's action 'had brought discredit on the Parliamentary Labour Party and had constituted a gross affront to parliament'.

Henderson also drew the NEC's attention to 'the unsatisfactory voting record of Mr Beckett'. There were reports that he was raising money to run socialist candidates against official Labour candidates at the next election. The committee decided to discuss with the ILP the problem of this increasingly impossible MP. John defended himself in the ILP publication, *The New Leader*. The protest was, he wrote, more successful than he could have dreamed:

The Press, usually blissfully oblivious of the sayings of dissatisfied Labour men, have been good enough to draw the attention of some millions of people to Parliament's disgraceful time-wasting.

For 14 months Parliament has been a grotesque and self-righteous orgy of useless point-scoring. Unemployment steadily grows, wages steadily fall. Armaments are increased and the intensification of British imperial tyranny goes on ... We cling without dignity or decency to office barren of power or prestige. The present government, with the support of the Liberal and Tory leaders, deliberately prevents the socialist viewpoint being put forward in the House. There is time for hours of backchat between Snowden and Churchill.

Time for voting huge sums of money for war. Time for ... endless ceremonials and bowing and scraping. Time for a summer holiday nearly three months long. No time for socialist motions or supplementaries on working class questions ...

Parliament may have been affronted, but Peckham seems to have been delighted. Two hastily summoned, but packed, public meetings cheered him to the rooftops, and a specially called meeting of the Peckham Labour Party passed a unanimous vote of congratulation. Fred Brooks wrote to me: 'It was a dramatic gesture of protest against the almost total lack of commitment by the government to the plight of the unemployed ... It won support and admiration from the people he had been sent to represent.'

It did not change the course of the government, though. The same month that Wheatley died and John stole the Mace, May 1930, the government threw out Sir Oswald Mosley's famous memorandum on unemployment, and Mosley resigned and published it. It called for a programme of public investment, protection of British industry with tariffs, an end to the export of capital for investment overseas, and a major programme of public works (which Lloyd George and the Liberals had advocated during the 1929 election).

Mosley spent the summer canvassing support for his proposals among MPs. John on his own account stayed aloof, sharing Maxton's distrust both of Mosley himself and of the proposals. John was certainly not among Mosley's supporters, although on 1 August 1930 Dalton wrote in his diary, rather bewilderingly: 'Beckett – Sandham – Mosley. The Posing Peacocks and the Booby. But against the Tired Timidity of Leaders, not a quite unnatural foreground.'

Nonetheless, John followed carefully the events which led to Mosley forming the New Party, which eventually became the British Union of Fascists. Strangely, given what was to happen later, John was not an admirer of Mosley. He thought him a spoiled young careerist, with more money and ego than sense, the sort of rich young aristocrat who impressed snobs like MacDonald but whom real socialists, like himself and Maxton, regarded with amused disdain.

He reports the formation of the New Party with a sort of disdainful irony which reads strangely in the light of what he himself did three years later. The New Party, on John's account, started 'in the fertile brain of W. J. Brown'. Brown was the ILP man who had been the other teller when John stole the Mace. He was secretary of the Civil Servants Association and an ILP loyalist. A small, delicate, fair man with a quick mind, John thought him the most stimulating conversationalist he had known, but did not take him seriously. 'The intense conviction with which he feels any idea which occurs to him during conversation makes him almost irresistible, but one yields to his arguments on Monday only to give him the trouble, on Wednesday, sincerely and convincingly of showing how wrong a view one holds.' So 'the shrewd laziness of Maxton and our natural iconoclasm usually prevented us from acting on his freely dispensed advice'.

One of the ideas was of a New Party, backed by Mosley, who would provide both the money and the charisma while Brown provided the ideas. Mosley and Brown were encouraged by two ILP men, Oliver Baldwin and Robert Forgan, as well as John Strachey, the old Etonian left-wing Labour MP, and John's Ulster Unionist friend W. E. D. Allen. Only Forgan and Allen were to follow Mosley all the way to fascism, and both were to play a crucial part in eventually recruiting John for that creed. As John was to write:

> There are several versions of the manner in which the debacle happened. The truth is that Mosley, after sitting on the fence for some weeks, declared at a small private gathering his willingness to proceed. Strachey and [Mosley's secretary] at once rushed into print with the news ... W. E. D. Allen resigned at once from the Conservative Party; Oliver Baldwin and Robert Forgan, followed two days later by John Strachey, resigned from the Labour Party; and a large number of Conservative and Labour members who had been hanging around the Mosleys for months rushed into print to say that they had nothing at all to do with it.
>
> Brown said that he could not take part because of the attitude of his union and his inability to forfeit their financial support. Mosley guaranteed him against financial loss, and went with Strachey to interview the union executive, who gave permission for Brown to participate. Brown then went to bed, ill. Mosley and Strachey rushed to Highgate to see him, but he was not well enough to be inter-

Dorothy Salmon, who married William Beckett in 1893, and was declared dead by her orthodox Jewish family for marrying out. This picture was taken in 1930, when she was 60 and already ill with the cancer which was to kill her at 62. (Beckett family)

John Beckett, the youngest Labour MP in 1925. (Beckett family)

Clement Attlee was Mayor of Stepney in 1920 when John Beckett went to live and work with him in Limehouse. (Anne, Countess Attlee.)

John's second political hero, and the only one who really mattered, was John Wheatley, housing minister in the 1924 government, and the real leader of the ILP. His exclusion from Macdonald's second government was 'a declaration of war on the left.' (Beckett family)

Left: John married Helen Shaw in 1920. (Patrick Beckett)
Below left: ... Kyrle Bellew in 1930 ...(Hulton Getty)
Below right: ... and Anne Cutmore in 1938, and again in 1963. (Beckett family)

The actor manager Arthur Bourchier who 'carried aload of debt big enough to over-burden a small nation, and lived in the princeliest style.' He told new directors: 'Now, my bloody boy, I've got seven bloody tricks, let me do those and I'll do everything else you say.' (Hulton Getty)

Jimmy Maxton, the Clydesiders' passionate and romantic leader and John's third political hero. But 'Maxton failed, as he was bound to fail in a crisis, because he does not want to lead.' (Hulton Getty)

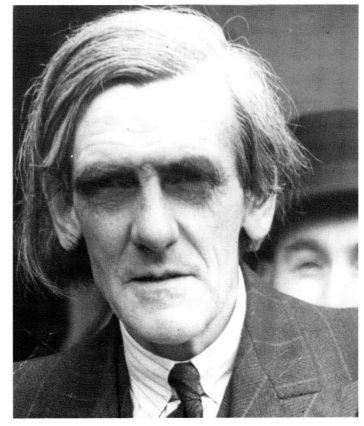

The chairman and secretary of the ILP, James Maxton and John Beckett, escorting their newest and youngest MP, Jennie Lee, on her first day at the House of Commons in 1930. The picture is in Jenny Lee's autobiography with a caption referring only to herself and Maxton: the large figure in the foreground is left unexplained. (Beckett family)

SCHOOLMISTRESS OF THE FUTURE (reading):
"SO, WITHOUT ANY OF THE DIGNITY OF THE GREAT CROMWELL, THE RUDE SOCIALIST PICKED UP THE DEAR MACE AND MADE OFF TO THE DOOR." —AND WHAT HAPPENED THEN, CHILDREN?"

JOHNNY: "PLEASE, MISS, PLAY WAS THEN CLOSED ON ACCOUNT OF THE BAD LIGHT."

Above: The cartoonist Low in Punch magazine on the removal of the mace. Ramsay Macdonald (head on table) and Philip Snowden were just as outraged as Low makes them look.

Right: An undistinguished stage career. John on tour in Treasure Island, in striped headscarf, as Honest Tom Watkins, with Vernon Fortescue. (Patrick Beckett)

Above: With his daughter Lesley about 1931. (Patrick Beckett)
Below: Open air meeting in the east end. (Beckett family)

1936: speaking in the east end for the fascist candidates in the London County Council elections. (Beckett family)

The Leader. "In every county are several dozen Mosley fans and whenever he speaks within 50 miles of them, they are harried by paid organisers sent on ahead, and pressed to collect parties and 'get there somehow' ... A far stronger brain than poor Tom's might well fail after five years' food for the ego of this description." (Friends of Oswald Mosley)

Left: William Joyce, later Lord Haw Haw.

Right: The Duke of Bedford, chairman of the British Peoples Party. (Beckett family)

Left: A. K. Chesterton in 1955, in Dublin to meet Otto Strasser, a former leading Nazi who had broken with Hitler in 1933. (Hutton Getty)

Right: With the author, in Pagham in 1949. (Beckett family)

Right: With the author's younger brother, mid 1950s. (Beckett family)

Left: Early 1950s. (Beckett family)

Below: The last friend. Fr Brendan Fox, at the head of the table, rubs his hands in the way he always did. Mid 1950s, John is second from left. (Beckett family)

viewed at any length. Mosley then broke down, and the new movement was ushered in with little welcome from its leaders and
inspirers. Mosley retired to bed in Smith Square the day after Brown
retired to his bed in Highgate.

... It is a queer system which drives men of honesty and independence of character to a hopeless and slightly ridiculous mutiny as
the only alternatives to the perorations of a MacDonald and the
narrow cunning of a Baldwin.

* * *

When Lord Rothermere's newspapers printed endless horror stories of
people getting a few shillings from the dole to which they were not enti-
tled, the ever impressionable MacDonald began talking of married women
turning up to collect dole in fur coats; and in 1931 the government
produced an Anomalies Bill in order, they said, to prevent abuses.

The ILP harried the bill unmercifully in an all- night session, nine ILP
MPs including John keeping the House in session until 10 a.m. the
following morning. John spoke with bitterness of his oldest friend in politics, Clem Attlee. In those early days in Limehouse, he wrote, 'it would have
seemed impossible to me that a kind, gentle, loveable man might be so
corrupted by the Parliamentary system that he could represent the people
of the abyss and yet vote for two shillings a week for their children; and
support the Anomalies Act, which swept them away from their meagre dole
like flies.' Attlee says in his autobiography that the ILP 'became more and
more irresponsible under the leadership of Jimmy Maxton'.

Unemployment rose from 1,630,000 in June 1929 to 1,912,000 in June
1930. Well before the end of the year it had topped the two million mark
and rising (it reached three million by the time the government fell.) By
now pretty well everyone shared John's low opinion of Jimmy Thomas,
who had been given the task of solving the problem. He was disintegrating
before his colleagues' eyes. A man who owed his political career to his
superficial joviality, he was petrified by the enormity of the task, and was
drinking too much and offering nothing but trite pieces of homespun
wisdom.

In the first few months of 1931 the financial situation grew worse
almost by the minute. British banks had taken short-term loans from the
U.S.A. and France, and lent to Germany at higher rates of interest. When

the German banks failed, they were left deeply in debt to the French and the Americans. By February Philip Snowden was telling the House of Commons: 'The national position is so grave that drastic and disagreeable measures will have to be taken.' Labour MPs knew he meant a reduction in unemployment pay.

The next month MacDonald set up a committee chaired by Sir George May, secretary of the Prudential Insurance Company, to recommend 'all possible reductions in national expenditure'.

In July there was a flight from the pound. That month also saw John's worst and most violent parliamentary scene. John McGovern, who had succeeded Wheatley as MP for Glasgow Shettleston, was, like John, fundamentally a rebel rather than a socialist. He came to the House one day burning with indignation about the harsh treatment apparently handed out to some lay preachers arrested for preaching on Glasgow Green without a licence.

McGovern, together with Maxton and the other Clydesiders, urged the Scottish Secretary to use his power to release the men. When they failed to get the undertaking they sought, McGovern refused to sit down. Ordered to leave, he again refused, and the Speaker had to despatch four attendants to remove him. There was then a pretty undignified scuffle. If you read John's account next to McGovern's, it looks like two quite different incidents. But it seems certain that McGovern wedged his feet into the paper rack on the seat in front, in order to form a lock, while Maxton, Beckett and some other ILP MPs prevented the attendants from reaching him. Maxton was knocked flying into the seats in front of him, and either John or McGovern knocked at least one of the attendants after him.

In the end, the honourable member for Peckham and the honourable member for Glasgow Shettleston were frog-marched out together, two attendants to each, holding their arms pinioned behind their backs while a Mr Rosbotham, Labour MP for Ormskirk, seized the chance to punch John in the face. The sitting was suspended owing to 'grave disorder'.

What on earth prompted John to get involved in this mess? He knew nothing at all about preachers on Glasgow Green. It was the sort of Scottish issue which a wise London MP would have stayed well clear of, and McGovern had given his colleagues no indication of what he intended to do. John knew little about McGovern, though he must by then have realised that this was not a man of the intellectual or moral quality of Wheatley and Maxton.

For John, however, the Clydesiders now represented the only decent force in Parliament. He always had to have people in whom he believed absolutely, who were right even when they were wrong. He needed someone to receive his absolute loyalty.

The Anomolies Bill was to be introduced the next week – the one bill they were most determined to fight – and their escapade seemed destined to ensure that they would be suspended and unable to take part in the debate. So Maxton immediately went into a series of meetings with Party leaders and the Speaker. John had a caravan beside the Thames at Hurley, and it was there that he, Maxton, McGovern and the rest met to decide what to do. MacDonald had told Maxton that, if he would agree to exemplary punishment for Beckett and McGovern, no action would be taken against anyone else. John wrote: 'As Maxton is the only political leader I ever met who was not anxious to pass responsibility to his followers in any moment of pressure, it never occurred to any of us that this offer should be taken seriously.'

Their apologies, every word of which had to be agreed by the Speaker, were grovelling. It was the bitterest medicine John had yet swallowed. But it was the price of being there for the Anomolies Bill, and listening, as John put it, to 'speech after speech telling of some Labour MP's relative or friend who knew someone else who had heard of a man who drew ten shillings a week in unemployment benefit when he actually did weekend work and earned a few shillings as well'. Maxton called the bill 'a surrender in the face of one of the meanest, ill-natured agitations that have ever taken place by the rich against the worst defences of the poor'.

John planned a strategy for the committee stage which he reckoned would enable the ILP group, now reinforced by Sir Charles Trevelyan who had resigned as Education Minister, to keep the House up all night. Trevelyan and others were sceptical. The Irish republicans, with all their experience of holding up the work of Parliament, advised that it needed more MPs than the ILP could muster. John wrote triumphantly afterwards:

The committee stage began at 3.45 p.m. and we kept the House going until just after 10 a.m. on the following morning. Nine of us made over 100 speeches, and there were over 40 divisions. No disorder of any kind took place. But every member of our small group worked in an orderly, disciplined manner, taking advantage of every legitimate parliamentary trick to embarrass the government.

The bill went through, and Parliament broke up for the summer. MPs went on their holidays, not knowing that this summer vacation was to be like no other, and that before they returned after their break the government would have fallen. John and Jimmy Maxton had planned a family holiday in John's caravan at Hurley, with John's daughter Lesley, Maxton's two sisters, and Maxton's young son Jimmy who, since the death of Maxton's wife, had lived with his sisters. It was a calm and comfortable few days beside the Thames, and neither man could have known that it was the last they were to have together with the same easy comradeship.

On 1 August the May Committee report was published. Sir George May said that the only possible solution was to save £97 million of national expenditure by cutting unemployment benefit and teachers' and police salaries by twenty per cent.

MacDonald and Snowden published the report without comment or policy statement, then went on holiday. Throughout August the drift from sterling accelerated, and the bandwagon for cutting unemployment pay, propelled by the newspapers, the banks and the Conservatives, rapidly became unstoppable.

There were, as the ILP pointed out publicly and some cabinet ministers pointed out privately, other ways in which the required savings could be made, without causing the hardship and bitterness among the poorest and lowest paid that May's proposals would entail. John's preference, typically, was to take it from the repayments of war loans – the money that those with capital had lent the nation in order to fight the First World War, and which was being repaid at a generous rate of interest. 'A cut of one per cent in war loan interest would solve the whole problem,' he said. The TUC wanted at least some of it to come from those who lived on investments or on property. They thought the rich ought to pay as well as the poor – including the city financiers, whose greedy strategy had collapsed, and who had then run to the government to demand that the unemployed and public servants should pay the price.

'The General Council are pigs,' said Sidney Webb to his wife Beatrice. 'They won't agree to any cuts of unemployment insurance benefits or salaries or wages.' But how could he have expected them to do so? The government was proposing the very measures that the TUC had founded the Labour Party to oppose.

By the end of August MacDonald and Snowden were sure that Britain's salvation depended entirely on obtaining a loan from a New

York bank. The bank demanded a ten per cent cut in unemployment pay as the price of a loan. The cabinet turned this down by twelve votes to nine. MacDonald, 'looking scared and unbalanced', according to Harold Nicholson in his biography of George V, went to the palace to advise the king to summon the other Party leaders. But Baldwin and acting Liberal leader Sir Herbert Samuel (Lloyd George was ill) believed the best solution was a National Government consisting of all three parties and led by MacDonald. If unpopular measures hurting Labour's natural constituency were to be introduced, it would be convenient to have Labour implicated. MacDonald put up a token resistance to the flattering idea that he was the indispensable man, and on 24 August told the cabinet that he 'could not refuse the king's request' to lead the new National Government.

For a few days John thought this just might be the moment they had waited for. Surely their old colleagues would now see that the ILP had been right all along? If that happened, then there would be no need of the new party he and Wheatley had planned just a year ago. The Labour Party could itself be made into the instrument which changed the world. He kept in close touch with Maxton and the Clydesiders in Glasgow, and Brockway in London, and established that the ILP would work with the Labour Party, without recriminations, if Labour would work with them.

But as soon as the Parliamentary Labour Party met with trade union leaders also present, it was clear that there was no chance of this. According to Gordon Brown, 'At the very moment when Maxton and the ILP could have seized leadership positions in the Labour hierarchy he chose to stand aloof ... Maxton misread the signs and was unable to grasp the opportunities presented to the ILP to recover its leadership of the Labour Movement.' Yet it is not as simple as that. Brown seems to suggest that a place on Labour's front bench was Maxton's for the asking, and perhaps even the leadership. But when Labour MPs met on 28 August, according to John's account:

Maxton's conciliatory speech was violently interrupted from its beginning, and a bitter attack upon us as the root of the trouble, made by an ex-cabinet minister, was roundly cheered. This minister was known to have hung about Downing Street for several hours in a fruitless attempt to see MacDonald after the dismissal of the Labour government, and the burden of his argument was that had we not criticised the Prime Minister so rudely he would not have left the Labour Party.

Sadly he does not name the minister, and there is no reference to this speech or to Maxton's in the fullest account we have on this meeting (in Hugh Dalton's diary.) However, the reference is probably to Herbert Morrison, who is known to have tried to get a job in MacDonald's new Conservative-dominated National government.

Still, Maxton could at least have stood for the now vacant leadership. In the event, 68-year-old Arthur Henderson was elected unopposed as Labour leader. At the meeting of the PLP, according to Dalton's diary, just five votes were cast against Henderson: Maxton, Beckett and three other ILP Scots – George Buchanan, Campbell Stephen and Jennie Lee. These were pointless votes, because they had no alternative candidate. No one, on either side, was going to forget and forgive. As John wrote bitterly:

Now the whole pack was in full cry. Here was an enemy upon which they could concentrate their chagrin at the early prospect of losing a general election. Arthur Cook tried to speak, and was threatened with physical violence. I succeeded in making a short speech pointing out that more important things remained to be done than to split the Party still further. A gentleman chiefly prominent for his ability to guess by which door any cabinet minister might be leaving, in order that he might open it, was so enraged that he rushed towards me, and when he was safely restrained by two colleagues, threatened violence.

The last six weeks I spent in the House were among the most miserable I had experienced. Until the last few days, the Labour Members believed that if only they did not oppose the National Government too strongly, there would be no general election, and daily they crawled past their lost leader in mute homage, uttering pleas for forgiveness because he had deserted them.

Mr Snowden, addressing the House one afternoon, paused for a few moments to survey the Labour benches thoroughly, and then remarked: 'I sat with my back to you for many years. Had I seen you as thoroughly as I do now I face you, it would not have been so long.' We sat on the benches below the gangway, and were able to watch the sickly and servile titters with which Labour Members greeted this.

Stripped of its bitterness, expressed here in John's usual pungent and unrestrained language, how honest is his record? John's account of that meeting of MPs, published here for the first time, has hardly anything in common with the only other version we have, which is Dalton's. The events reported by both of them probably occurred. It is their selection, and the flavour they attach to it, that makes the difference.

Most of John's charges, in fact, and also Maxton's, can be seen, seven decades later, to be accurate. Labour MPs knew that MacDonald had it in his power to destroy their careers by calling an early election, in which many of them would lose their seats. They also knew that there was very little difference between the policies MacDonald was now pursuing, and the policies he had previously pursued with their support. If MacDonald's policies were a betrayal, then they were all guilty.

There are very few Labour people who come out of the 1931 crisis with any credit at all. Jimmy Maxton, John Beckett and their friends may not have handled themselves with much political skill, but they were consistent and they were honest.

Lingering hopes that MacDonald might not call a snap election were swiftly dashed. The government secured the American loan; went off the gold standard which it had been formed to safeguard; and, of course, made the reductions in unemployment benefit and public service pay which MacDonald's Labour colleagues had refused to make. Then, six weeks after he had formed his National Government, MacDonald dissolved Parliament for an election.

The public had been badly scared, and with some justice blamed the incompetence of the Labour government. The fact that the two chief figures in that government were Prime Minister and Chancellor of the Exchequer in the National Government mattered little, because now they stood alongside the reassuring figures of Stanley Baldwin and the Liberal Herbert Samuel.

The Labour Party's first concern seemed to be to get its ILP rebels in line. Maxton and others were sent a form to sign, promising not to vote against the whips under any circumstances. Most of them refused to sign it. They were therefore denied endorsement as Labour candidates.

One of them was never sent a form. John Beckett was not even to be given this last chance to redeem himself. The Labour leadership was determined that, whatever the fate of Maxton and the rest, Beckett at least was to be got rid of.

Peckham Labour Party nominated John enthusiastically. But on nomination day they discovered that Labour Party headquarters had declared a Captain Beaumont, someone of whom they had never heard, to be the Labour candidate for Peckham. It turned out that the London Labour Party – then as now the most conspiratorial of bodies – had organised a secret meeting of five local members, together with Lewis Silkin, who had lost the nomination to John for the 1929 election. They announced their nomination of Captain Beaumont, and Transport House declared them to be Peckham's official Labour Party. A MacDonald National Labour candidate was also nominated.

Although other ILP MPs were refused endorsement, only John Beckett and John McGovern were actually opposed by official Labour candidates. This was partly because they were the two who were most hated. But there seems to have been a more cynical calculation. It was no good opposing Maxton and George Buchanan – they would easily hold their Glasgow seats against anyone. And there was no need to oppose the ILP MPs in English seats – they were likely to lose anyway, given that the tide was running against Labour. But Beckett and McGovern seemed likely to win if they were left alone. Should the Labour vote be split, there was a reasonable chance that the Conservative could win.

John had no money to fight the election. Since Captain Beaumont was the official Labour candidate, it was against their own rules for trade union branches to finance John's campaign, though they refused to finance Beaumont's campaign. John, who knew a thing or two about the law of libel, wrote afterwards: 'The origin of the £600 with which Captain Beaumont's expenses were paid is still a close secret. He told me that he was not a man of means, and his expenses were being paid for him. His only constant supporter was Mr Silkin, who succeeded him in the candidature when the unpleasantness of the campaign was over.' It need only be added that Lewis Silkin, a wealthy lawyer and a friend and colleague of John's old enemy Herbert Morrison, became at the next general election the Labour MP for Peckham.

To add to John's troubles, the communists decided to devote all their considerable energies in London to ensuring that he was not returned. His views were closer to theirs than those of any other London Labour candidate, and that was why they opposed him so fiercely. The Communist Party in 1931 believed that its first duty was to destroy other people and parties of the left, because they competed with it for the allegiance of the working class. It is an absurd and self-defeating way to behave, but it is the way in which several left-wing groups, such the Socialist Workers Party 50 years later, buried and destroyed the ideals for which they fought.

Their main tactic was to destroy John's meetings. They would turn up en masse where he was due to speak, and sing and chant to prevent him from doing so.

For John this was another staging post on the road to fascism. His response was to organise a defence force and to put in charge of it a well-known local boxer. It was the first sight in British politics of the type of bodyguards for which, within three years, Sir Oswald Mosley was to become notorious.

For the last time, John threw his hurricane-like energy and imagination into a furious parliamentary campaign, hampered as never before by lack of funds. His supporters seemed sure of winning right up to the declaration, but John sensed victory slipping from his grasp in the final three days.

The Conservative, Viscount Borodaile received 19,458 votes to John's 11,217. The MacDonald Labour candidate received 1,442, beating Labour's official nominee, Captain Beaumont, into fourth place with 1,350. The turnout was low, and John was sure that, without the issue being confused by the intervention of two other Labour candidates, he would have won. As it was, he wrote bitterly, 'The machine had triumphed, and although it was a Pyrrhic victory, the Labour Party had the satisfaction of seeing Peckham represented once again by an orthodox Party man instead of a socialist.'

The National Government returned to Parliament with 556 seats and a majority of 500 over all opposition parties. Labour won just 46 seats. It was the most crushing defeat imaginable for a Party which, just two years earlier, had become the largest in the House of Commons. Of the ILP rebels, only Maxton, McGovern and George Buchanan remained in Parliament. Of John's list of 53 Labour MPs who had voted against the 1929 government, only nine were left. Labour's leadership was decimated. Its leader Arthur Henderson lost his seat, along with a huge swathe of his colleagues, including Herbert Morrison and Hugh Dalton. Veteran left-winger George Lansbury, who had made his peace with Labour's leadership a few years previously and was now 72, became leader, and the only other survivor with any ministerial experience, Clement Attlee, who had become Post-master General just five months before the Labour government collapsed, became deputy leader.

It was another thirteen years before Labour was to hold power again. In 1945, led by Attlee, it was elected with an overall majority and for the first time started to implement its own agenda, instead of simply administering that of its opponents.

The game of historical 'what if' is a fascinating one, though not really approved of by academic historians. The 1931 result has provided the material for endless rounds. What if Herbert Morrison, or Hugh Dalton, had held their seats in 1931? Dalton and Morrison tormented themselves with this scenario, probably for the rest of their lives, and their biographers followed them. Either of them, they believed, would have become deputy leader instead of Attlee, and Prime Minister in 1945. Personally, I think they were wrong. Attlee would have beaten either of them.

Another commonly played version is: what if Oswald Mosley had stayed in the Labour Party? Would he not have retained his Birmingham seat and become leader, and Prime Minister in 1945? Again, my own view is: no, Attlee would still have led Labour.

But I have my own version, which I think is more fascinating than the usual questions. What if John Wheatley had lived?

After Wheatley's death, the small ILP parliamentary group began to fall apart, and its parliamentary influence to diminish. By the time the government fell, people like Fenner Brockway – idealists, but practical politicians and democrats too – were beginning to distance themselves from an ILP group which was starting to look increasingly desperate, afloat on stormy seas without a rudder. The group was now the Clydesiders, plus John Beckett.

When the 1931 crisis came, Maxton seems to have been frozen by indecision. Should he try to lead the Labour Party, or forge a new political force out of the ILP? Effectively, he did neither. After the 1931 election, the ILP broke away from the Labour Party and was, within a few years, an irrelevance. Its supporters scattered: John Beckett and Robert Forgan, eventually, to fascism; John Strachey in the direction of the Communist Party. Others, like McGovern and Jennie Lee, stayed in the ILP as it dwindled into an ineffectual fringe, and they eventually rejoined the Labour Party.

If Wheatley had lived, the ILP's nineteen parliamentary rebels would have behaved very differently in the last year of the Labour government. Wheatley demanded, and received, discipline from his followers. He had once reduced Maxton almost to tears for failing to prepare properly for an important meeting. He would never have allowed them to dissipate their energies and credibility in pointless scenes over preachers on Glasgow Green, nor would John Beckett have run away with the Mace.

In Parliament the ILP would have worked in the disciplined manner in which it opposed the Anomolies Bill, and would have avoided the shambolic scenes created by McGovern and Beckett. McGovern, of course, would not have been an MP (he inherited Wheatley's seat) and Beckett would have been Wheatley's loyal and able organiser.

When the crisis came, the ILP would have made itself strong enough outside Parliament to be a real and credible threat to the official Labour Party. It could not have been excluded without real danger. Wheatley would have been a key power-broker after the 1931 election, and quite possibly Labour's leader in preference to George Lansbury.

For John Beckett the difference would have been stark. He would probably have kept his seat in 1931. If not, he would have stayed loyal to Wheatley, and would probably have returned to Parliament at the 1935 election. After 1935, Labour under Attlee extended the hand of friendship towards those rebels who remained, so much so that the ILP's George Buchanan became a minister in 1945. John would have returned to the mainstream of events. After the 1945 general election, he would probably have been awaiting a call from his old friend Clem Attlee to tell him which cabinet post he was getting, instead of being newly released from prison, jobless, destitute, and under conditions which MI5 described, accurately, as house arrest.

CHAPTER SIX

DYING ON STAGE

The election nomination papers in Peckham in 1929 record that John Beckett, Labour candidate, was by profession a theatrical agent. Back in 1925, a young, handsome and glamorous newly elected Labour MP began a love affair with a theatrical profession which was itself entranced by the radical politics of the time. The 1917 Club saw young socialists such as John Beckett and Fenner Brockway forming close friendships with left-wing actors and actresses.

John's first and closest theatrical friend was Arthur Bourchier, one of the last great actor-managers and the lessee of London's Strand Theatre. John drew Bourchier into the work of the Labour Party, persuading him to open the Strand Theatre on Sundays (when it was illegal to perform plays) for Labour meetings which attracted large audiences from all over London. Bourchier drew him into the work of the newly formed Actors Association, an actors' trade union and the predecessor of Equity.

Perhaps because of his friendship with Bourchier, a few months after his election to Parliament John found himself, rather improbably, sharing a platform at Wyndham's Theatre with George Bernard Shaw, the actress Sybil Thorndike, and the Irish author Conal O'Riordan, discussing the real meaning of Shaw's *Major Barbara*.

Somehow the whole thing got on his nerves. He disliked studied theatricality. He was irritated by Shaw, who 'having gained a reputation for wit, suffers agonies in his efforts to retain it.' He thought his audience 'either Hampstead pseudo-intellectual, or the kind of fan which makes itself a pest at theatrical garden parties, and places where there is an opportunity to intrude its petty ego upon hard-working people whom it could not possibly interest'. He loathed 'the air of genteel sympathy with the working classes'. So he made a speech of violent class hatred, designed to irritate both his audience and his hosts (who, he later admitted, had deserved better treatment) and left. He was followed out by a tall, magically good-looking young man who introduced himself as Denis Neilson-Terry, a matinee idol of the day, who had loved the speech. By the evening they were friends. Neilson-Terry, from one of Britain's oldest and most distinguished theatrical families, wanted to make contact with the real world outside the privileged theatrical one in which he had been brought up, and spent long periods in Gateshead with John, meeting miners and Labour Party activists. For John it was a glittering friendship, and when one day someone saw the two of them together and remarked how alike they were in appearance, his cup of happiness overflowed.

Within months John was doing more than moving in theatrical circles. He became Bourchier's partner as promoter of a show at the Strand Theatre, and, still married to Helen though no longer living with her, was having a scandalous semi-public affair with Bourchier's glamorous actress wife Kyrle Bellew. She had starred opposite the great man in many of his later productions, and was much younger than Bourchier but four years older than John.

After Bourchier died in 1927, Kyrle Bellew inherited his lease of the Strand Theatre and John began to take an active part in its management. He also started investing the money he had made with Bourchier, but now without Bourchier's hand to guide him. He invested in *The House of the Arrow* by A. E. W. Mason at the Vaudeville Theatre, and seems to have been involved in every aspect of the production. This is less surprising than might appear: the producer was Kyrle, and it was her first venture outside acting.

For the next four years John and Kyrle must have lived in each other's pockets. He came into her world, increasingly managing as well as publicising her work. She came into his: a long-standing Labour supporter, she was elected as a councillor in Peckham after John became Peckham's MP, and became a loved and admired local figure of whom Peckham Labour Party was exceptionally proud.

John's managerial duties seem to have ranged from helping select Denis Eadie to play the main part, and taking the certified box office returns to Eadie after each performance (stars in those days were paid a guaranteed salary plus a proportion of the gross takings), to comforting and guiding his highly strung leading lady, Valerie Taylor. But after three weeks' run, Eadie died suddenly, and the show was doomed. The next year John was equally involved in *Appearances*, by Garland Anderson, the first play by a black writer to be presented in London

That summer John and Kyrle rented a houseboat near Henley. Paul Robeson stayed one weekend, together with the actor Edmond Gwenn, and they introduced John to a vigorous and exhausting American game called

Bumble-puppy. Robeson was playing Othello in the West End that summer, and the *Daily Mail* – later to endorse Sir Oswald Mosley's fascists – asked his Desdemona, Peggy Ashcroft, what she felt about having to kiss a black man on the stage. Miss Ashcroft treated the question with the contempt it deserved, but her quote was enough for a prurient little news story: 'I consider it a great honour to be acting with Mr Paul Robeson, and any discussion about my kissing and being kissed by him seems merely silly to me. I have thought no more about it than I would have would have done if I had to kiss an Englishman on stage.'

John became a sort of parliamentary spokesman for live theatre, introducing a bill to give local authorities the power to fund the establishment of a local repertory theatre and getting all-party support for it. The government, as is the way with governments, did not allow even so minor a backbench initiative any parliamentary time. When the government introduced legislation to allow Sunday opening of cinemas, he put down an amendment extending this to theatres. But the churches lobbied heavily against this, and it lost in committee by a narrow margin. Speaking to the committee, John noted sardonically that the religious bodies opposing him 'have never spent an effort or bought a stamp to urge parliament to feed their lambs, or to protest against the systematic malnutrition of women and children in a Christian state'. He was right, of course, but the atheist Clem Attlee and the Catholic John Wheatley would have avoided making unnecessary enemies of such powerful organisations.

The campaign brought him into contact with the great comedian Leslie Henson, who lobbied tirelessly for the reform, and Henson became another close theatrical friend. 'Off stage, like most comedians, Leslie is not a very cheerful person,' wrote John. 'A visit to his dressing room after the show is often enough to convince one that life is not worth living.'

Henson became the source of many of those anecdotes which John loved so much and told all his life. Henson, he said, was generous in big things and remarkably mean about small things. He remembered sitting in conferences all morning where everyone, in turn, passed their cigarette cases around the room. Henson's case would not be seen except when, occasionally, he would finish the cigarette he was smoking, glance round the room to see that no case was doing the rounds, then carefully extract one cigarette from a well- filled case and replace it in his pocket. It reminded John, a very heavy smoker and instinctively open-handed, of an old Labour Party friend, the miners' leader Bob Smillie, a pipe smoker who claimed that he never had a decent smoke. When he used his own tobacco, he filled his pipe too loose, and when he used someone else's he filled it too tight.

After losing his seat in 1931, John had more time to devote to the theatre. On the face of it, it was a most enviable existence, far better than the average MP who loses his seat and scratches for a way to make a living. He was an established theatre manager, his wife was a famous actress, they lived in considerable style, and he liked and admired theatre people – so much better and more straightforward than the greasy politicians he had associated with at Westminster. For a while at least a part of him thought that this was how he would spend the rest of his life.

He helped revive Bourchier's Christmas tradition of a production of *Treasure Island*, with Tod Slaughter playing Bourchier's role of Long John Silver and Kyrle as Mrs Hawkins. The show flopped, a backer let them down and disappeared leaving huge bills, and John, Kyrle and Tod Slaughter were pursued by creditors for months afterwards – an unhappy omen for what was to come.

They salvaged something from the wreckage by taking *Treasure Island* on tour with another actor, Vernon Fortescue, as Silver. John managed the tour, and in those weeks, forgetting politics briefly, he was as happy as he had ever been in his life. He loved moving about the country, he was growing to enjoy golf and was able to play (badly) on a different course each week; and he loved the freedom and lack of convention of being among theatre people, so different from the stilted, suspicious company of politicians. He worked hard in the evenings and spent the days on a local golf course.

He even made his first appearance on the professional stage. When some of the cast left and funds were running low, he cast himself as Honest Tom Watkins, who appears in a short scene alone on the island with Silver, refusing to take part in Silver's nefarious plans, announcing his incorruptible honesty, and getting killed after a dramatic struggle. It was a three-minute scene and he loved it, but it taught him that he could never be an actor. This, typically, he put down to the fact that he was a great orator, and the two talents, he decided, were incompatible.

John and Kyrle had a wonderful time on tour, and were able to salvage something of their finances, so a few months later they went on another tour, again with John as manager. They thought that if they did what Bourchier had done, and presented a play as nearly as possible in the way that it had appeared in London's West End, there would be an audience for it.

They learned the hard way that the touring theatre in England was almost dead. For the first five weeks, *Firebird* lost a fortune every week, and John had to decide whether to cut his losses and pay a heavy forfeit to the theatres with which he had contracts. He decided to carry on, but to reduce expenses.

One of the ways of doing this was to take on a small part himself, that of a famous actor who, after a passionate love scene with the heroine, is shot dead. For the second and last time he died on stage. This time his character, conveniently, wore a dinner jacket, so it was a simple matter to play his part, exit, clean the make-up from his face, and go out front to continue the managerial job of counting the house.

Playing the part was less simple. The heroine had to rescue his performance most nights. The heroine, of course, was Kyrle, and she seems to have become irritable as, night after night, he ruined the scene with his stage fright and his inability to remember his lines. On his first night, his nerve and memory failed him so badly that he clung to a balustrade repeating any nonsense that came into his head.

In the summer of 1932 Kyrle, as the proprietor of the Strand Theatre in London's West End, appointed John as its manager. It wasn't an easy assignment. The mortgage on the theatre cost £250 a week to service, an enormous sum in those days which had to be found even if the theatre was shut. The job would have taxed someone who knew the theatre inside out and had an excellent head for business. For John, it was a disaster, not helped by the fact that he had the sort of manner which convinced everyone, including himself, that he knew exactly what he was doing.

His first play, called *Sally Who* and starring Jessie Mathews and Sonny Hale, flopped, despite good notices. It was a poor start, and he felt sad for his two stars as well as himself, but he had to take the show off at the end of June. He had great hopes of a new farce, starring Sydney Howard, but it was not due to open until November, and how was he to fill his theatre during the summer? He found, at a small theatre in a Paris suburb, a Mexican company performing a kind of musical revue. He took to them at once, and, with his usual method of reaching decisions, agreed terms that evening.

It was a terrible mistake, as he must have begun dimly to perceive the very next week when he travelled from London to Newhaven to meet his new company. The American manager with whom he had negotiated turned out to be a casual acquaintance whom the Mexicans had picked up in Paris. None of the rest of the company spoke any English. He had not bargained for them bringing an army of wives, children, relatives, friends, two mothers and one grandmother. Most of the company expected to sleep in the theatre with the baggage, except for the principals who went to the Waldorf Hotel next door, and he had to collect them from their various dugouts and find them digs in and around Covent Garden. He lost three, who emerged the next day from the cellar under the stage. All the financial references they had given him in Paris turned out to be fake; the company possessed no funds whatsoever. John had to advance large sums of money for the production if it was to appear at all.

When they started rehearsing, he realised with horror that, instead of performing the routines which had succeeded in other countries, they were rehearsing entirely new routines they had thought up on the boat across – and the show was due to open the next week.

They must have noticed his growing agitation, because at last their stage manager, with an understanding gleam in his eye, drew John to one side. 'We all most grateful to you, Mr Beckett,' he said. 'All the company wish to show their gratitude. Any lady, any gentleman, show their gratitude, Mr Beckett.'

John had invested too much in his Mexicans to let them fail. He set up a press reception at the Waldorf next door, and was delighted to see some key journalists there. But no Mexicans appeared. At last his assistant came in to say that they were rehearsing a new number they had just thought of, and could not be persuaded to break off. He rushed next door to the theatre and hustled and bullied them into the press conference, but it was too late. The key journalists had left, in a bad temper.

The show was appalling, and the press notices said so. He had the reviews translated to his company the next morning. On the second night, he says, 'They gave one of the most beautiful performances imaginable in a theatre containing 40 people who had paid for their seats and 100 dead-heads whom the box office manager had whipped up to "dress" the house and prevent general recognition that the show was a flop.' After three weeks they took it off. There were still two months of summer to get through.

Now the theatre, and its manager, were in serious trouble. Each morning he crept into the premises by a different route, avoiding creditors and writ servers. Kyrle went to the countryside in what seems to have been some dudgeon, and it may be guessed that she was getting a little impatient with her new manager. John eventually locked up his theatre, wrote a few newspaper articles to provide some sort of income, rented a small country bungalow, and retreated there to await November and Sydney Howard's farce.

Then he heard that Howard had been taken seriously ill, and there would be no farce.

It looked like the end. But John was saved, for the moment anyway, by what he called 'one of the few acts of really disinterested generosity which I have met'. Leslie Henson was rehearsing for a new musical which he intended to take to the Palace Theatre. He brought it to the Strand instead, even though the building was far too small for this lavish spectacle and he would make much less money out of it. In October he opened with what became one of his most famous shows, *Nice Goings On*. It kept the theatre full until Easter 1933.

All was right with the world again. That Christmas John again involved himself in *Treasure Island*, with Kyrle again playing Mrs Hawkins. This time Malcolm Keen played Silver, and John and Keen got to know each other well, playing golf together and going to theatrical first nights and to boxing matches. Winter 1933 was calm and untroubled. But in March 1934 Kyrle opened in the lead in a play called *The Bride*. It was another disaster. On the second night, fewer than ten people paid for seats, and it closed in less than a week.

John's own account of his stewardship of the Strand ends on a high note in Christmas 1933, and *The Bride* is not mentioned at all. I think he and Kyrle blamed each other. Certainly they were by now constantly bickering. He told me that her spendthrift instincts caused their disaster. She had never had to worry about money, he said, and she had always led him to believe there was, more or less, a bottomless pit. It was, he maintained, a terrible shock to discover suddenly that there was nothing at all to fall back on. She, on the other hand, seems to have believed that the failure was caused by his bad management and poor choice of plays. My suspicion is that they were both right. The truth, probably, was that they took on Arthur Bourchier's legacy, but lacked his professional instincts.

Whatever the reason, it was the final disaster for both of them. They insisted on trying to repay all their debts, and it ruined them. John was declared bankrupt early in 1934.

All their money was gone. Her reputation was damaged irreparably. She never again appeared in the West End, though two years later we find her at the Alhambra, Glasgow, and she worked successfully with several touring companies.

She still had a profession, however, and the remains of what had been a great reputation in it. He had nothing. He was broke, homeless, and jobless. He had been quite rich for nearly ten years, and had forgotten how a poor man lives.

Perhaps the person who suffered most was his daughter Lesley, now thirteen. Until then John had sent her mother Helen regular money, and paid for Lesley to go to an expensive private school. Lesley's visits to her father and her glamorous stepmother seemed like visits to fairyland, in a succession of pleasant riverside homes. One day Kyrle, about to travel to Paris in style, asked Lesley what she should bring back for her. Lesley timidly asked if she might have a pair of silk stockings of the type she had seen Kyrle wear, and was amazed when Kyrle returned with six pairs.

At the beginning of 1934 the money, and the visits to fairyland, stopped abruptly. Helen was forced to take Lesley away from the school, and could not even send her to the local grammar school (whose entrance exam Lesley had passed) because she could not afford to buy the uniform. Lesley left school two years afterwards, and in later years, although she did quite well, she often wondered what she might have become if she had been able to finish her education. I suspect her father remembered his own childhood and education, blighted by his own father's bankruptcy, and never forgave himself.

What was John to do? He might have revived his dream of being a lawyer, or looked for work in journalism – there were still people who remembered that he had a talent for turning a sentence, even if it was most often used for invective. The trouble with those options was that they might take a little while. More or less destitute, beset by creditors, he did not feel he had time.

The choice he made while he was cornered destroyed the rest of his life and the whole of his reputation.

In the three years from 1931, when he lost his seat in Parliament, to 1934, when he lost all his money, a great deal happened, both in the world outside and in John's own life. Soon after the 1931 election, Jimmy Maxton took the ILP out of the Labour Party and on to the long road which led to its oblivion, and Oswald Mosley turned his New Party into the British

Union of Fascists. Maxton's main lieutenant was now John's old ILP friend Fenner Brockway, who had also lost his seat in the 1931 election. Mosley's deputy was another of John's ILP 'parliamentary suicide club', a Scots GP called Dr Robert Forgan, and he, too, lost his seat in 1931. Another defeated rebel, John Strachey, was moving towards the Communist Party. The left was splintering madly in all directions.

For John, the theatre absorbed a great deal of his energy. But politics was in his blood now. When he thought of Ramsay MacDonald and the Labour establishment, or of the communists, or of the poor who had expected so much of organised labour, he could still feel so angry that I guess he found it hard to breathe. He still wanted to change the world; and he still had friends and admirers in politics. One of them was a young Oxford under-graduate named Barbara Betts, better known later as Barbara Castle, who wrote to me: 'I certainly remember meeting your father who was a bit of a hero of mine in my young days, not least because of his stealing the Mace as a protest against the rising tide of unemployment. He certainly had guts.' When we met she added, 'I had a bit of a crush on him, you know,' but refused to elaborate.

In the first few months after the election, the Peckham Labour Party was fiercely loyal to John. One activist, Fred Brooks, wrote to me that taking the Mace 'won respect and admiration from the people he had been sent to represent'. Mr Brooks thought him 'a very sincere man whose one ambition was to do all he could to help the working class. I recall that he had an expression which he used often to describe the Conservatives: "Moral perverts." ' Kyrle too was admired: 'She was one of the finest people ever to take her seat on the council,' wrote Mr Brooks. 'Her care and compassion for the poorer folk within her ward would be hard to surpass and she was literally loved by all.'

So it is unsurprising that for a time, Peckham Labour Party defied Labour's ruling national executive and continued to support John, insisting that he would be their standard-bearer at the next election. When, in 1932, Labour's executive announced that Lewis Silkin would be Labour's official candidate for Peckham, all except two of the members of Peckham's Labour Party decamped into two ILP branches formed by John and Kyrle. John was starting to create at a local level the great new party of the left which he and John Wheatley had planned in 1930 as a national party. Locally, it was not called the ILP but 'the Beckettite party'.

Local historian Dave Russell writes: 'Regular meetings were held at the

Old Kent Road Baths and at the Central Hall, Peckham, where Beckett could be heard "preaching firebrand politics to rapt audiences."'

But it was no good. The left did what it always seems to do in times of crisis: it degenerated into sectarian squabbling. You could hardly have a better example of the left at self-destructive play than the demonstration against unemployment in February 1933. The chief preoccupation in Peckham seems to have been, not 'How many people can we mobilise?' but 'How do we make sure more people march under our banner than under the banners of our rivals on the left?' There were three competing banners: the official Labour Party, the National Unemployed Workers Movement (a communist front organisation), and the ILP.

John wrote later:

> I had hoped that the ILP, freed of its Labour Party commitments, could act as an independent revolutionary socialist party, using parliamentary action for the purpose of creating a socialist common-wealth upon British lines and by British methods. The stress of the fight with the Labour Party, however, had worn down a great many members who would have been invaluable, and the Communists had skilfully penetrated the movement with men and women who, while they obeyed every instruction of the Communist Interna-tional, denied any connection with the Communist Party.

The most dangerous communists, he wrote, were those who were not open about their membership. 'I know one of our most prominent journalists, holding a key position on a national daily paper, who is often bitterly attacked in the *Daily Worker* [the communist newspaper], and who has been an outside member of the Communist Party for many years.' This is the only reference in John's memoirs to a man whom he saw much of in those years, another strange and foolhardy mixture of idealist and repro-bate, Tom Driberg.

It was the communists, he believed, who in the end wrecked his party, and he was at least partly right. The communists were still in the grip of the Moscow-driven policy called 'class against class' which required them to attack other left-wing parties far more ferociously than they ever attacked the supposed class enemies. We now know that Moscow, and Britain's top communists, many of whom had been John's friends and comrades in the heady days of the early 1920s, were now, in the early 1930s, filled with fierce sectarian bitterness and paranoia, and that they deliberately targeted the ILP because its policies were closest to theirs.

Of all the ILP people, John was singled out for special attention by the communists, paradoxically because they saw him as the most left-wing, and therefore the one most likely to lead the working classes away from the true faith.

Douglas Hyde, who was to become one of Britain's top communists before he defected to the Catholic Church, has recounted how, under instructions from communist headquarters, he joined the ILP 'as a means of taking my communism into the enemy camp'. He became ILP secretary in North Wales. When the ILP left the Labour Party, he demanded that all his members (many of them elderly folk who thought of Ramsay MacDonald with affection) should tear up their Labour Party cards. They refused, as he knew they would, and he expelled them from the ILP. When it had no more members, he closed the branch. He arrived soon afterwards in Surrey to perform the same service for the ILP branch there.

Caught between the Labour Party hammer and the Communist Party anvil, it would have taken exceptional leadership for the ILP to survive. Perhaps John was right, and his hero Wheatley could have provided that leadership. At any rate, Jimmy Maxton could not offer it, and for the first and only time John speaks harshly of his friend and comrade: 'Maxton failed as he was bound to fail in a crisis because he does not want to lead; he has no political ambitions, and justifies his lethargy behind a curious philosophical theory that the rank and file should always lead.' Of his other old friend Brockway, now ILP secretary, he writes:

> He is the hardest working man I know; but he works in a circle, without vision, and instead of devoting his organising ability and influence to the creation of a militant political party, trails pathetically after the Communists, appealing to them not to abuse him.
>
> Had Wheatley lived, we should not have lost this great opportunity to create a workers' party. In his absence was illustrated how erroneous is the belief that the time produces the man.

In May 1933 Peckham trades council narrowly carried a motion of support for Silkin. Gradually, but inexorably, the political machine was winning back Peckham, and John announced that he was leaving the ILP for 'business reasons'. He had decided to give up politics, and in May 1933 the theatre must have looked like an attractive way in which to use his talents and energies.

There was, he was now sure, no hope at all in democratic politics, 'the sacred principle of nose-counting'. There was, however, another sort of politics, the sort where you find a great leader to take decisions, and leave matters in his hands. Three years earlier, in the summer of 1930, just after Wheatley's death, John had visited Italy, partly for a holiday, and partly to see how fascism worked.

As a holiday, it was a disaster. On the train to Naples, where he planned to stay, he felt an appalling pain in his stomach. He had with him Kyrle's teenage son, who suffered badly from asthma (he was to die of an asthma attack during the Second World War, while John was in prison). John's pain got steadily worse throughout the train journey of several hours, and the long taxi run to his hotel some way outside Naples. His stepson had a severe asthma attack. The two lay in their hotel room for days on end, both thinking they were going to die. A local doctor visited them and, apparently, injected morphia, using an infected needle, into the scar of the old war wound in John's right arm (which, months later, caused a swelling so serious that it looked briefly as though the arm might have to be amputated.) The doctor put a bottle of laudanum beside the bed and told John to drink some if he could not sleep, but 'happily I retained enough sanity to realise the danger of this advice'. On the fifth morning they both felt a little better, but they were very frightened, and John was terrified to find that when he lifted his fingers to his face, they were like matchsticks.

His stepson was well enough to go and find the British Consul. 'Late that evening he returned with the Consul and an English doctor, well groomed and in clean white suit. Never in my life have I so wanted to sing Rule Britannia.'

But as research, John's holiday proved much more rewarding. He found that 'the working people looked on Mussolini as their man, and seemed quite certain that, in any reasonable dispute with the employers, the fascist decision would always go in their favour'. English conservatives living in Italy told him they thought Mussolini's working-class sympathies were too great. 'The fact that both conservatives and workers regarded him as the champion of the underdog made me revise my opinions fairly drastically.'

The intense nationalism of fascism, which turns so quickly into racism, was no trouble to him at all. He always felt sure that some races were better than others, and that the English were a good deal better than most. He never liked his Labour colleagues' desire to dismantle the Empire. The next year he had had some long private talks with Ghandi, then in London to lobby for independence. John wrote afterwards:

> Remember that he is an Indian, with the poor physique of the natives of the lower part of the country, that he was trained in England as a lawyer (which seems poor equipment for sainthood), and that he has the greatest personality and one of the most obtrusive egos imaginable. Remember that after living to the age of 48 and having had several wives and a large family, he formed an Order of Celibacy for young men … A curious exhibitionism led him to walk about London streets and appear at English functions in a quite unsuitable piece of white linen … I thought him a slightly better type of charlatan than the average British statesman because his will and fanaticism gave him strength to undergo hardships which the average Tory and trade union politician could not endure.

Despite his sympathies, it was another four years before he began to work for the British Union of Fascists. There are certainly several reasons, but the one of which he never spoke to anyone, must be that in 1931, when Mosley formed the BUF, John's Jewish mother Dorothy was still alive. It is true, of course, that she had rejected her Jewish religion and been declared dead by her family, but she must nonetheless have known who she was – and known that fascists were enemies of her people.

John was devoted to her, and I think that her death in March 1932 left him utterly forlorn and utterly lost – orphaned, almost, even though his father was still alive. She died, after a long, painful illness, of breast cancer. In 1930 he had lost John Wheatley, and in 1932 he lost Dorothy. John had no one left to him with the sense and moral authority to shout: 'Stop!'

Although he kept in touch with very few old parliamentary colleagues, he did see two. Had he known a fraction as much about them as the researches of historians have since uncovered, perhaps he night not have allowed them, gently and flatteringly, to guide him towards Mosley and fascism.

The first was W. E. D. (Bill) Allen, an Ulster Unionist MP from 1929 to 1931 and the heir to the W. H. Allen publishing empire. 'Allen, more than any other man I have met, seemed to represent the spirit of modern chivalry,' he wrote, which shows not only the G. A. Henty notions which were already rather quaint in 1932, but also his capacity for completely misjudging his man, and giving his trust and friendship without sufficient investigation. (The sentence was written in John's memoirs in 1938 and crossed out after the war, so perhaps before he died he suspected that Allen was not what he seemed.)

Allen, he said, was not only sensitive and physically good-looking, but in Parliament had been 'the recognised spokesman for a group of young Conservatives who took "noblesse oblige" in a practical form, and to whom patriotism and imperialism meant care for the British and Imperial peoples, rather than a careful network of financial intrigue cloaked by wild waving of the Union Jack'.

Allen was also one of the few MPs who not only joined Mosley's New Party, but stayed with it when it became the British Union of Fascists. He was personally close to Mosley, and was still supporting him when war broke out in 1939. He paid the salaries of some of Mosley's staff and financed Mosley's highly secret attempt to set up a pro-German radio station. But when Mosley, Beckett and the rest were interned in 1940, Allen was not. We now know why.

He was, throughout the time that John knew him, MI6's chief informant on the BUF, reporting directly on John and his friends to the security services. He reported continuously on John's movements long before John had anything to do with fascism: there is even an MI6 report that John went to have tea in the House of Commons with Jimmy Maxton in 1932. The security services, then as now, were very keen on spying on the left, and may well have been quite happy for one of its agents to help to convert a socialist into a fascist.

John did not know of Allen's MI6 connections, but Mosley, apparently, did. He let it continue, he said in later years, because he considered Allen a Walter Mitty character who would provide unreliable information. But Allen also pumped his own money into the BUF and helped to arrange for Mussolini to pump money into it. Allen managed both to spy on the BUF and to be a convinced fascist, and as with most spies, the distinction between spy and *agent provocateur* became remarkably vague.

Those interested in Bill Allen catch up with him again in 1956, when MI5 was at last closing in on the Soviet agent Kim Philby, and Philby had been fired from the Foreign Office. Allen, back on the family estates in northern Ireland, offered Philby a bolthole, and Philby stayed with Allen for several months, out of the eye of the storm. He was also for a time MI6 Head of Station in Ankara.

Like most spies, Allen probably never knew himself whose man he was. The business of spying, then as now, is full of men such as Allen, to whom the game and the secret power it gives them over people's lives are all the reward they want. They do no end of harm.

The other former parliamentary colleague was Dr Robert Forgan, one of the small band of ILP rebels whose activities John had organised in the 1929–31 Parliament, who had gone with Mosley into the New Party and was now deputy leader of the BUF. Everyone who knew Forgan seems to agree that he was charming and terribly handsome. John thought him intelligent, too, but Brockway described him as 'a charming if rather naïve Scot', although he also considered him sincere in his socialism: 'He had been a doctor in the Scottish slums and had seen the effects of malnutrition.' He had also been an army medical officer in the war, and was an international authority on the treatment of venereal diseases.

In 1933 and 1934 he took the lead in persuading John to join the British Union of Fascists. John could not have known – no one knew until, 60 years later, Professor Geoffrey Alderman examined some Jewish records in New York and published his findings – that by the early summer of 1934 Forgan was more or less offering his services to the Board of Jewish Deputies as a spy in the Mosley camp.

He was supposed to be acting as Mosley's emissary, negotiating a *modus vivendi* between fascists and Jews. In fact, he told Board Chairman Dr. Laski that he found it impossible to work with Mosley, that despite protestations to the contrary Mosley was deeply anti-Semitic, and that he intended to leave. But Mosley was paying him £700 a year, he had a wife and children, and he had to earn a living. Also, though he did not mention it to Laski at the time, he had serious personal problems. His wife had attempted suicide, and he had sent his daughter to stay for several months with another fascist leader, William Joyce, and his wife.

Forgan probably never really had the totalitarian fascist frame of mind, and joined Mosley largely from personal admiration and friendship – he was godfather to one of Mosley's children.

Laski told him rather sharply that the Board of Deputies did not buy opponents. Laski instinctively distrusted a man who left a party – any party – in so underhand a way, and his note of the meeting records: 'I did mention that a normal method of changing parties was to write a letter to the leader of the party which was being left giving reasons for its abandonment.' Three months later Forgan left Mosley and returned to medicine.

None of these doubts surfaced during the series of lunches Robert Forgan held with John Beckett and his wife Kyrle in 1933 and early 1934. John's main concern seems to have been Mosley. If you are joining a fascist party, you need to be pretty confident of the leader, and John had always considered Mosley to be insincere and foolish. Forgan told him that Mosley had changed: 'He takes his mission extremely seriously, and is now grown up.'

Forgan had a new, temporary and very pretty secretary called Anne Cutmore, and on an instinct he invited her to make up a four at the lunch, and then at several subsequent meals. He told her to be charming: John Beckett was, he said, a key figure, a clever and charismatic former MP whom they were very anxious to win to the party. His real view, he confided in an interview 40 years later, was rather different: 'I did not believe in Beckett as a political leader. Did not think he had it in him. He was prepared to take all sorts of risks. In fact he might have been a dangerous leader.'

Anne Cutmore was an aspiring actress who had learned shorthand and typing so that she could live while not working, and had registered with Pitmans, which farmed out temporary secretarial staff. They had sent her to fascist headquarters to work for Dr Forgan, and, her theatrical career not prospering, she stayed for several months. She had no idea at all what she was getting into: she thought it was just another job to tide her over until she could get another part.

Forgan had an eye for a pretty girl, and they got on well together, but for Anne, the lunch changed her life. She could see John's and Kyrle's marriage literally disintegrating in front of her eyes – it must have been about the time of the Mexican fiasco at the Strand – and could sense John's immediate and keen interest, both in her physical charms and in her lively and literate conversation.

The next time they met, John came to the office. Forgan was tied up on the telephone and John said: 'You know, you and I between us could turn Bob Forgan into something.' That, she said, impressed her: that John could see the emptiness beyond Forgan's charming façade, yet want to build him up, not tear him down. John, by this time, had fallen hopelessly in love again.

Forgan and Allen talked John out of his distrust of Mosley. After that there were several meetings with Mosley himself, and later in 1933 another visit to Italy confirmed John's view that 'here was a great new conception of civilisation … Italy was achieving all those things which I had hoped for from the Labour Party in this country.' Italian fascists were, he thought, eliminating class differences, national credit and the power of money. So with twentieth- century power of production, it would be able to organise a life of reasonable comfort for all its citizens.

He did not mind the nationalism – in fact he rather liked it. 'Progress in Britain need not wait for the Zulus to join their union and the Japanese to become members of the third international.' Nor did he value democracy: 'My experience in the Labour and trade union world confirmed my distrust of any organisation pretending to be democratic.' Democracy meant giving votes to the ludicrous Colonel Blimps who were the mainstay of the Conservative Party, and even to the appalling communists who disrupted his meetings, 'slouching in untidy files through the streets of our cities … they bear banners urging war in Asia or Spain or some other place where they suspect the prevalence of a spirit of patriotism, discipline or decency'. Was he joking when he added that they should be put in 'well run labour camps where, properly fed and efficiently educated … they could be restored to mental and spiritual health'? I like to think so. But I am not quite sure. Perhaps he was not quite sure, either.

On his return from this second Italian trip, Forgan provided the last push. He told the Italian press that John Beckett was about to become a fascist. According to a report from the British ambassador in Spain to the Foreign Secretary, 'the "conversion" of Mr John Beckett, late MP for Peckham, was given large headlines by many papers, which represented the incident as an important political event'. British newspapers picked it up from them, and when he landed in England he found a battery of reporters asking him about his conversion.

Years later John told me: 'I thought, I'm getting all the odium of people thinking I'm a fascist. I might as well be hanged for a sheep as a lamb.' So he confirmed the story.

However, he was still an inactive member. His boats were not completely burned. But in early 1934, after the failure of *The Bride*, the sad and stupid fact is that he was suddenly bankrupt and entirely without resources, and Mosley offered him a salary. He admitted this to Colin Cross, author of *The Fascists in Britain*, but not, as far as I know, to anyone else. His usual account of the moment at which he became an active fascist is, naturally, rather more elevated.

It happened, he said, when he went to a meeting at Paddington Baths. Mosley was ill, and the meeting was taken by a young man called William Joyce, of whom John had never before heard. He described the effect three years later, in a pamphlet called *National Socialism Now*: 'Within ten minutes of this 28 year old youngster taking the platform I knew that here was one of the dozen finest orators in the country. Snowden's close reasoning and unerring instinct for words were allied with Maxton's humour and Churchill's daring.'

After that meeting he ordered a black shirt, from Forgan's tailor, naturally.

He wore it first to address a meeting in Uxbridge in March 1934. He was, he says, feeling 'extremely self-conscious and uncomfortable' in the shirt, but not, unfortunately, uncomfortable enough. He would not, I am sure, have been wearing it at all had his mother not died two years earlier. Even now his faithful and much-abused friend Brockway could find an excuse, telling me 40 years later: 'I'm sure John thought, I've tried Maxton's romanticism, Frank Wise's intellectualism, let's see what Mosley can do.'

These are the jumbled events that led to the moment which ensures that John Beckett today is remembered, when he is remembered at all, not as a charismatic and fluent, if muddled, idealist, burning with righteous rage on behalf of the underdog, which he undoubtedly was; but as a racist bigot, which he also was.

CHAPTER SEVEN

FOLLOWING THE BLEEDER

'During my life I have roamed a good deal,' wrote John Beckett on the front page of Mosley's newspaper *Fascist Week* in March 1934, explaining his conversion to the cause. 'I have lived in Limehouse and Mayfair, have known intimately dockers and big business men, Boers, Indians, Australian and English Tommies, all sorts and conditions. In the Parliamentary Labour Party I discovered a new low level … Those who mattered would have disgusted Tammany and nauseated a cosmopolitan crook. Some sold themselves openly for a job. The majority succumbed to a double whisky and a condescending nod from a real "gentleman".'

A Labour government, John wrote in the *Fascist Quarterly*, 'means spineless government by nonentities without any guiding principles'. And he was quoted, in a fawning biography of Mosley written at the time by A. K. Chesterton (*Oswald Mosley – Portrait of a Leader*) as saying: 'Mosley had the worst possible temperament for success of Westminster. He suffered fools badly. He wanted to work – not to listen for hours to the wearisome babblings of decrepit trade union leaders sent to the House of Commons as a place of pension …'

From all of which we might gather that John's main motive in joining the fascists was his loathing for the Labour Party establishment: a loathing so intense that he could not see clearly for the fog it created in his mind. But there was also a philosophy of sorts, though it, too, rested on the failings of his former political home. In an article in the *Fascist Quarterly*, John said that there were three basic ideas: fascism, communism and social democracy. Social democracy had failed in every country where it was tried: 'It not only failed to effect the peaceful transformation from predatory capitalism to socialism, but it failed to provide the slightest check on the robber.' It attempts to have things all ways: 'Promise the rich and poor alike that you will be their friend. Abolish the slums and dine with the slum-owner.'

The problem was the democracy bit. The working class did not want to govern. They wanted comfort and security, and could get it by discipline. 'If the nation is to be reorganised and regenerated,' he wrote later, 'either

Parliament must be reconstructed first, or we must face the inevitability of extra-constitutional methods.'

So he put on his black shirt, submitting, so he said, to the discipline that it demanded. The reality, of course, was that submitting to discipline of any kind wasn't what he was best at, and fascist discipline required an uncritical acceptance of authority compared with which the Parliamentary Labour Party was positively liberal.

'Beckett, a tall red-faced handsome man with a tendency to lose his temper, was among the most interesting figures who attached themselves to Mosley,' wrote Colin Cross in *The Fascists in Britain*. 'His career inside and outside politics has been marked by a combination of recklessness and an intelligent instinct for self-preservation. Over a somewhat arrogant belief in his own abilities lies a jovial charm and a boyish delight in elaborating an anecdote. His native ability might have carried him to a leading place in the labour movement, but, like Mosley, he was a casualty of the 1929–31 parliament.' I think it's a pretty good assessment (with some reservations about the 'intelligent instinct for self-preservation.)' Nicholas Mosley describes him as 'histrionic and pugnacious' and adds: 'A good public speaker, in the hierarchy of BUF speakers he soon gained a position second only to Mosley and William Joyce.'

That year, 1934, was when the BUF peaked. It had the support of Lord Rothermere's newspapers, the *Evening News, Sunday Dispatch* and *Daily Mail*, which acclaimed it in January 1934 with a famous front page lead headline HURRAH FOR THE BLACKSHIRTS. It had perhaps 40,000 members. But it had failed to make much impact on the working class and the unemployed (which no doubt was why Mosley was so anxious to get the left-wing hero John Beckett) and its headquarters was sinking under the weight of its own bureaucracy.

It reached a watershed three months after John joined, on 7 June 1934 at an Olympia meeting addressed by Mosley. Police records now available show that the Communist Party and its allies carefully planned to disrupt and destroy the meeting, but the fascist reaction to the threat was sinister and equally deliberate. As he heard interruptions, Mosley would stop speaking while the searchlight sought out the perpetrators. Stewards then advanced on them and removed them with ostentatious violence, and some of them were then beaten up in the foyer.

The following month Rothermere withdrew the support of his newspapers, citing the BUF's growing reputation for violence as well as its burgeoning anti-Semitism. By the time 1934 was over, Mosley had made it clear that fascism in Britain was going to be, like its continental counterparts, racist. It lost its respectability, it lost its influential newspaper support, it lost any chance of bringing in the left, and it became increasingly reliant on anti-Semites and Blimpish ex-army officers. After Olympia, the hostility of organised labour was implacable, but ex-officers and former public schoolboys queued up for two days outside the Black House headquarters to join.

By October 1935 the best estimates we have suggest the BUF was down to 5,000. The movement John had chosen now relied on the people who had broken the general strike, and the spirits of his Gateshead constituents, in 1926. Bob Forgan, the last former MP in its leadership apart from Mosley and John Beckett, left six months after John arrived.

For John, though, there were still a few familiar faces in its ranks. The most prominent was John Scanlon, a left-wing journalist and an old Glasgow chum of Maxton's. Scanlon's book, *The Decline and Fall of the Labour Party*, was the political history of the twenties and early thirties according to Maxton and the ILP. He continued well into the thirties writing for fascist newspapers under pseudonyms, and was still working with John when the war came.

But John did not behave as though he had joined a lost cause. 'Beckett threw himself into his new career with gigantic enthusiasm, addressing 100 meetings in the first six months, leading his stewards in two-fisted battles against violent opposition,' writes Colin Cross. He spoke all over the country, at small street corner meetings, in large halls, on village greens and at open air rallies. He claimed that his speeches 'were practically the same as those I had made in the ILP, because my change of organisation had no effect on my socialist convictions'. Fenner Brockway would have recognised them: no policy, just punch and hit, very effective.

John always maintained that the violence at his meetings came from fascism's opponents:

Blackshirt speakers were always assured of a good audience, but almost as soon as they began to speak, a small section of it would begin to shout or sing, and if it was thought that the speaker was alone or only had a few companions, the platform would be rushed and often considerable physical damage done. Some half a million hooligans in this country have taken it upon themselves to decide what speakers may be heard, and what meetings shall be closed down.

At Marylebone, a lump of lead narrowly missed his head. A meeting at Plymouth degenerated into a free fight before he had even begun to speak, and John went down from the platform to rally his stewards and lead them to the rescue of four of them who were on the floor. He was felled by a flying rugby tackle and his head was being beaten on the floor when the police arrived. When order had been restored, he gave his speech. He might just as well have remained an MP: he could have had all that in the chamber of the House of Commons, shoulder to shoulder with John McGovern.

As often as not, Anne Cutmore went with him, and he remembered all his life one open-air meeting in the East End at which he had to climb down from the roof of his loudspeaker van and make his way through hundreds of opponents who looked and sounded as though they were ready to tear him to pieces at any moment. Anne, a diminutive but elegant figure, wormed her way to the front of the crowd so that she could walk beside him, and though there was much shouting, the crowd parted to let them through and no one touched them. 'I think,' he would say jovially in his comparatively mellow old age, 'that they thought: he may be a bastard, but he's got a nice wife.'

In the north-east, he was greeted with cries of 'Traitor Beckett' in his former Gateshead constituency and ran the gauntlet of (on police estimates) 2,000 protesters, many of them throwing missiles, to get to his orderly ticket-only meeting; he addressed friendly meetings in Durham mining villages; and, in Newcastle, he was the key figure in what may have been the biggest pitched battle the fascists ever fought.

Accounts from both sides of the barricades, and the police and local press, agree on the essential details of what happened. Local fascists were holding Sunday meetings at Cowan's Monument, a well-known Newcastle landmark. The local Anti-Fascist League was determined that these meetings should stop, the more so after fascists had disrupted an ILP gathering, and the last four meetings before John arrived had ended in fighting.

John went to see the deputy chief constable, who told him that the trouble was caused by the presence of uniformed fascist stewards. John asked: if he were to go to Cowan's Monument alone that Sunday, would the police protect him? He was told that they would. So that Sunday he mounted the monument alone.

A vast army of people on one side of the platform – all estimates put it at about 1,000 – moved ominously towards him, shouting abuse, and for a few seconds he felt something like panic. He looked for the police: he could see two constables and an inspector on the outside of the crowd, far too far away to help even if two men were of any use. But in the front of the crowd, although he did not know it, were six fascists in plain clothes, sent up from London to see how it all went. 'I truly believe that to these men I owe my life,' he wrote afterwards. John was pushed off his platform, which was smashed to pieces, and the policemen advanced through the crowd and ordered him to close the meeting.

Then the fascists literally fought their way, inch by inch, through the streets of the city to their own headquarters, carrying two of their comrades who were unconscious, and reinforced by twenty or so more. Sometimes they had to rescue a colleague who was lying on the ground and being kicked; sometimes they would themselves dart into the crowd and set about an opponent. The official report claims that the police escorted them, but both John and his enemies seem agreed that it as the other way round: the fascists escorted the police. 'The crowd was particularly incensed against Beckett and were determined not to allow him to speak,' states the police report.

A *Newcastle Journal* reporter inside the headquarters that day described it as 'exactly like a first treatment centre behind the line'. About fifteen injured fascists were helped or carried inside, and the floor of the big meeting room was covered with blood and groaning men.

John told me about Cowan's Monument in the 1950s. He said that the story had appeared in A. K. Chesterton's hagiography of Mosley, and that when the book was reprinted, after John had left the BUF, it no longer contained the episode. He felt indignant, and I remember telling him how naïve his indignation was. 'I'd still done what I'd done,' he grumbled. Even at the age of ten or eleven I knew something about totalitarianism which my father went to his grave without understanding properly. I knew that it writes apostates out of its history.

He never, as far as I know, mentioned one detail which I think is almost unbearably sad. Most of the anti-fascists, when they dispersed, went to the Palace Theatre, to listen to his old friend Jimmy Maxton.

Within a few weeks John and Mosley were speaking in Hyde Park, and a meeting in opposition was being addressed by other old friends, Fenner

Brockway and John McGovern, together with communist leader Harry Pollitt. Police estimated that 60,000 people were there – pro-fascists, anti-fascists, and curious onlookers. His own speech, or those parts of it the police reporter could hear, still contained passages that could have been delivered had he been sharing the platform with Brockway but others that could not: 'Thousands of men and women here today defying the mob ... Declaration of war against poverty ... Some of them are misguided enough to let the poison from Moscow get into their veins; many of them are decent English working men and women, but lots of them, thrown out of the sewers of Moscow ...'

Despite the battles – perhaps partly because of them – he was happy on the road for those six months. He had probably never enjoyed politics so much since he stomped the country as one of the roving band of ILP speakers, before he went into Parliament.

He returned to London and occupied an office in the huge, grandiose headquarters Mosley had bought for his movement, the Black House in King's Road, Chelsea, which was a social centre for fascists as well as a political headquarters. There he put the energy which had served him so well on the road into his schemes for reforming the BUF's organisation.

In headquarters he found a mess, that particular sort of mess which goes with a totalitarian organisation revolving around a leader whose pronouncements are considered infallible:

A huge staff of badly paid and useless people had been gathered together, and there were probably at least 200 full time organisers and speakers, paid anything from ten shillings and their keep to two pounds a week. They made trouble wherever they went, and their only qualification seemed to be their cheapness and extreme servility. Some of the senior officers seemed quite happy if they could sit at their ease while a few underpaid hacks clicked their heels and saluted ... A part of national headquarters staff were unbelievably like the caricatures of fascists in the *Daily Worker* and the *New Statesman*.

A successful businessman came to Black House offering voluntary service. He was kept waiting for a long time, then shown into the office of a young blackshirt officer who, a few months previously, had been a door-to-door salesman. The businessman took a seat and the young fascist shouted:

'Stand to attention when you are talking to me.' John himself tried to recruit a prominent Catholic, arguing that if you accept the authority of the Pope, why not that of the fascist leader. 'I don't mind the Pope laying down a dogma every thousand years,' said the Catholic, 'but I'm not having Tom Mosley lay one down every five minutes.'

John heard these horrors, but did not see that they came with the creed he had embraced. He thought they could be solved by better administration if only Mosley were made to understand; and once back in London, he told Mosley what he thought, several times, in person and by memorandum, in his trenchant and rather tactless way. Mosley came to resent his counsel, according to Colin Cross, but 'it would not have occurred to Beckett to stop giving advice'.

At first he thought he had been successful. The Black House was sold in 1935 and, in the new and more modest Great Smith Street headquarters, Mosley set up a Central Council, including John and the two men who, after Forgan's departure, John liked best: William Joyce and A. K. Chesterton. A famous military strategist, Major General J. F. C. 'Boney' Fuller, arrived to sort out the organisation, and John felt optimistic. Fuller had been chief of staff to the British Tanks Corps in 1917, and later Military Assistant to the Chief of the Imperial General Staff. He was a short, abrupt military man with the sort of army officer's political opinions that can so easily spill over into fascism, coupled with a nutty sort of theology which led him to the view that 'mentally and morally, the Jew does not fit into the Christian World Order'. He was also associated with Aleister Crowley, the self-styled apocalyptic 'beast', and through him my father was introduced into that circle. He talked of it very little, and wrote not at all, but I know he saw things which frightened him, and left him convinced that, in some ill-defined way, he had seen an evil spiritual force at work.

'We understood,' wrote John, 'that this council would discuss the whole work of the movement, and although there were also a number of bureaucrats on the council, they were not gifted men, and we felt confident, once we were sure of being consulted, of our ability to sway Mosley by the force and sincerity of our arguments.' I am quite sure that John wrote this rubbish entirely seriously.

Mosley spent much of 1935 in Italy. He was there when Italy invaded Abyssinia, and John effectively took control of strategy and propaganda, launching a campaign against intervention under the slogan 'Mind Britain's Business'.

One purpose of Mosley's long Italian sojourn was to ensure that Mussolini continued to fund his movement. The BUF, we now know, received £40,000 in 1933 and 1934 from Italy, probably £3,000 a month throughout 1935, and £1,000 a month in 1936, until Mussolini grew disillusioned with Mosley and stopped the money in 1936 or 1937. These were huge sums in those days. As Richard Thurlow (*Fascism in Britain 1918–1935*) puts it, 'The Mind Britain's Business campaign ... was a true quid pro quo, the price of foreign funding.'

But the implementation was John's. He invented the slogan, and he took the opportunity to drop the fasces symbol, a picture of several sticks bound together, which Mosley had inherited from the Italian fascists. Instead he adopted a flash and a circle, designed by a member, which became the movement's symbol from then on, and soon became known as 'the flash in the pan'. Leaflets were issued, meetings were organised, members were encouraged to chalk 'Mind Britain's Business' on walls throughout the country, and a cable was sent to Mosley in Italy asking him to return, which he did within a week.

John became director of publicity, editing the BUF's two weekly magazines, *Action* and *The Blackshirt*, and controlling the rather heavier quarterly, as well as handling all publicity material. He assembled a small staff of younger people, and acquired a reputation as a maverick.

Mosley asked him to form what he called 'an anti-libel front'. In Germany, he said, Nazi propaganda chief Dr Josef Goebbels had fought dozens of libel actions and been bankrupted several times before his party achieved power. All it needed, he said, was to ensure that publications were run by an official who did not mind being made bankrupt, and to arrange that publishing and printing were done by companies with no assets. Then, when he received a writ for libel, all the editor had to do was to go into court and make a propaganda speech repeating all the libels. The BUF would incur no costs, and the paper would appear the next week with another printer and publisher.

John considered it a splendid idea. He, of course, had no money or assets at all, and had already been bankrupt once. He thought it would enable him to expose scandals which could not be proved in court. He set up the trust so effectively that, when he was fired two years later, he realised it would be a waste of time to sue his employer for the money he was owed. He lost a libel action to eight members of the Amalgamated Engineering Union, whom he accused of corruption. But he was not slow to use the libel laws himself, and won £700 damages for a false accusation that he had converted funds from the National Union of Ex- Servicemen for his own use.

He was, as Clement Attlee and the Gateshead Labour Party had discovered, a propagandist of something like genius. He understood how to make a newspaper at one and the same time a propaganda vehicle and a paper that people really want to read. It is a hard trick to pull off, and few can do it, even today. Most people either fall into the marketing trap, and produce wall-to-wall breathless good news which no one wants to read, or they produce journalism which forgets that it is also supposed to be propaganda.

John was proud of pushing the circulation of *The Blackshirt* from 13,000 to 23,000 and that of *Action* from 5,000 to 26,000, and bleakly satisfied that, a year after he left the papers the former had been discontinued and the latter was down to 14,000.

He discovered, nevertheless, that the reality of power inside the BUF was very different from the appearance. The real power lay, not with the flamboyant figures like himself and William Joyce, but with the BUF Trust Ltd, which controlled the money.

The BUF headquarters was now split into two factions. Thurlow writes:

> The dispute was between those who saw the BUF's future in terms of a military organisation appealing to law and order, and emphasised a style of disciplined marches and demonstrations, and those who saw a need to expound propaganda and convert the masses to fascist ideology. The first faction was led ... by ... Neil Francis-Hawkins (the chief administrator) and Ian Dundas, the latter group by William Joyce, John Beckett and A. K. Chesterton.

Francis-Hawkins was the key figure among those John called the bureaucrats. A short, stout former maker of ophthalmic instruments, in the 1920s he had been in a small fascist group, the British Fascists, a bitter group of right wing anti-Semites who had argued that the way to deal with unemployment was to lower income tax so that wealthy people could hire more servants. (We should not laugh too loudly. Some perfectly respectable mainstream politicians make essentially the same argument today.) Like most of the British Fascists, Francis-Hawkins transferred his loyalty to Mosley in 1931. He was a bachelor and a workaholic, and said he preferred working with unmarried men because they could give more time to the cause. He was, unsurprisingly, rather popular with the regiment of Colonel Blimps who attached themselves to fascism.

Joyce, too, came from the British Fascists, and perhaps the two were working out antagonisms first developed in this tiny, obscure and rather ridiculous organisation, for Joyce and Francis-Hawkins were as different as two human beings could be. Joyce, remembered today mainly as Lord Haw Haw who broadcast for Hitler from Germany during the war, was a remarkably effective platform orator, and between 1933 and 1937 he addressed hundred of meetings all over the country, to great effect. He could have been a fine writer, too, if some stylist had found him early enough and trained out of him a certain wordy sententiousness.

He was an Irishman from Galway, though he had been born in Brooklyn, and had a first class honours degree in English literature from Birkbeck College, London, where he had been president of the university Conservative Society.

In private Joyce seems to have been affectionate and likeable. At home he regularly consumed huge quantities of a cheap Spanish drink called Segovin, but he was not an alcoholic: he could go for weeks without alcohol. When people came round and talked politics, his wife Margaret said he had become 'segovinned'. His daughter, Heather, who was 17 when he was hanged in 1946, remembers a loving and affectionate father who would deal with his explosive temper by taking long walks, from which he returned quite calm.

In public he was pugnacious and aggressive, and people thought him stiff and unapproachable. With the British Fascists, he was fighting street battles with communists as early as the early 1920s, and he had a long scar down one cheek which, he said, was inflicted when two communists held him down and a third slashed his face with a razor.

Joyce was a passionate opponent of Irish Home Rule. This had brought him, early in his life, in contact with the British security services in Ireland, and, perhaps, with the Ulsterman Bill Allen; for Joyce, too, was providing information on the BUF to the security services, in his case to MI5 and the appalling Maxwell Knight, in the early 1930s, though he was never as important a spy as Allen, and unlike the latter, he did not have the serpentine qualities which the best spies need.

Joyce was a generation younger than John, too young to have fought in, and been shaped by, the Great War. But A. K. Chesterton, born in 1899, arrived as an officer in France in the spring of 1917, and the things he saw and did stayed with him in nightmares all his life. Eleven years later, reviewing R. C. Sherriff's First World War play *Journey's End*, he became carried away with his memories:

> Think of the effect on a man of seeing friends, fellows who he has learned to love during the sharing of unspeakable experiences, following each other post haste into screaming death, while he himself must go marching on, watching the world become a vast Necropolis, keeping his head the while, leading his men, enheartening them, planning his defences and waiting, waiting, waiting for the day when he too will be a stinking corpse, grinning at the moon.

Chesterton was awarded the MC after leading his men in seven hours of hand-to-hand fighting in the German trenches in September 1918. After taking the trench he returned to inform his commanding officer, and reached his objective almost without touching the ground, which was covered by a vast carpet of German and British bodies. For years he had a recurring nightmare of walking over a mass of dead bodies stretching to infinity.

Like many First World War officers, he made the trenches bearable by drinking whisky. He became an alcoholic, and alcoholism alternated with long periods of total abstinence for the rest of his life.

Chesterton, a cousin of G. K. Chesterton, spent the 1920s as a journalist with literary tastes, a drama critic, and something of a Shakespeare scholar. The theatre in Stratford was burned down in 1926 and Chesterton played a prominent part in the campaign to have a modern theatre erected in its place. In 1933 he met Mosley and, for a while, was mesmerised by him, seeing him as the last representative of the spirit of the Tudor aristocracy. In his first three years at BUF headquarters he was frequently too inebriated to work, and John remembered several times, when Chesterton had been missing for a few days, touring his known haunts, finding him, drunk and filthy in some dive, and returning him to his wife to be cleaned up. Eventually Mosley paid for him to go, throughout the winter of 1936–7, to a special clinic in Germany where they specialised in alcoholism. After that he was dry until half-way through the Second World War.

Chesterton was tall and thin, with piercing eyes and a faintly aristocratic manner. He was brought up largely in South Africa, and believed all his life, though he might not have put it like this, in the superiority of the white Anglo-Saxon, and among white Anglo-Saxons, the superiority of the Briton.

Sitting on top of the heap, because it was his money which had founded the movement and which, together with Mussolini's, maintained it, was the extraordinary figure of Sir Oswald Mosley.

Mosley's image has been given a careful make-over in recent years. He emerges from Robert Skidelsky's biography, from his own autobiography, from a biography by his son Nicholas Mosley, and most of all from an extraordinary television biopic, as he might have hoped history would see him: a politician of genius, a man of passion, the most attractive platform figure of his generation: with flaws of course, fatal flaws perhaps, but fundamentally a great wasted talent. Six feet four inches tall and apparently irresistible to many women, he has been presented as somehow different from the brutal dictators and would-be dictators of Europe in the thirties, more civilised, less likely to send his foes to concentration camps. He was, after all, a peer, an army officer, an Olympic fencer, a sophisticated, cultivated and educated Englishman. Even after the Second World War he could still count millionaires, dukes and top politicians among his friends and admirers. So, the theory runs, he must surely be superior to a brutal Bavarian corporal who slaughtered millions of Jews.

Yet many of those who worked with Mosley, and knew him closely, describe something much more sinister, and that should not surprise us. Fascism requires its followers to subordinate their own views utterly to those of the Leader (it always has an upper case L in these circles). If that requires a remarkable faith in its followers, it requires a far more remarkable trick from the leader. He has got to believe, really believe, that he is infallible, and that is as good a definition of madness as I know.

'I have finished with those who think. Henceforth I shall go with those who feel,' said Mosley when he founded the movement. But of course, that meant his followers had to feel, and to leave the thinking to him. Clement Attlee thought Ramsay MacDonald guilty of something like fascism in 1931, with his call for a 'doctor's mandate', a call which the nation was sufficiently panicked to heed; and it was that panic on which Mosley, at first, hoped to capitalise. Attlee thought that what distinguished fascism was the absence of an ideology and a programme, other than a belief that the leader knew what he was doing.

John seems to have thought that the creed might have worked if the leader had not, unfortunately, been mad. The trouble is that the creed is the leader. When he described Mosley, John, without knowing it, described exactly how an authentic fascist leader must be:

> Mosley ... has enormous personality which dominates any conference or committee. He is capable of inspiring great love and great enmity. Yet ... during the whole of his career not one person of intellect and integrity has remained his associate, although his brilliance and magnetism have drawn to him the best of his generation. This is the fault of his enormous ego, combined with a peculiar shallowness of judgement and ability to deceive himself. The man who brings him good news is his friend, the carrier of unwelcome tidings slowly becomes his enemy.

Richard Thurlow confirms this: 'Those who had access to Mosley's ear realised that ... the best way to advancement was to tell him what he wanted to hear, whether it was true or not.' But Thurlow, like John, seems to think that this was some personal weakness of Mosley's. In truth, a fascist leader has to be like that. Think of Hitler in that bunker in Berlin in 1945, taking furious revenge on any subordinate who suggested that the war might be lost. A fascist leader has to believe that he is always right – must, in some mystical way, always be right. If he did not, the strain would blow him apart. John goes on to describe the public image:

> Several times a month, [Mosley] addressed large audiences, and saw hundreds of members and great enthusiasm. He did not realise, and I suppose does not realise now [1938], that a great part of this is a stage army which attends him everywhere. In the north the same 100 or so have been his 'brothers in arms' in every place at which he speaks; in the south, Bethnal Green and Shoreditch fascists have represented the growing strength of fascism in every town south of the Trent. In every county are several dozen Mosley fans and whenever he speaks within 50 miles of them, they are harried by paid organisers sent on ahead, and pressed to collect parties and 'get there somehow'. They are given reserved seats in the front rows, and they behave as hysterically as film star fans.
>
> The Communists ... stage flattering scenes outside his meetings. He drives through streets alive with opponents shouting his name and calling attention to him, to a hall where admirers greet him with

enthusiasm all the more boisterous because of the 'dangers' which their hero has just escaped. A far stronger brain than poor Tom's might well fail after five years' food for the ego of this description.

The only people he valued were those who gave him absolute and uncritical admiration. When I started to research this book I went to see a man whom I shall call John Christian who as late as the 1990s was still running an organisation called The Friends of Oswald Mosley, a supremely loyal man who said to me: 'When I was young I thought OM [Mosley] was a god. Now I realise that he wasn't a god, but he was the nearest thing to a god that I'll meet in this world.'

Only a man like Mosley could, without a trace of humour, call his associates by their unadorned surnames and expect them only to call him The Leader. John, who in the House of Commons had, like his other parliamentary colleagues, called him Tom, started the habit of referring to him behind his back as The Bleeder, a of gentle abuse in those days.

The Central Council, in which John had foolishly placed his hopes, turned out to be a weekly waste of time. Apart from General Fuller, himself, Joyce and Chesterton, 'the other members sat silent and stupid, occasionally starting up with fury when it occurred to them that someone was arguing with The Leader. After three months General Fuller declared he had no more time to waste, and attended no more.'

The year 1935 saw unrelenting trench warfare in BUF headquarters, chronicled in detail by MI5. In January 'John Beckett is spreading rumours that the Blackshirts are finished and it is all the fault of F. M. Box' (an ally of Francis-Hawkins). By July Mosley is censoring Beckett and two others for 'having aired their grievances among themselves instead of "coming forward in a fascist and comradely spirit"'.

The detail of the MI5 notes show that their spies must have served them very well, and it seems likely that they had other spies in addition. There was hardly a meeting or discussion of the smallest importance which they did not record, and you sometimes wonder, looking through their reports, whether, without the MI5 agents, fascism in Britain could have caused even the small ripples it did cause. The security services' men in the BUF included not just W. E. D. Allen and (erratically) William Joyce, but also the BUF chief of intelligence, P. G. Taylor, who was in reality an agent named James McGuirk Hughes. Mosley is thought to have known this, but considered Hughes to be 'on our side', presumably because Hughes had a history of helping with strike-breaking operations and stealing documents from communist offices. His enthusiasm for fascism seems to have been quite genuine, and he re-emerged in John's life after the outbreak of war.

Researcher John Hope has shown that the strange and sinister spymaster Maxwell Knight, responsible for monitoring fascists, communists and their sympathisers at MI5, had in 1924 been a member, with Joyce and Francis-Hawkins, of the British Fascists, and had become their director of intelligence. Mosley's own secretary is now widely believed to have been another MI5 agent, although the evidence in inconclusive. The distinction between spy and sympathiser was even more blurred than usual in the case of the BUF.

By 1936 John was certain that Mosley had finally lost all touch with reality. For the rest of his life he would tell the story of the moment he came to this conclusion. It happened during the new king, Edward VIII's abdication crisis. Both John and Mosley had met the king, as Prince of Wales, and taken to him. As socialists they had been impressed by the fact that he was visibly shocked at the poverty and malnourishment that was allowed to co-exist with great wealth in his future kingdom. On a visit to south Wales, shocked at the condition of miners' families, he had caused anger in establishment political circles by saying, 'Something must be done.' To them, the young, handsome king represented their generation, and his enemies, principally Prime Minister Stanley Baldwin, represented the old men who had profited from the war and stifled their dreams.

So John and Mosley threw themselves into a campaign to rally public opinion on the king's behalf. John again designed the campaign under the slogan 'Stand By The King', wrote the leaflets and pamphlets, organised chalking on walls and produced a special newspaper called *Crisis* which sold 37,000 copies.

It was, of course, doomed, and John must have known it. But Mosley, apparently, did not. Here is the story in John's words:

> When the crisis became front page news Mosley was in Liverpool, and had to stay overnight for a conference. He telephoned to London and asked Joyce and I to drive there and discuss the position with him. A Bentley was placed at our disposal, and we reached his private suite at the Adelphi Hotel at about seven. Mosley was in a state of great excitement. He claimed to be in direct communication with the court. The king, he said, was strengthened by the knowledge of the support of him and his movement, and for this reason

would accept Baldwin's resignation and call upon Mosley to form a government.

Standing in the middle of the room, he detailed his plans for governing without parliament until the budget, pointing out that the financial estimates until then had already been passed, and he strode about the room in excitement as he explained that millions of pounds would be available to fight an election in such a cause, and that as Prime Minister he could broadcast as often as he wished. This, he was certain, could not fail to turn the electorate in his favour.

At this point a telephone call came through from London. Explaining that this was an important call for which he had waited all day, he seized the instrument and began rapidly speaking in back-slang. When he replaced the receiver he turned to us and explained that he had received most important news from court. He apologised for speaking in cipher, but said that he always used it because his calls were intercepted by the CID.

I had learned this simple method of talking at school, and Joyce said that he thought every London schoolboy understood it ... I am sure that Mosley really believed he was on the threshold of great power. The conversation confirmed my suspicion that he was deluded, and was dangerously near the borderline between genius and insanity. I knew the man to whom he had spoken. He was a dilettante society friend of Mosley's, who lived in as fictitious a world of grandeur as Mosley himself ...

We left Tom that night convinced that he already believed himself in charge of the nation's affairs, and agreed that his powers of self-delusion had finally conquered his sanity. He could not realise that nobody except himself and the comical little group of ex-peddlers and humourless ex-officers with whom he was surrounded took him at all seriously.

Edward VIII abdicated and married Wallis Simpson. It moved John to searing anger at those who had forced him out:

They are the preachers of Christianity without Christ, of churches without charity, of humanity without dignity ... Paying lip service to the Cenotaph and the Unknown Dead, these crabbed, aged and wartime stay-at-home heroes hunted, in a self-righteous pack, the finest symbol of the living whom they had betrayed ... Always in my heart, as in the hearts of millions of my generation, we shall think regretfully of the dethroned king who represented the new ideas of the wartime generation and was crucified by malice and hatred disguised as righteousness, and hypocrisy enthroned as principle.

As for Mosley, perhaps, in the light of what we now know about Edward VIII, he was not quite as deluded as his publicity director thought. Edward VIII had some sympathies with Hitler and the German Nazis, and during the Second World War the Duke of Windsor (as he became after his abdication) made efforts to secure peace which seem to have bordered on the treasonable. After the war the duke and duchess's closest friends in their Paris home were their near neighbours Sir Oswald and Lady Diana Mosley.

In 1937 the BUF mounted its first electoral challenge, putting up candidates in three East London council elections. Right up to the count, Mosley, against all the evidence, was certain of victory, telling John the canvass results proved it. John said his reading of the results was that they could not possibly win. Mosley was furious, and later severely reprimanded the man who had showed John the canvass returns. William Joyce picked up, and passed to John, an authoritative rumour that Mosley wanted to be rid of both of them.

The results were an utter humiliation. John and Mosley were together as they came in. Mosley sat at his desk working out figures for some time, then looked up with an air of triumph. 'I've got the stuff for the papers, Beckett,' he said. 'The percentage of our vote is slightly higher than the percentage Hitler polled at his first big election.' John pointed out that the BUF figure was in three carefully selected constituencies, whereas Hitler's was over the whole country, and left his leader drafting a preposterous announcement of victory on percentages. Mosley was quoted in a German newspaper: 'Our position is now nearly equal to that which was formerly in existence with you in Germany ... In the east end of London we have now gained the absolute majority ... Our struggle against the Jews ... has ... helped us to win ... Britain and Germany must be in the closest possible alliance.'

The security services, always very well informed about the BUF, noted:

Beckett is very bitter about the conduct of the campaign. He stated quite bluntly that he considered Francis-Hawkins and Donovan to be utter fools and that if Sir Oswald Mosley was not as great a fool as they are, he is certainly far too complacent; that perhaps the shock ... will induce Mosley to place less credence on the counsels of Francis-Hawkins and his friends ... The headquarters staff who went to east London ... were worse than useless ... Raven Thompson [the BUF ideologue and philosopher] is a dangerous idiot who frothed about the Jews and boasted that he would soon be elected and giving orders ... Beckett ... confided that he felt so exasperated at the incompetence and lack of realism ... on the night of the election that he had very nearly resigned from the movement ... Headquarters officials who were sent down to work did nothing but sit around the fire in the election agent's room ... and order or bully the voluntary workers.

Five days later, in a cull of full-time staff, Mosley fired John, William Joyce, and, according to John, 'every other man or woman on his staff who had ever reasoned with or contradicted him or his henchmen'. An MI5 report said: 'The significant feature of this upheaval is the complete victory of the Francis-Hawkins "blackshirt" clique, which has practically eliminated those who were opposed to its conception of the BUF as a semi-military organisation rather than an orthodox political machine.' It also noted that cuts were needed because Mussolini had stopped funding the BUF after its failure in the East End. After Beckett and Joyce had gone, Chesterton could not last long. His wife told David Baker that John was Chesterton's closest friend in the movement, sharing a sense of humour with him: 'John was roguish in the endearing sense.'

Years later, after the holocaust had so discredited anti-Semitism that no politician could profit by it, Mosley found it convenient to suggest that all three were fired for their anti-Semitism. It has proved a remarkably durable myth. Skidelsky swallowed it, and so did Nicholas Mosley. It was even repeated unthinkingly as late as 1996, in relation to Joyce and Beckett, by Chesterton's biographer David Baker.

Such a motive was never suggested at the time. It does not figure in the lengthy, self-serving explanation Mosley sent to his district leaders at the time, which says that they were dismissed 'for reasons of economy only'.

The truth is that that Mosley himself was the leader and inspirer of the BUF's Jew-baiting campaign. The likelihood, in the cases of John and Chesterton at any rate, is that they became much more anti-Semitic than they had been before as a result of absorbing the atmosphere of the BUF.

Neither of them had been particularly anti-Semitic when they joined, by the standards of the 1920s (an important qualification, because the 1920s was a very anti-Semitic decade).

Chesterton was brought up in South Africa, a good place to learn theories about the superiority of white Anglo-Saxons. His embryonic anti-Semitism was fed before the First World War by the Marconi scandal, which his famous cousin G.K. Chesterton had helped expose, and he had absorbed the anti-Semitism of the Chesterton-Belloc circle. But his most strongly anti-Semitic writings were directly inspired by Mosley, who commissioned a special task from him: to research 'the Jewish question'. David Baker's remark about Chesterton is even more applicable to John: 'What is often ignored ... is the degree to which he gained his more extreme ideas from within the movement – as a result of concentrated exposure to these beliefs. This process of socialisation must have been important as there is little evidence of such extreme or systematic anti-Semitism in his pre-fascist writings.'

John, no doubt, had imbibed the standard ideas of the turn of the century imperialist from his own father, as well as the mild anti-Semitism of Labour leaders such as Attlee, Dalton, Morrison and Bevin in the 1920s. He had, in a vague and unfocused way, felt that war profiteers like Sir Alfred Mond were most often Jews, and had certainly felt that there were powerful Jewish interests in the London theatre in his time. But up to the time of his beloved mother's death in 1932, he was not, and could not have been, the rabid anti-Semite that he later became, under Mosley's tutelage. All his life he clung to the increasingly absurd conviction that he was not anti-Semitic, he just opposed international money power which happened to be controlled by Jews.

From the time he lost Rothermere's support, Mosley seems to have decided that he had everything to gain and nothing to lose from constant and brutal assaults on the Jews. At one fairly typical meeting in Manchester in late 1934 quoted by Colin Holmes (*Anti-Semitism in British Society*), he talks of 'sweepings of the continental ghettos hired by Jewish financiers', 'these Jewish rascals', 'this little crowd brought here by Jewish money', the 'yelping of a Yiddish mob', 'alien Jewish finance' and the 'alien faces' in his audience. From then on, few Mosley speeches were complete without many if not all of these references.

International Jewish finance was 'that nameless, homeless and all-powerful force which stretches its greedy fingers from the shelter of

England to throttle the trade and menace the peace of the world ...'

Fighting the 1937 East London council elections, Mosley, according to police reports, was telling East End audiences:

> The Jews already in this country must be sent to where they belong ... You have seen the foreign Jews brought in here and making the goods under your noses ... No more of admitting foreigners into this country to take British jobs and those who are already here can go back to where they belong ... There are many people in the East End of London who have received notice to quit from the Jews, but this time you are going to give the Jews notice to quit.

There was a rumour around that Mosley's wife's mother was Jewish. It was probably incorrect, but it always provoked violence at fascist meetings whenever it was repeated. In Hornsey town hall one evening, drunk BUF stewards singing the Horst Wessel song attacked a man and a woman who shouted out the rumour. Mosley stopped speaking each time he was interrupted, telling his stewards to eject the hecklers 'with old-fashioned fascist courtesy'.

Internal BUF documents which fell into the hands of the security services show that the policy decision had been made to put 'the Jewish question' at the heart of the campaign.

Mosley, the man who said of the Abyssinian crisis 'Stronger even than the stink of oil is the stink of the Jew', did not dissociate himself from anyone because he was embarrassed by their anti-Semitism.

None of this, of course, excuses any of them. Whatever John or A. K. Chesterton were when they joined Mosley, they were both racist bigots by 1937. Joyce is a different case, because he seems to have been pathologically anti-Semitic all his adult life. His anti-Semitism corroded his whole personality, and touched everything he said and did. Nonetheless, Mosley's post-war repudiation of Joyce – 'that horrid little man' – stinks of hypocrisy. Joyce's anti-Semitism was not expressed in language any more extreme than Mosley's, and Mosley had never once attempted to curb it. Nicholas Mosley, in a mostly honourable attempt to come to terms with his father's life, suggests that Mosley simply failed to restrain Joyce's anti-Semitism, but there is no evidence that he ever tried, and every reason to suppose that the violence of Joyce's tongue suited Mosley's purposes at the time. If there is a difference between Joyce and Mosley, it seems to be that Joyce was utterly sincere in his hatred, while Mosley may simply have made the cynical calculation that there might be political mileage in stirring up hatred against Jews.

The truth is that the split had nothing to do with policy. As Colin Cross put it, William Joyce and John Beckett were bad at taking orders, and therefore bad fascists. A week or so later, according to a police report, Joyce's friend John McNab went to see Mosley to complain about the treatment of Joyce: 'He thought Mosley was going to strike him or have a seizure. Mosley went livid and thumped the desk and shouted that Joyce was nothing but a traitor; that he would never rest until he had broken him; that he would roll him in blood and smash him. He also threatened he would smash (McNab) and everyone else who acted as a traitor.' McNab, apparently, returned to his own room, and a uniformed guard appeared. He was given ten minutes to clear his personal belongings and then escorted to the main entrance.

Under totalitarian regimes, apostates are written out of history. Even half a century later, when his existence could, with difficulty, be acknowledged, the BUF's official historian, Richard Reynell Bellamy, wrote of John rather as Stalin's official biographer might have written of Trotsky: 'A clever and able man, who held the mentality of the masses in contempt, and who was well versed in serving up what his readers wanted, had been editing *Action* with success, and adding to his own reputation.'

Others in the BUF remembered mainly his jokes and his stories. Many remembered him telling the story of the Mace, and how it was so light that he almost fell over backwards – 'He made it sound hilarious,' writes one. They remembered his breezy manner and scabrous jokes. William Joyce's six-year-old daughter Heather remembered hearing one of the adults tell her mother, 'That John Beckett, he's got a filthy tongue', and the next time Heather met John, she watched him, hoping he would stick his tongue out so that she could see what a filthy tongue looked like.

Soon afterwards, Lord Camrose, the owner of the *Daily Telegraph*, sued the fascist weekly, *Action*, which John had edited, for suggesting that he was, in the words of Camrose's barrister, 'a Jewish international financier with no loyalty to the crown and no sense of patriotism, and that in his conduct of the *Daily Telegraph* he allowed his duty to the public to be subordinated to his own financial interests'. John was not named in the action, but he turned up in court anyway and asked to make a statement. He said he had been given the information by 'a titled friend' (obviously Mosley) and now accepted it was false and wished to apologise: 'To me, to tell a man that he is a Jew and that his financial interests are far greater outside this country are two of the greatest insults that can possibly be offered ...'

John had two objects. The first was to damage Mosley, and he succeeded. Camrose was awarded £20,000 damages and costs. Beckett still had nothing, and could pay nothing. *Action*, still owned by a £100 company, went bankrupt, and Beckett told the press of his disgust at a man who could hide behind a £100 company – the very scheme he and Mosley had contrived together as a 'libel-proof front'. But one hardly grudges him this victory. It is one of the few ways in which the very poor can take revenge on the very rich.

But his second objective is not forgivable. He wanted to establish that it was insulting to call someone a Jew. He thought: we will not attack the Jews. We will simply establish that the word 'Jew' is an insult. It was the idea of a brilliant propagandist whose brain had been scorched and distorted by disappointment and hate, and it was utterly, irredeemably wicked.

John's anti-Semitism was different from the pure hatred preached by Mosley and Joyce. John, who in everything else used the bludgeon, in this used the rapier. His method was the indirect one, the sneer rather than the assault. Attacking trade union leaders in the fascist quarterly, he analysed the expenditure of the miners' unions, ending with an item called 'Fees and grants', and translated this for his readers as 'Hungry Jews etc.'. At one meeting, according to an observer for the Board of Deputies of British Jews, he talked of the national press and 'delighted his audience with stressing the Jewish names of the persons either owning or being part owner'. He also said that most of Britain's moneylenders and shady businessmen were Jews. I like to imagine that he went in for this uncharacteristic way of doing things because his heart wasn't in it. I have no idea whether I am right.

Few people can make as many mistakes as John had made, and still get yet another chance. John was getting one, if only he could have seen it. Not a particularly good chance, certainly, because he was more or less destitute, his salary was gone, and for most of his old friends he was now beyond the pale. But he had his native talent. It was a chance to rethink and remake his life. What would he do with it?

His personal life was more complicated than ever. By now he was living with Anne, but Kyrle refused to divorce him. His solution was typical. He told Anne, 'We'll tell everyone we're married, and it'll be just as though we were married.' It worked brilliantly. For the rest of their lives, no one seems to have had any idea that they were not, legally, man and wife. I certainly didn't. They even had a wedding picture taken, with William Joyce and John McNab as witnesses. She suggested changing her name by deed poll, but John said no: it would only draw attention to the situation. She should just call herself Anne Beckett. She did, and as far as I know, no questions were ever asked.

The BUF had become a much bigger part of Anne's life than she had expected when she went there as a temporary secretary to Robert Forgan. She was not a fascist at all. Set her apart from John, and you would not find any of the racism or the fanaticism that a fascist requires. Even after she had lived with him, listened to him and been loyal to him for 30 years, when she herself spoke about politics, it was surprising how little of it she understood. She was an early, determined and thoughtful feminist, but apart from that, politics just wasn't her field.

She must have ignored the advice of Mosley's mother, who had an office in BUF headquarters and, according to an internal report quoted by Nicholas Mosley, 'kept a motherly eye on some of the less staid and prettier ones and warned them of the hungry looks being cast in their direction by appreciative Blackshirts, and by one high-ranking officer in particular who was both an experienced politician and an experienced womaniser'.

Whether this was John, Forgan or Mosley is uncertain; it could truthfully apply to all three. At any rate, Anne had enjoyed Forgan's company, and then become part of a circle of intellectual young men in the BUF. They went to theatres, to the country, to clubs, they talked and danced, and they took their politics just seriously enough to be a common intellectual base, but not so seriously that they had to examine them. She was especially close to a young composer named Selwyn Watson, who wrote the music for the song which was intended to become the British version of the Horst Wessel Lied.

John made her the drama critic for all the fascist newspapers, and when Forgan left, she went to work for the chief of staff, Ian Dundas. She thus became one of the few people who knew for certain that Mosley was being funded by Mussolini, because Forgan and Dundas both boasted about it to her, and showed her the cases full of banknotes. She was the sort of woman who has that effect, quite unintentionally, on rather vain men.

Born in 1909, fifteen years younger than John, she was 28 when they left the BUF together in 1937. She was small and dark and, like both his other wives, very beautiful, with an oval face and a smile that lit it up. Her first name, which she hated and never used, was Doris. It sounded a little like Dorothy, the name of John's mother, so he often called her Dorothy Anne. In later years, she sometimes thought that with different breaks (and perhaps a different husband) she might have been a considerable actress. She received an offer of a season at the Shakespeare Memorial Theatre in Stratford-upon-Avon but got laryngitis that winter and could not take it up. She was certainly a talented mimic, with a lively, mobile face and voice, and her writing was stylish and fluent. Like John, she had a tongue which could make enemies, and she was sometimes cruel and caustic, though an essentially kind person.

Anne, in her own way, was even more of a casualty of the First World War than her husband. She remembered with dreadful clarity how in 1916 her father arrived home from work and announced that he was going to volunteer to fight in France.

James Cutmore would not have been conscripted: he was 40 years old at the time, a legal draftsman, with three daughters. He had tried to join up early in the war, out of a sense of duty and guilt, but was turned down because he was short-sighted.

That day in 1916, while walking home to Clapham from the city, a woman came up to him and gave him a white feather. Guilt overwhelmed him, and he spent the next day persuading the army to let him in. It was not hard. By 1916 they cared nothing for short sight. They just wanted a body which could stop a shell, which he duly did two years later. Anne never forgave that woman, whoever she was.

Anne and her mother kept all his letters from the front. They were long, in his fine law writer's script, and he only commented on what the children were doing, never a word about his own doings because he didn't want his wife and daughters to be sad or frightened, except once when he sent a registered letter to Anne, and all it said was:

Celer et Andax
Domine Dirige Nos

The nine-year-old girl cannot have had any idea what it meant, but she must have known it mattered, because she kept it through a difficult and muddled life in its original envelope, in which I found it after her death. Anne always remembered his last leave, early in 1918, when he was so shell-shocked that he could hardly speak to her, and her mother spent every day ironing his uniform in the vain hope of killing all the bugs.

He died in France in April 1918 of wounds received several days earlier. Anne's mother, in deep shock, sold their South London home and took the family to New Zealand, where she had relatives. When they returned to London, Anne was a grown woman.

When she met John, Anne was still mourning her father. The grief never left her. In her last years, with her brain crippled by Altzheimer's, when she had forgotten everything else about her life, Anne still remembered her father and his useless death. She carried to her grave the unconditional love that the luckiest fathers inspire in their nine-year-old daughters. It seems likely that she was, unconsciously, looking for an older man, a man who knew the world and its ways and could instruct her in them, as her father would have done had he lived.

She wanted guidance. John needed guidance. Neither of them got it. She took a job, working for the Corvinus Press, which published rare books, seeing all the books through the press. He, I think, waited for something to turn up, and she told him that while he was waiting, he should write his memoirs for publication. He wrote them, very quickly, with all his usual verve and lack of restraint, and at least two publishing houses expressed an interest in them. On John's own account, one of them wanted to change them for use as Conservative propaganda, the other to change them into Labour propaganda, and he turned them both down. Whatever the truth, they remained unpublished, and have been the principal source for this book for the years 1920–37.

What turned up was his old comrade William Joyce, with a pot of gold. He had been to see a man called Alexander Scrimgeour, a rich admirer of Joyce's who was said by MI5 to have contributed at least £11,000 to BUF funds. Scrimgeour was willing to fund a new fascist party fronted by Joyce and Beckett. Or rather, not so much a fascist party as a Nazi party. Thus was born the National Socialist League. Within a few months Chesterton, too, had left the BUF. The NSL published his pamphlet attacking Mosley, and he spoke at several of their meetings.

Anne loyally tried to like John's new hero William Joyce, but she only saw a small, square, pugnacious man drinking constantly to keep away the pain behind the eyes. Her younger sister saw a man who tried too hard to please: 'I was introduced to him once and he said, oh, I've heard of you, of course, and of course he hadn't at all. I didn't think a lot of that.'

One old BUF hand recalls going to see them in their Vauxhall Bridge Road office:

> Up several flights of uncarpeted stairs. The HQ was on the top floor in a single room, also uncarpeted, the only furniture a desk and two or three chairs. In a corner of the room were a couple of piles of … leaflets. When I went in, having knocked on the door, both Beckett and Joyce were there. I told them I wanted to hear their side of the argument. They sat me down and for the next half hour they explained the policies in great detail.

A few weeks later he saw, at a street corner, a portable platform with one of them (he could not remember which) standing on it and speaking, and the other heckling – a standard way of trying to attract an audience to an open air meeting. 'What a terrible comedown from the great meetings I had heard them speaking at!'

But Joyce's anti-Semitism was by now so violent, bitter and obsessive that it frightened away both John and Chesterton, neither of whom were particularly squeamish about such things. Joyce's attitude to the danger of war worried them too. At one meeting, Chesterton reported:

> He brought the meeting to an end by calling for the National Anthem to be sung. That done, he shouted the Nazi cry of triumph Sieg Heil. I did not attach much importance to the episode, if only because the unpredictable little man was quite as capable of closing the meeting in Icelandic or Old Norse, both languages, incidentally, which he had mastered … [At another meeting] I expressed my concern at the growing danger of war. Joyce arose vehemently to dispute my contention. 'There will be no war,' he thundered. 'I trust Adolf Hitler to see to that.' Something had happened to Joyce's clarity of vision …

Perhaps Joyce had changed: he had parted from his wife in 1936 and shared a flat with his friend John McNab, who had left the BUF with him, and he was drinking more heavily than before.

Quietly, John parted from Joyce. Joyce wrote to his members to tell them of 'the resignation of Mr Beckett, who felt that greater moderation was necessary, especially in relation to the Jewish problem'. But the NSL was declining irrevocably, and Joyce, scratching around for a way to earn a living, found his way to Gabbitas Thring in Sackville Street, off Piccadilly, a firm which for generations has provided teachers for private fee-charging schools and tutors. They sent him enough private pupils, whom he taught in the South Kensington flat he shared with John McNab, to keep body and soul together for a while.

CHAPTER EIGHT

THE ANTI-WAR FACTION

We tend to think that from the moment Hitler took power in Germany in 1933, the Second World War was inevitable. It did not seem so then. Europe had Hitler at its centre, Mussolini to the south, Stalin to the east, and the bitter and brutal Spanish civil war was a test-bed and training ground for a war between the great powers. The generation of 1918 splintered in extraordinary and unpredictable ways, and a substantial section of it was against fighting Hitler.

In 1914 many of them had rushed loyally to the trenches to defend civilisation against what they were told was a German antichrist led by a mad and evil Kaiser, only to discover afterwards that they had been told lies. So why, they reasoned, should they now rush out to fight because the same elderly and comfortable statesmen told them about a German antichrist led by a mad and evil Führer?

Fascists, socialists, right-wing conservative peers and pacifists stood shoulder to shoulder against the threat of another war, and were joined (and sometimes, it seemed, almost outnumbered) by a set of grubby extreme right-wing spies and *agents provocateurs* from MI5.

Preventing the outbreak of war was now John's main political aim. His next creation was the British Council against European Commitments (BCAEC), founded at the time of Munich in 1938 and bankrolled by Lord Lymington, a Conservative MP between 1929 and 1934 and later to become the Earl of Portsmouth. Lymington had been a leading figure in English Mistery, a right-wing group of wealthy farmers and landowners which praised 'tradition' and 'race' and condemned 'moneyed interests' and 'aliens' (no prizes for guessing who that meant). In 1936 English Mistery had split, and Lymington now led its more pro-Nazi faction, The English Array. Lymington believed that a war against Germany 'would benefit no one but the Jews and the international communists'.

John often took something of value from the people with whom he associated, and from Lymington he took an abiding belief in organic farming and a hatred of farm chemicals. I expect he also told his new landed friends, in his loud, cracked, street-corner orator's voice, all about the Cheshire Becketts and his 'yeoman ancestry', and, like the English gentlemen they were, they hid their contempt beneath polite expressions of interest.

John was secretary of the BCAEC. The socialist who had fought for starving miners and East End slum dwellers had come a very long way in a few years. He also, presumably, produced the one-off newspaper on 1 October 1938 welcoming Chamberlain's trip to Munich to confer with Hitler, though it was not done with his usual flair. It was headed, in huge capital letters, WAR CRISIS, and its lead headline was:

> BRITAIN ON THE BRINK OF DISASTER!!
> PATRIOTS! SMASH THE WAR CONSPIRACY!

It also contained an article called 'What War Means to Women', signed simply A. C.

> In the spring of 1918, my father came home after ... service in France. A quiet man, and a scholar, he returned a shell-shocked and physically ruined man, who could neither recognise a neighbour nor write his own name. At the end of fourteen days leave he went back to the battlefields of the Somme, to be blown to pieces by a shell.

Her heartbroken mother, wrote A. C., had then been forced to work in a kitchen to feed her three children while the War Office quibbled about her pension, and then struggled to bring up the children on the meagre pension ultimately provided.

A. C., of course, was Anne Cutmore, and the story was true, but I believe someone got hold of her article and put a lie in. According to the article as printed, the kitchen Anne's mother worked in, belonged to 'one of the Rothschilds'. Many of the anti-war faction were unable to see any evil that did not have Jews at the bottom of it.

The newspaper's appeal was to avoid a repeat of 1914–18, and a powerful appeal it was too. An article by-lined 'A. K. Chesterton MC' began: 'After 20 years of the fullness of peace you will now be suitably fattened for the slaughter which last time you were fortunate to escape.' John Beckett's article recalled Ramsay MacDonald saying at a meeting in 1918 that the dismemberment of Germany and Austria was laying the seeds for future wars. 'At the same meeting Jerome K. Jerome talked, amidst great applause, of "the devil's kitchen at Versailles brewing the bones of the future's youth".' Yet now, 'with the exception of Jimmy Maxton and his ILP group, they are all clamouring for another "war to end war".'

In poured the leading lights of the far right. Major General Fuller and A. K. Chesterton joined. So did Admiral Sir Barry Domvile, a former Director of Naval Intelligence and the founder of the biggest and most successful pro-Nazi group called The Link. Domvile's racism was of the upper crust military sort. At one meeting, he wrote in his diary: 'A dirty little Jew called Leon got up afterwards and made a speech about his beastly little race instead of asking questions.'

From the National Socialist League came William Joyce. From the Imperial Fascist League, the most extreme of them all, came Arnold Leese, who had always refused to have anything to do with Mosley, whom he denounced as a 'kosher fascist'. Leese, a former vet, had been inspired to an anti-Semitism even more violent and obsessive than William Joyce's partly by disgust, apparently, at the kosher method of slaughtering animals.

In too came the members of all the strange little pro-Nazi and anti-Semitic bodies which sprang up in the 1930s, some of whose names bear witness to their extreme nuttiness: the Anglo-German Brotherhood, the Nordic League, the White Knights of Britain, the Militant Christian Patriots, British Vigil, The Britons, the English Array.

So too did Jimmy Maxton's old ILP chum John Scanlon, as well as another Labour Party figure, Ben Greene. A cousin of the novelist Graham Greene, during the thirties he had run a successful campaign to change the Labour Party's voting system so as to give less weight to the views of the trade unions and more to the views of the ordinary Party member. It was an important battle, making Greene for a time a key player in Labour Party politics, earning him the dislike of the Party's great power-broker Ernest Bevin and enabling the Labour leader, Clement Attlee, to bring in much-needed reform. Greene's importance in the history of the Labour Party has rather been sadly overshadowed by his subsequent association with other former Labour Party left-wingers like John Beckett and John Scanlon.

Greene was a huge, fat man, six feet eight inches tall. He and his cousin Graham had been at Berkhamsted public school at the same time as A. K. Chesterton, when Graham's father Charles Greene was the headmaster. All three of them hated the place, and Ben Greene had a sort of constant melancholy lying underneath his surface panache. His size made him feel something of an outsider. My mother thought he was always running away from himself. 'If Ben was in London he would say he could not stand it, and rush off to Scotland. But then he couldn't stand that either, because he took himself with him.' He was a Quaker and a pacifist, and had done famine relief work with the Quakers in the Soviet Union and Germany.

The BCAEC, in fact, was a front organisation for every fascist, neo-fascist and anti-Semite in London, and a way in which they could link up with socialists, pacifists and anyone else who might be recruited to the anti-war cause in the wake of the Munich agreement. It lasted only about six weeks, but the coalition it represented stayed more or less together until most of the leading figures were imprisoned.

After Munich, Lymington bankrolled a new monthly magazine, *The New Pioneer*, which John edited. It tried to be the thinking right-winger's paper – a kind of *New Statesman* of the anti-war faction. 'Let us not blind ourselves,' it editorialised with studied moderation just after Munich, 'to the fact that something of the old Prussian spirit of Weltmacht is still extant, and we must be prepared for any eventuality if the present regime of Herr Hitler should be overthrown'.

It contained literary and theatre criticism by Anne Stone (a pseudonym for Anne Cutmore) although the review of a film of *The Mikado* was naturally signed J. B.: 'It cannot possibly injure the susceptibilities of even the most traditional Gilbert and Sullivan follower.' It offered several pages of review of political books, many of them signed A. K. C. But John chose to review a biography of Ramsay MacDonald by MacDonald's former PPS, L. MacNeill Weir.

Weir was unsparing about his old master, writing that everyone of any decency and humanity pleaded with MacDonald to raise the allowance for the child of an unemployed man. John wrote: 'On December 3rd 1929 Miss Jennie Lee and I moved an amendment ... to increase this figure. Not only Mr MacDonald, but Mr Attlee, Mr Greenwood, Sir Oswald Mosley and some 200 other Labour members voted against any increase, and in the 37 who voted for "decency and humanity" the name of MacNeill Weir was conspicuous for its absence.' Ben Greene and John Scanlon also offered sad and disillusioning reminiscences of Labour Party politics, and Major General Fuller offered gloomy assessments of Britain's military strength.

It cannot have been easy, even with memories of the First World War in your mind, to enter 1939 still believing in the goodwill of Adolf Hitler, after the destruction of the synagogues on Kristallnacht and the invasions of Austria, Czechoslovakia and Poland, but Beckett, Greene, Lymington and their friends seem to have managed it. Greene actually went to Germany, saw persecution of Jews for himself, and came up with the extraordinary idea that the way to help them was to send money into Germany for them. The certainty that this would have been confiscated at once, as their own property had been confiscated, does not seem to have occurred to him.

They kept it up even after Hitler's march into Prague in March 1939. In fact, the very next month John founded his last political party, the British Peoples Party (BPP), bankrolled this time by the Marquis of Tavistock, the future Duke of Bedford.

This was quite unlike all the other fringe anti-war groups at the time, with their predictable right-wing enthusiasms for the English countryside, class system and racial purity. Tavistock was an enthusiast for social credit and for monetary reform, and the BPP put social reform at the top of its agenda. It rejected fascist totalitarianism, insisting that change must only come about in the democratic parliamentary way, and John was now insisting that he was no longer a fascist.

He had, I think, at last realised, as Churchill once put it, that '... democracy is the worst form of government, except all those other forms that have been tried from time to time'. Mosley, he said later in his appeal against imprisonment, had cured him of dictatorships:

> One feels one must put up with this one-man dominance for the sake of the objective, then when you get inside it cures you of all that. You realise you must have democracy, otherwise you get palace politics ... A leader sitting in a room in the palace by himself, as happened in the bad old days with kings, with the courtiers intriguing in the outer rooms.

Many of the BPP's ideas would not have been out of place in a left-wing party, and its most prominent leaders had started their lives on the left: John Beckett, John Scanlon, Ben Greene. They married this, however, with a delicate dose of anti-Semitism. This was not to be the raucous hate of a Joyce or a Mosley. At its inaugural meeting, John, defending the BPP from barracking by Mosley supporters, was quoted as saying that more could be achieved by refraining from direct attacks on Jewry: a campaign against 'usury' would bring about the same results. 'From now on,' writes Richard Griffiths in his recent book *Patriotism Perverted*, 'we shall find the terms "usury" and "money power" used continually by people such as Beckett and Greene, as a coded reference to Jews, to be understood by their members.' It joined the other code-words for Jews which had been common among British anti-Semites for decades: aliens, cosmopolitans and others.

The month after the foundation of the BPP, May 1939, saw the first appearance of the Right Club, started by the Conservative MP for Peebles, Captain Archibald Maule Ramsay, another aristocratic back-to-the-soil pro-Nazi and anti-Semite. If the BPP was designed to take the anti-war message to the left, the Right Club was to take it to the right. Its first object, wrote Captain Ramsay, was 'to enlighten the Tory Party and clear it from any Jewish control'.

In July the BPP put up a candidate at the Hythe by-election, to fight on an anti-war ticket. The candidate, in retrospect, was a fascinating choice. He was Harry St John Philby, who had a long association with the Middle East, starting in Iraq during the First World War. Arabists do not, of course, have to be anti-Semites, but many of them are, and Philby was. Today Philby is much less well known than his son Kim, who, it later transpired, was at this time embarking on his career as a Soviet spy at the heart of the British establishment. Kim Philby had also worked for the Anglo-German Fellowship in order to spy on it, publicly breaking with left-wing friends so that he could do so, and associating closely with people like Domvile and Fuller. The anti-war camp was stuffed full of spies, English, German and Soviet. Without them there would not have been enough people to get the work done.

John was the election agent, responsible for trying to mould the strange coalition of racists and pacifists that turned up in Hythe to support Philby into some kind of campaigning machine.

What on earth was John thinking? He had never taken any particular interest in the Middle East, nor in land reform. Even with his catholic tastes in human beings, he cannot have been excited about the peculiar right-wing grandees he had to work with, even less that of the pacifists whose support he had to try to obtain.

He had not, this time, found a leader. Lord Tavistock was no powerful and brilliant politician such as John Wheatley, no glittering charismatic figure like Oswald Mosley, not even, as William Joyce had been, a man with sufficient force of personality to enable John to imagine himself, if he tried very hard, in the presence of greatness. For the first time John never had any illusions about his new leader.

Was he thinking single-mindedly about the cause, putting in the same work rate and the same passion that he had once put in for Clement Attlee among the slums of Limehouse? Apparently not. In Hythe, he was the most neglectful election agent ever, unable to bring himself to make any real effort for the doomed cause of getting St John Philby elected to Parliament. Meeting Anne for canvassing, she thought she was in for a hard and dreary afternoon. But he took all her canvass cards from her, filled them in on the spot, writing 'Conservative' against some names and 'Labour' against others, and said, 'That's done. Let's go to the pub.' It is doubtful whether even his old energy could have improved much on Philby's 578 votes.

He had a well-grounded horror of war. He claimed to have great hopes of Chamberlain, who he thought was determined to avoid war. But he cannot have enjoyed his campaigning, and cannot have thought the Hythe by-election was going to do much for the cause.

He was probably able to convince himself that he believed in what he was doing. More than that, he was in love, as fiercely as when he first fell in love as a soldier in 1915. That made him despair about his life. He knew his past would damage Anne's future.

'I know I ought to leave you alone to make the best way you can in this vale of tears,' he wrote to her. 'But I DON'T WANT TO. Here's the five pounds. I'll send the rest when I can.' And, in another a letter dated simply Monday, 11.30 a.m.:

Here's the dough, precious, and after great difficulty, Ann Black had no money, I succeeded in getting Lewis to cash the fiver so can now get away to Middlesbrough.

Have I mentioned that I am wildly, devastatingly, most passionately and really generally very much in love with you ...

Bless and keep you, sweetheart, I'll only really be human again when I get back to you.

Yours only and ever, John.

One day, about to rush off to another pointless meeting, he paused and looked at her. 'I wish I could just go and do an ordinary job,' he said, and was gone. But the Marquis of Tavistock was very rich, he needed John, and John was still broke. He took his first wife Helen out to lunch and told her of his despair.

His heart had gone out of his work. But, in the frantic and self-deluding circles in which he was now moving, no one knew it, least of all the spies.

He was, however, not quite so lost to sense as to listen to the next proposal that came his way. Some time between the Hythe by-election and August, William Joyce told him secretly that, if war broke out, he intended to go to Germany and offer his services to Hitler, using an old German Embassy contact, with whom they had both associated, as an introduction. Would John go with him? John never gave the idea a moment's serious consideration.

Joyce was not very happy. He was short of money. His National Socialist League was failing and he was living in a bachelor flat in South Kensington with his friend John McNab. He was having constant rows on the telephone with his first wife Hazel, who, with her new husband, had remained loyal to Mosley. She was now refusing to allow him to see his children. The oldest, Heather, still remembers the happy weekends they had spent in his flat until her mother stopped them, and how, curiously, he used to tell her tales of Germany mythology.

Joyce, we now know, had advance warning on 24 August from his MI5 contacts – possibly direct from Maxwell Knight – that the Emergency Defence Regulations were to come into effect on 26 August, giving the government power to intern anyone who might harm the war effort; and that his own detention order had already been signed. Joyce and his second wife Margaret left for Berlin on the morning of 26 August.

War was declared on 3 September. At first the anti-war campaigners seemed inclined to give up, but soon they were making plans to stop the war even at this stage. John and Ben Greene began the campaign for a negotiated peace by attending a Peace Pledge Union conference. On 19 September, they had lunch with Admiral Domvile and then drove straight to a flat owned by Captain Robert Gordon-Canning, another old BUF hand, now a key supporter of the BPP and an admirer of Hitler. There they met five of Domvile's key supporters in The Link, and the plans were laid.

Thus was founded the British Council for a Christian Settlement in Europe (BCCSE) to work for a negotiated peace. Lord Tavistock was chairman and John Beckett secretary. The headquarters were in Ben Greene's Berkhamstead home. The intention was to create a broad front of everyone who, for whatever reasons, wanted to see a quick end to the war.

All the usual suspects attached themselves to it, including Harry St John Philby and the writers Henry Williamson and Hugh Ross Williamson. But so, too, did Christians and pacifists with no connections at all with the pro-Nazi right. The Peace Pledge Union supported it, as did the Revd Donald Soper, Eric Gill and Laurence Housman. So did the Labour MP Richard Stokes, who the next month brought together a group of Labour MPs to oppose the war, providing a link with some more of John's old friends, the ILP MPs Jimmy Maxton, George Buchanan and John McGovern. McGovern especially was a strong supporter, and it is likely (though there is no proof) that he and John met several times in this period and co-ordinated their efforts. Landed gentry were well represented, the outright pro-Nazis now being reinforced by some of the foremost peers in the land.

It even brought in the anti-war faction of the Conservative Party, and its views were faithfully represented in a monthly magazine called *Truth*, which was secretly controlled by Sir Joseph Ball of the Conservative Research Department, the principal adviser to Prime Minister Neville Chamberlain, and edited by a friend of John's and A. K. Chesterton's, called Henry Newnham.

In December 1939 the BPP produced a pamphlet, *The Truth about This War*. No author was given, and historians have variously ascribed it to Beckett, Tavistock and Greene. They are all wrong. It has a literary style which none of these three could have managed, and it was in fact written (to a brief, no doubt) by Anne Cutmore. The next month the German government published an exact translation into German. It was a prelude to a series of 'peace initiatives', of which the best known was a deal discussed between Lord Tavistock and the secretary to the German embassy in Dublin.

There were still two factions outside the BCCSE: Mosley's BUF and Captain Ramsay's Right Club. In October Domvile started to try to bring them all together, hampered by the fact that Beckett and Mosley were not on speaking terms. They had not met since John's departure from the BUF, and were never to speak to each other again, not even when they were incarcerated in the same prison. Mosley always referred to Beckett as 'that crook'. It seems likely that they refused to be in the same room, because all meetings recorded by MI5 contained one or the other, but never both.

Perhaps for this reason, negotiations floundered, and the anti-war movement fractured and splintered, as tiny extreme groups are liable to do. Ramsay, feeling dominated by Mosley, stopped meeting him. Domvile worked mostly with Mosley, reporting to him privately on his meetings with Beckett and Tavistock and complaining that Beckett 'talked such rot'.

But the anti-war campaign was reinforced from two unexpectedly main-stream sources. There were John's old friends in the now-tiny ILP group of MPs, and there was Lord Beaverbrook. In March 1940 three ILP MPs, Jimmy Maxton, Campbell Stephen and John McGovern, were invited to Beaver-brook's home, where he put to them an extraordinary proposition. If they would introduce a 'peace candidate' into every parliamentary constituency in the country, Beaverbrook would pay all the election expenses. Beaver-brook told McGovern that 'the nearest approach to peace we were and will ever be able to have was when the Marquis of Tavistock tried to arrange an honourable peace'.

I think that McGovern kept in close touch with John throughout this period, but if they met, it was with great care and in secret, because the meetings do not figure on MI5's comprehensive records. John knew he was being followed and had techniques available for secret meetings. He intro-duced McGovern to Tavistock, and McGovern's support for Tavistock's peace efforts was well known. When Beaverbrook made his offer, it must have excited both of them, but especially John. Perhaps he thought that it might afford, for him, a way back from the extremist ghetto to which he had condemned himself.

It came to nothing, of course. What John called Maxton's 'shrewd lazi-ness' would probably have killed it anyway. But two months later Churchill appointed Beaverbrook as Minister of Aircraft Production, and suddenly Beaverbrook was anxious to pretend that the meeting with the ILP had never happened, which he did successfully until 1941 when McGovern revealed it.

This might help to explain why John always regarded Beaverbrook as one of the very few truly evil men he had ever known – an opinion shared, curi-ously, by an old friend from whom he was now utterly estranged, Clem Attlee.

McGovern (though not Maxton) was certainly willing to be publicly identified with the BCCSE, and spoke at several of their meetings, strongly supporting the 'Tavistock peace proposals'. One was at the Kingsway Hall. John Beckett was in the chair, and the speakers were Tavistock, McGovern and Hugh Ross Williamson, a well-known Catholic writer and historian. It seems to have been a peaceful occasion. Both Beckett and McGovern were older and stouter, if not wiser, than when they had forced attendants to frogmarch them off the floor of the House of Commons

The breadth of the anti-war coalition was evident that night. You approached the packed hall past communists selling the *Daily Worker*,

Peace Pledge Union members selling their publications, as well as pro-Nazis selling theirs. I suspect that for a moment, John might have believed he was on the road back to the mainstream. The delusion cannot have lasted long.

It is unlikely to have outlasted the arrest of two members of Captain Ramsay's Right Club, Tyler Kent and Anna Wolkoff, for spying. The Right Club by early 1940 consisted, as Richard Thurlow puts it, of, approximately, 'Ramsay, Kent, five women with eccentric views and three MI5 agents'. Kent was an American, a cipher clerk at the US embassy with extreme anti-Communist views, and in 1940 he took to smuggling large quantities of documents out of the embassy and handing them to Wolkoff, a Russian émigré with similar views. These documents included secret cables between Winston Churchill, the First Lord of the Admiralty, and President Roosevelt, as well as between Roosevelt and his London ambassador, Joseph Kennedy. Wolkoff took Ramsay to Kent's flat to see the documents. Ramsay intended to use them in Parliament to expose the links between Churchill and Roosevelt. But Wolkoff passed them to the Italian government; and although Italy was still neutral, its security services traded information with the Germans. Thus Rome learned that Churchill and Roosevelt were in correspondence – at that time one of the most closely guarded secrets of the war, because of the domestic harm it could do to Roosevelt.

Wolkoff was trapped by one of the Right Club's MI5 agents, and she and Kent were arrested on 20 May 1940, less than a week after Churchill had become Prime Minister and formed a coalition government. On 22 May the security regulations were tightened, and the police came for John on 23 May. As Labour leader Clem Attlee moved into No. 11 Downing Street his one-time friend and agent John Beckett was moving into Brixton prison.

In Whitehall another former friend, now in the government, was gloating. Hugh Dalton wrote in his diary: 'Ramsay's arrest announced by the Speaker. It is ironical that the first MP to be jailed should be a Tory. Later announced that Mosley, Beckett and others also in jug. This is some compensation for the loss of Boulogne! Ruth (Dalton's wife) says "We had to lose Norway to get rid of Chamberlain, and to lose Boulogne to get rid of Mosley." '

From his bunker on the verge of extinction, John had been watching old friends go to fight the war against which they had campaigned so long. A. K. Chesterton joined the army. John laughed hollowly, saying that no one had been more emphatic than Chesterton about the immorality of fighting

Germany. The morning of his arrest, he received a letter from General Fuller who wrote that he had taken a war office appointment and could not therefore proceed with the new campaign they had planned together – an ex-servicemen's movement, like the one John founded after the great war, to ensure 'that the young men who are fighting should not have the empire pawned behind their backs, as was the case last time'.

John half despised Fuller and Chesterton for taking the respectable option. And he half envied them. He himself had joined the home guard a few days earlier, and rather hoped that would protect him from prison. Nonetheless, he had made preparations for arrest. He had worked out how to ensure that the BPP membership lists and his contact files were not taken when he was; and he had acquired character references a few months earlier, from Jimmy Maxton, Robert Forgan and Major General Fuller.

He knew he had been watched, and had some idea who the spies were in his camp. He also knew by then the policeman who came for him, Detective Sergeant Joss, and rather liked him.

About 11 a.m. on 23 May, Katherine Greene, Ben Greene's sister, bounded up the stairs of 13 John Street, near Victoria Station, which was the BPP office and which had a flat on the top floor where John and Anne lived during the week. (At weekends they lived in a small cottage in Berkhamstead rented from Ben Greene.) She was shouting, 'John, the police are here!' In a well-rehearsed manoeuvre, John's secretary took the files with many of the BPP's names and addresses along the parapet and into the empty adjoining building.

That night, Anne picked them up and dumped them in the pond at Hampstead Heath. Sadly, in the rush, most of John's correspondence over the years went with them.

While the documents were disappearing, John was meeting Joss and two other plain clothes men on the landing.

'John, we have come for you,' said Joss.

'Have you got a warrant, and what for?' John took Joss through the formalities, to make sure his secretary had plenty of time.

'It's under Regulation 18B and here is the Home Secretary's certificate.'

'What can I take?'

'You are not an ordinary prisoner. You can wear your own clothes and smoke and so on. It won't be for long.'

Anne helped John to pack in their flat above the office. The police opened the empty filing cabinets, and, unsurprised, shut them again, taking what there was to take. John came down with his suitcase and Joss asked, 'Would you like to go by taxi?'

'If you pay for it,' replied John, and Joss said, 'That will be all right.'

John and Joss went to the street to look for a taxi, while Joss's two colleagues stayed to ransack the office. John stopped the taxi in Kingsway to buy a large supply of cigarettes, and they drove on to Brixton prison.

John was sure Joss was right – it wouldn't be for long – and he had never been inside an English prison. He liked new experiences. He had no idea, as the great iron doors slammed behind him, that he had seen the last of freedom and of Anne for almost four years, and that he would come out ten years older and with a prison pallor that was never to leave him.

They drove into the yard and Joss took him to a little bare room with a counter at the end of it. Behind this, a small man in uniform signed for John as though he were a parcel and said, 'This way, Beckett.'

Now, the familiar figure of the policeman gone, doors clanging shut behind him, I think John began to feel very alone. He went with the little uniformed man through a long, grimy passage, on each side of which were doors which started at about two feet off the ground and were about five feet high. These were the reception cells, and John was locked in one of them. And suddenly, he was terrified. There was barely room to stand up, no room to walk, and only a small wooden ledge, about four feet long and fixed to the back of the cell, to sit on. He thought this cell was where he was to be kept.

After an hour, someone handed him over the top of the door a greasy tin with something inside which made his stomach seize up, and said, 'Here's your dinner.' By this time he knew he was not alone: 'Voices all round me proclaimed the presence of what my friend A. K. Chesterton has so aptly described as the "Mosley Circus". I had not heard them for three years – had I never heard them again it would have been too soon. And yet, in all their pompous raucousness, I heard them shouting comments from their various dens.'

After the meal had been consumed, the door opened and another man in uniform said, 'Come on, Beckett.' They went along a corridor and into a small, bare room with a weighing machine and several warders. John stripped and was weighed.

'I suppose you had a bath this morning,' remarked the chief warder, and allowed him to dress. In the next room, they shut him in another small pen for a couple of hours, then a warder took him outside and told him to strip again for the medical examination. He lined up with a few others and 'an extremely shabby and weary little man shuffled in front of us with a stethoscope hanging from his shoulders and said to each of us in turn "You all right?" '

They let him get dressed, and someone said, 'Come on Beckett' and took him to his cell. His watch had been taken from him, but he heard 6 p.m. chime on a church clock. 'The weary prelude to incarceration had taken all day.'

An hour later, 'I had a pressing call of nature, and seeing a bell by the door of my cell, I began to ring it. It rang loudly through the hollow prison, and after intermittent ringing for nearly an hour, I heard a voice outside: "What's the matter with you?" and saw a baleful eye looking at me through a tiny peephole in the centre of the door.

' "I want to go to the lavatory."

' "Well, you don't bleeding well ring, you use the tin thing under the washstand", and with various imprecations the voice died away in the distance. Making it as best I could in the small filthy utensil with no lid, I settled back to look at the bible which was the only printed thing in the room, and examine the wooden board with two or three unhygienic-looking blankets on it, on which I was supposed to sleep.'

He was woken the next morning by his cell door being flung open with the cry of 'slop aat'. 'On looking out I saw my fellow prisoners, in various stages of undress, coming out of their cells and along the corridor, carrying before them with careful dignity small tins just like the one to which my attention had been drawn the previous night. As I joined them, Captain Ramsay MP, whose cell was one away from mine, passed with his burden. The other side, Sir Oswald, surrounded by several miniature followers, was engaged in the same useful task.'

Two years earlier, reflecting on his visit to Poland a decade before. John wrote: 'In considerable wanderings around the world I have come to consider the right of immediate trial one of the greatest assets of Englishmen. Any government having the right to keep people in prison indefinitely without trial, will abuse that right ...' That is true, and no less true because John admired regimes which had that right, and did abuse it. The British government, in suspending habeus corpus and imprisoning John and hundreds of others in May 1940, had removed a key civil liberty from its people.

Yet it cannot have been easy for the government, faced in May 1940 with imminent invasion, to distinguish between those, like Ramsay, who had connections with spies, and those, like Beckett and the majority of the internees, who did not. The Tyler Kent affair helped to persuade the government to act when it did. They must all have seemed very dangerous people to have running around free at a time when the Germans had swept through Norway, Holland and Belgium, and France was on the point of surrender.

More than 700 were imprisoned, including Mosley, Ramsay, Greene, Harry St John Philby, John McNab and William Joyce's brothers Quentin and Frank Joyce. Tavistock and Lymington remained free, perhaps because they were peers.

John's situation was pretty unpleasant. Not only was he locked in a tiny cell for twenty hours a day: in his brief time in the exercise yard, he was surrounded by bitter enemies, the Mosley loyalists. They looked at him, he felt, as though they longed to back him up against a wall and break his bones. He did not think the prison guards would rush to protect one fascist from attack by other fascists.

In those first few months in Brixton, he and the obsessive, anti-Semite Arnold Leese became close to each other, mostly, I imagine, because they both, for different reasons, loathed Mosley. He recalled standing with Leese in the exercise yard and watching Mosley and his supporters walking up and down. 'There goes Tom Mosley and his bunch of kosher fascists,' said Leese loudly. My father told me this story admiringly, and I remarked it was a rather stupid thing for Leese to have said. 'Yes, but it was very brave,' he replied. 'There were twenty of them and only two of us.'

One day, a member of Mosley's entourage broke away from the group, presented himself in front of John, and gave the fascist salute.

'Hail Mosley. The Leader says that at this time of danger for our nation, past disagreements should be put to one side. He offers you a place in his provisional government.' John, whose many faults never included lack of a sense of humour, simply laughed. The man turned away, but returned a few minutes later.

'Hail Mosley. The Leader says, if that's your attitude, you shan't be in the provisional government at all.'

As at the abdication crisis, John's contempt for Mosley's dreams may have been misplaced. Hitler's plans for Britain are thought to have involved Lloyd George as figurehead Prime Minister and the Duke of Windsor, the former Edward VIII, as king, with Mosley as deputy Prime Minister and the real power in the land. Mosley must have known something of this, for he always cast Lloyd George as Britain's Quisling, and he may have known something of the Duke of Windsor's near-treasonable relationship with the Nazis at this time, for he and Lady Diana Mosley were always very close to the Windsors. But if that were to happen, it seems likely that John Beckett would have seen a firing squad before he saw the cabinet table. He was sure of it, telling the appeal against his internment:

> Probably more than anyone I have reason to fear a German invasion here ... I can produce three reliable witnesses to tell you that I was put on the 'to be shot' list two years ago. Mosley has told these personal friends of mine, one of them known to you ... My name has been at the top of that list for two years, ever since the Camrose case.

When the blitz began that summer, and each night the air was dark with German bombers dropping their deadly cargo over London, the inmates of Brixton prison were perhaps the most frightened people in the city, for they were locked in their cells. They did not think that, in the event of a bomb falling on them, the guards were likely to risk their lives to free their prisoners.

Some of the men went to pieces very quickly in prison. Joe Beckett, former British heavyweight boxing champion and former Mosley body-guard, had a cell close to John, and night after night John and the others could hear him crying and weeping to be let out. John was always rather proud of the fact that he coped better than most. He did it by feeding his mind, by discovering reserves in himself which he could enter, and ignore his surroundings. He found he could read anything at all and absorb himself in it, however trite it was or however often he had read it before. When the governor stopped prisoners lending each other books, the bible and old newspapers did fine for a while. He played chess constantly with the German in the next cell. They did this by drawing chess boards on the floors of their cells with pieces of chalk, and working out an elaborate code so that they could convey their moves to each other by knocking on the wall. By the time they were both transferred out of Brixton they had played over 100 matches, and the German was two or three games up because his play was more careful. John approached chess rather in the way that he lived his life, with a certain flair but a fatal disregard for the consequences of his moves.

A radio would have helped, but his request to have one was turned down. Mosley's request, on the other hand, was agreed, and night after night he could hear Mosley's radio from a few cells away. It was too distant to make out the words. He found that maddening: too loud to ignore, too soft to hear properly. But he was hardly on the sort of terms with Mosley where he could ask him to make his radio louder or softer.

Jimmy Maxton came to visit John, and Mosley as well, and spent an hour or two with John. The visit caused a serious row on the ILP National Council. 'God's truth, Jimmy, how could you lower yourself – especially to visit that bastard Mosley?' said one of its members. John McGovern, who had known all about the visit, writes in his autobiography: 'I do not think any other person in the party would have got away with it so easily as Jimmy, but his personal popularity allowed him to ride the storm.'

On 10 July John's appeal against internment was heard by a committee set up to hear such appeals under Norman Birkett KC. Birkett asked him about William Joyce, now broadcasting for Germany:

Q Joyce is Lord Haw Haw, I am told. Have you listened to Lord Haw Haw?
A Very often.
Q Do you confirm it?
A I cannot confirm it, but I think it is very likely.
Q Not that it matters, but we are told that it is so. We know Joyce has gone to Germany.
A He is in Germany. Of course, he was never a British subject.
Q Was he not?
A No. He was an American subject, he was born in America, but I did not find that out until after we had parted.

This exchange was the first time that anyone mentioned the defence Joyce was to use at his trial. It is almost as though John was preparing the ground for his friend.

They asked him about a letter he and Joyce had written to Dr Christian Bauer of the German embassy when they left Mosley saying they were 'most anxious that our German friends should know the truth'. He told them:

Mosley had spent a great deal of time in Germany and the Germans looked upon his as being the great head in this country for the kind

169

of doctrine they believed in ... Bauer was ... a press correspondent over here ... Mosley is a very vindictive man if you disagree with him, he told the press a lot of stories about us here and I expected worse in Germany, and I was keen to see Bauer so that he might know why we had left Mosley.

His experience with Mosley, he said, had convinced him that, after all, governments should be democratic; and he was able to show that the BPP constitution, which he had drafted, made it an ordinary democratic political party.

Over a full day of questioning, John was taken through pretty well every word he had spoken and written in the previous three years. His account of himself, though sometimes self-serving and occasionally economical with the truth, is for the most part clear, honest and fluent. He could not change his private views, he said. He was not a pacifist or a Christian, as Tavistock was; he just did not believe in the rightness of this war. But he had stopped all anti-war propaganda, and issued instructions that the BPP was to stop it, on 12 May. The so-called phoney war was over and the real war had begun and 'I could not go in front of an audience whose young men folk were fighting, and take all the heart out of them by telling them exactly what a swindle I thought they were fighting for.'

So, if they were to order his release, this is what he would do: 'I have enough land at Berkhamstead which I have already dug up and cultivated ... to keep me fairly active, and I have a very cheap cottage there which I very much like and where we live whenever we can.' He would live there, dig his ground, join the home guard – 'I was a sergeant instructor of signals when I was discharged, I know all about signalling, and so I can instruct in signalling.'

But of course none of that mattered, and both John and Birkett knew it. The justification for locking him up was contained in one paragraph of an MI5 report which Birkett had in front of him, and which read:

In conversation, Beckett has been more frank. In January 1940 he stated that he was making efforts on behalf of his organisation to get in touch with the men in the forces, so that, when the time was ripe, they would 'turn their rifles in the right direction'. Quite recently he has stated that he would like to join the local Defence Volunteers so as to obtain a rifle and ammunition, and he reproved his associate,

Greene, for refusing to do so when given the opportunity, on account of pacifist principles. Finally, he has stated that the names and addresses of members of the fifth column, among whom he ranks himself, are recorded in Germany for use when the Germans arrive.

Of course, this was terribly serious. If even half of it were true, the government would have been grossly negligent had it allowed him to walk the streets.

But not a word of it was true. He knew exactly where the first part of the story came from, and told Birkett's committee. In January, 'A man I had known for some time, I had met him first in the Mosley movement, came to see me, and he told me a long story about his own illegal activities, of which I did not believe a word, and he then told me a long story about Mosley's illegal activities, of which I did not believe a word either, and then he leaned forward to me and said: "I hope you are doing something of the sort, what are you doing." He is a man I have suspected for a long time of being some kind of agent.' John had not used the words quoted, 'but I am quite confident he would have gone off and said I did'.

Birkett asked the name and he told them. It was James McGuirk Hughes, alias Major P. G. Taylor, Mosley's head of security and the man whom Mosley knew was an MI5 agent in his organisation. Hughes, as researcher John Hope put it in *Lobster* magazine in 1998, 'was of central importance to the organisation and development of the BUF ... During the crisis which engulfed the BUF following its dismal performance in the local elections of 1937, it was to Hughes that Mosley first turned to salvage the disaster.' Hughes was Mosley's emissary to Ramsay and the Right Club, and 'threw himself wholeheartedly into the intrigues in which Ramsay engaged in 1940'. Hughes was Maxwell Knight's man and Mosley's man, and on behalf of MI5, he provided lying evidence to fit up Mosley's enemies for internment.

John did not know where the second part of the story, about the fifth column, came from. We know now. It was invented by a young German who spied for MI5 called Harald Kurtz, who also provided false evidence on which Ben Greene was imprisoned. Greene was able to prove that it was untrue, and was released. But for John, the entirely false allegations reappear over and over again in MI5 documents explaining why his continued detention was necessary, with embellishments. By 1941 it was being confidently asserted that he believed Kurtz to be a Nazi agent and that he 'openly refers to himself and his colleagues ... as members of Hitler's fifth column'. There is nothing glamorous about spies, even your own spies.

John was desperate to get out. He told the committee that his whole view had changed when France fell. He added that he dreaded a German invasion, and this was certainly the truth, if only because, as he put it, 'The associations I have been forced into during my imprisonment have strongly sharpened my fears of the consequences of defeat, and I am genuinely anxious to do my part in avoiding this disaster.'

It didn't work. In theory, the allegations of Taylor and Kurtz were discounted, but they must have influenced in the decision. 'The committee considered the whole of the evidence in this case with the most anxious care,' they reported to the Home Secretary. 'They were not unimpressed by the personality of Beckett, who gave his evidence in a very frank and attractive way. They entertained no doubt that Beckett was a politically minded man who held his views with great tenacity, and was not lacking in courage in expounding them.' But they concluded:

> The history of Beckett's political activities indicated a great element of instability in his character ... It was impossible to be quite sure that a man so unstable in his mental and political outlook would not be led into activities which would cause great trouble. The committee also considered the fact that Beckett had been associated with Joyce in the public mind ... Whilst they did not regard Beckett as a highly dangerous man, or one who would willingly do injury to the country's efforts, they yet felt that if they were to recommend his release, it would be done with very considerable misgivings ...

In September 1940 John heard the committee decision, and was moved to Stafford jail. The next month he had even worse news. With London being bombed heavily, Prime Minister Winston Churchill brought a famous Londoner to the Home Office to oversee the improvement of air raid shelters: Herbert Morrison. And the only person who could order someone to be arrested or released under regulation 18B was the Home Secretary. There were no checks, no other legal process. The Home Secretary did not have to listen to his advisory committees and did not have to give a reason for his decision.

John and Morrison still loathed each other. Twice during the hearing before the committee, John's emotions ran away with him, and both times it was because he had somehow managed to remind himself, in passing, of Herbert Morrison:

'I have known Morrison a long time, I knew him in the last war when I was a soldier and he was not, and I do find something extraordinarily wrong in a man who was a conscientious objector when he was of military age ...' It was one of the few occasions when the tribunal interrupted to bring him back to the point.

The same point was made in Parliament by Labour MP F. J. Bellenger, who quoted from a first world war pacifist leaflet Morrison had written: 'Go forth, little soldier. Though you know not what you fight for, go forth. Though you have no grievance against your German brother – go forth and kill him. Though you may know he has a wife and family dependent on him – go forth and slay him; he is only a German dog.'

'A man who could write that stuff in the last war' thundered Bellenger, 'when many of us were defending our country and he was not, is not the man to be the judge of subversion on this occasion.'

John had two mortal enemies in politics. Mosley was the first, and John believed that he was still in prison because of the lies of Mosley's friend and confidante James McGuirk Hughes. Morrison was the second, and I believe he pictured Morrison laughing at him as he jangled the keys. He felt sure that Morrison's vindictiveness would keep him in his cell. For the first time he realised that he was likely to spend a long time behind bars. Despair mixed with a sort of black anger.

He had been moved from Brixton to Stafford prison. The governor of Stafford Prison minuted in November:

Beckett was on report on three occasions:
(a) On 14/10/40 he was reported for (1) Causing a disturbance during an Air Raid Warning and (2) Insolence to a Principal Officer on 13/10/40. For these offences he was deprived of privileges for 3 days.
(b) On 16/10/40 he was reported for (1) Disturbing the quiet of the Prison and (2) Threatening an officer with the Governor. He was deprived of privileges for 7 days.
(c) On 12/11/40 he was reported for attempting to pass a letter to his wife during a visit on 11/11/40. He was deprived of privileges for 14 days.
His general conduct during the time that he was in my custody was such that I have every reason to suppose that he would be a nuisance

in a camp and his detention at Brixton Prison as a disciplinary case would seem to be merited.

'I have twice travelled to Stafford from London,' wrote Anne to the new Home Secretary, 'to find on my arrival that I could not see him because – for some action the wrongness of which he was not even aware – he had been deprived of "privileges" which included my fifteen minute weekly interview. He is quite willing to give his guarantee not to take further part in political work for the duration of the war – and to this I would add my own guarantee and most earnest request for a reconsideration of my husband's case.'

CHAPTER NINE

MR MORRISON'S PRISONER

To the end of his life, John was convinced that Herbert Morrison used his power as Home Secretary to keep him in prison, as an act of revenge for humiliating Morrison on Hackney council twenty years earlier. Was he right?

When John was arrested in May 1940, a German invasion, for which Britain was not at all prepared, was expected at any moment. But from the autumn on, the justification for keeping men and women locked up without trial became thinner, especially those like John who were clearly not spies or fifth columnists, and did not want a German victory. It became clear that the fifth column was a myth.

The authorities recognised this by starting to release some of the internees. But many remained inside, including some of the best-known names: Mosley, Domvile, Ramsay, Leese – and Beckett. In March 1942 a Home Office memorandum suggested that some of them should be taken off the review list and interned for the duration of the war. This should apply to Mosley, Ramsay, Domvile, Leese – but not Beckett.

John's lawyers repeated his assurances about his behaviour, and yet another old political friend was found to back them up, because they wrote to Morrison: 'Mr Beckett is prepared to take no part in politics and he understands that Mr Frank Owen, editor of the *Evening Standard*, will guarantee this if it is necessary.'

John wrote to Morrison that he had never knowingly been associated with anyone connected with a foreign government, or done anything to help a foreign government. Yet 'I am in a prison, and, with some slight amenities, treated like a convict. My letters and visits are severely restricted, my wrist watch and razor have been taken away and I am not even allowed to have the writing pad and pencil I brought with me. I am locked up in a cell for eighteen hours a day, cannot tell the time, and am not even allowed to leave my cell to satisfy the demands of nature. I am told to use a very small tin receptacle which makes the cell thoroughly beastly ... Does the government really desire to inflict vindictive punishment on those who disagree with it?'

It did not help his sense of grievance to discover that Mosley was no longer sharing these hardships. He spent most of his time of internment in Holloway, where he lived in a small flat with his wife in an otherwise empty prison, and the governor took to drinking brandy with them after dinner. It is not clear why, but it may have had something to do with the deference due to a wealthy baronet.

The advisory committee heard John again in 1942 by which time he had been moved to the Isle of Man. They spent a long time questioning him about a report that, in the prison camp where he was one of the elected 'house leaders' responsible for organising one of the houses, he had said to another house leader: 'Why do you keep your house so clean? It is toadying to the authorities.' This, apparently, was supposed to show that he still had a bad attitude and should remain in prison. He denied it, and so did the man to whom he was supposed to have said it. A secret Home Office minute complained that John should not have been told who accused him: 'This disclosing of an informant's identity seems quite wrong, and it is only natural, now they are together in Brixton, that Hudson should deny having given the information against Beckett.' MI5 had placed spies among the prisoners, so that they should never know whom to trust.

Early in 1943 he had to have an operation and was allowed to spend a month convalescing in Robert Forgan's home. When he was due to return to Brixton, Forgan, who had returned to medicine after his ill-fated time in politics, wrote personally to Morrison to ask for an extension. John Beckett's health was still very poor, he said. He even offered a financial guarantee for John's behaviour.

The prison doctor responded that the main trouble now was not the aftermath of the operation, but the heart disease, and that the prison hospital was just as healthy a place as Forgan's home. Morrison minuted: 'I can only be influenced by medical evidence, and it must be medical evidence in which I have confidence' – presumably his way of saying what he thought of his old parliamentary colleague Forgan.

About the same time, the advisory committee heard John again. They were told that he had developed a heart condition in prison, and saw for themselves that he fainted and collapsed as he left the hearing. Forgan treated him, and again wrote asking for his release on medical grounds, offering to put him up in his own house and guarantee his good behaviour. The committee reported to Morrison: 'Health considerations are not to be ignored, but apart altogether from these … Beckett does now consider that there is no alternative to the course upon which the nation is set ... The committee think that Beckett could now be released and they recommend that he should be released.'

Home Secretary Herbert Morrison overruled them, and decided that John should stay in prison.

The committee's recommendation to Morrison was secret. All the same, some of John's friends suspected the truth. John McGovern, still an MP, reproduced in his autobiography a letter he wrote to Morrison that September: 'In enclosing a letter from Mr John Beckett, Brixton Prison, I ask you to seriously consider – free from personal bias – the releasing of this man. Surely when the position has so seriously changed, and that Beckett was not acting with the Fascists, you can do one just act. Do not allow personal spleen to operate in this case ... Please do the generous thing in this case, as he will give any reasonable undertaking concerning the future.' But Morrison could argue that he was following the advice of the security services. MI5 was determined that John should stay behind bars, and did everything possible to influence the Home Secretary.

An eight-page paper for Morrison, signed G. R. Mitchell (a key MI5 figure over many years), asking him to reject the committee's recommendation for release, began with a highly selective collection of quotes from John's pre-war articles, showing what everyone knew: that up to May 1940, he advocated a negotiated peace.

Mitchell stated that, appearing before the advisory committee, 'Beckett made no secret of the fact that all he did in May 1940 was to abandon the public advocacy of negotiations, and not his view that peace ought to be negotiated'. On this question he was 'quite frank'. And so he was. He said that he could not change his private views, but would not speak of them publicly. Mitchell was arguing that private views, even if never publicly expressed, are a sufficient reason to lock a man up. Thought policemen are not confined to dictatorships.

Every letter John had written to Anne and everyone else had been opened. Mitchell boasted: 'We have copies of dozens if not scores of these letters in our files.' None of them contained a seditious word, Mitchell admitted. But 'it should be remembered that Beckett is not a fool, that he very much wants ... to be released from detention, and that he has always known that his letters were subject to scrutiny'.

So they set him up. 'He thought he had succeeded in smuggling out a letter to his wife.' Yet even then they got nothing on him. 'He says in the letter: "It is nice to write and to know nobody but you will see the letter" and the rest of the letter is purely personal, its tone is even more affectionate than usual, and there is no political or military comment at all.' Nonetheless, the letter remained in the files of the voyeurs from MI5.

In the absence of anything incriminating from him, Mitchell turned to Anne's letters. There was not much more there either. The best Mitchell was able to find was a plea to John not to criticise the government in case it affected his chances of release.

The only serious evidence Mitchell could find was a pro-German entry in an autograph album. The fellow detainee who offered it turned out to be another of MI5's prison spies. John told the advisory committee that this was written in a fit of temper after hearing that his previous application for release had been turned down. The committee believed him. Mitchell said that MI5 did not. They said it proved that he wanted a German victory.

Mitchell, knowing his audience, took care to point out 'the virulent invective which Beckett has expressed over the past three years against the Prime Minister and the Home Secretary in particular'. It dwelt lovingly on quotes from purloined letters intended for Anne in which John said unkind things about Morrison. Mitchell, one supposes, knew – or thought he knew – his Home Secretary.

I find it impossible to read Mitchell's paper without feeling that I have touched something unclean. It reminded me strongly of a witch-hunting Comintern paper I read when I was researching Britain's communists, written about the same time, which began: 'The leadership of the Communist Party of Great Britain contains a number of people who were formerly connected with enemies of the people' and it was devoted largely to statements they had once made which Stalinist loyalists would consider politically unsound.

There is the evident pleasure in the secret power Mitchell has over the life of another man. There is the calm assumption that it is right to lock a man up because you think that secretly, though he says nothing, he harbours unreliable opinions. Quotes are manipulated in the safe knowledge that they will not be examined publicly, and that no right of reply is available to the victim. Possessing the man's love letters to his wife is an occasion for prurient gloating.

Perhaps the creepiest thing in the document is the sly way in which it makes sure Morrison understands that John Beckett has, and expresses, a low opinion of Morrison. These are clearly intended to influence

Morrison's decision. This does not, of course, prove that Morrison would keep a man behind bars for saying rude things about him; only that Mitchell thought he would.

The document is the most eloquent argument for never allowing anyone to be locked up without trial, for that places them at the mercy of men like G. R. Mitchell. Secret at the time, the document is now available in the Public Record Office in Kew (since Mr Mitchell is no longer with us) and it is worth reading in full if you are ever in danger of forgetting how fragile our liberties are.

Morrison's civil servants pointed out that the government had been obliged to release Ben Greene because the evidence of the MI5 informer Harald Kurtz was found to be unreliable, so they could no longer use Kurtz against John. Nor could they use the evidence of McGuirk Hughes, alias P. G. Taylor, because the Advisory Committee had recommended that it was not safe. This left a legal problem which John himself summed up for them: 'Everything I am accused of here, if it were all true and all proved to the hilt, would be roughly that I was concerned with two organisations and one publication which it was not in the national interest to allow to continue ... The 18B Regulation was not intended to deal ... with such cases.'

A civil service brief to Morrison stated that, nonetheless, there was a case for keeping John Beckett in prison. It was likely that he still privately would like to see a negotiated peace. There were, still at liberty, an ill-assorted collection of eccentrics who wanted the same: the Duke of Bedford, Lymington, the Peace Pledge Union, and others:

These people have hitherto been harmless, partly for lack or organising ability and political experience, partly because they have often been too obviously fascist, and partly because the idea of a negotiated peace has been so unpopular. It is not beyond the bounds of possibility, however, that some of them might be organised by a man such as Beckett to form a far more effective crypto-fascist party than we have yet seen ... Beckett is opposed to Mosley and the dictatorship principle and is not, therefore, tarred with the BUF brush. He has the skill and plausibility to take advantage of such a feeling ...

There was 'no evidence that Beckett or the Duke contemplates such a thing'. But 'to release a man of Beckett's views and abilities would be to risk more than a mere increase in anti-war propaganda'.

Morrison seems to have had two civil service briefs, one recommending release, the other agreeing with MI5 and recommending continued detention. Morrison wrote on one of them in his own hand: 'I think the reasons are so substantial that detention is necessary.' And that was that.

They eventually let him out in October 1943, well after Domvile and Gordon-Canning and just a month before Mosley. Even after he had left prison, the battle continued and the Home Secretary continued to take a personal interest in it. John was under a sort of house arrest, not permitted to travel more than five miles from Dr Forgan's house where he lived. MI5 opened all his letters, even his Christmas cards, in order to obtain ammunition with which to argue that his five-mile restriction should remain. G. R. Mitchell, who had fought so hard to keep him in prison, and whose name John probably never knew, wrote: 'The card sent to J. A. McNab, William Joyce's friend, contained the following verse:

'God send us men with hearts ablaze
'All truth to love, all wrong to hate,
'These are the Patriots Britain needs,
'These are the Bulwarks of the State.'

Added in ink were the following words: 'So Plutocracy put them in Concentration Camps.' At the end of a series of similar rather innocent quotations Mitchell wrote: 'We quote the above passages from intercepted correspondence, but we most particularly request that no hint of the source of our information be given to Beckett at his hearing ... They are not apparently aware that their correspondence is subject to scrutiny ...'

Morrison went out of his way, in a speech in Parliament in 1943, to drag his old adversary into a debate about the imprisonment of Mosley:

There was the case of John Beckett in connection with which a number of people approached me, not only on this side but in other parts of the House as well, to let him out ... John Beckett is a man I have known since 1920. He was a troublesome left wing member of the Hackney Borough Council when I was its leader. He is not a wealthy person; he is a proletarian gone wrong. He is what I would call a political organiser and lives as best he can ...

I am sure John thought this was a coded way of telling him that Morrison had had the last laugh.

Morrison seems to have interested himself in the most trivial aspects of the matter. Incredibly, a decision as to whether John might be permitted to travel to London for the day to see his optician because he had broken his glasses went right up to the Home Secretary. And by the time it reached Morrison, it had been considered by four civil servants. The first, G. W. Sturt, wrote a long briefing which began: 'It is clear that Beckett intends to get up to London, on one excuse or another, as frequently as possible.' He had already been allowed to London to visit his mother-in-law in hospital. 'This seems most undesirable, both on account of the very grave view taken of this man by the security services, and from the point of view of possible reactions upon political or public opinion and morale of allowing this traitor free access to London and elsewhere.' There was no justification for the word 'traitor', but John could never see the document or know the word had been used, so presumably it was not thought to matter what was said.

The minute suggested telling him that if he were ever allowed to travel to London, it would be under escort and he must meet the costs. They knew he had no money, and that this would therefore ensure no further requests. Meanwhile, the request should be refused.

Morrison's minute reads: 'I agree. He is being vexatious if not frivolous in his excuses. I rather liked the escort idea of Mr Sturt except his proposal to charge police expenses. Try to tighten up on Mr Beckett within fairness and reason.'

After the war, when Forgan applied to rejoin the Labour Party, he was turned down more than once by committees on which Morrison had an important voice. In March 1946, with Morrison present, the Party's Elections Subcommittee looked at his application. 'The National Agent reported on conversations with Dr Forgan concerning his present political outlook and his entertainment of Mr John Beckett following Beckett's release from prison.' On that basis they turned him down. Morrison, as wartime Home Secretary, had only released John on condition that Forgan would put him up. Morrison, as a key member of Labour's National Executive Committee, was now punishing Forgan for doing exactly that.

On the face of it, these facts suggest a spirit of mean-minded vindictiveness, as well as an abuse of power. The least one can say of Morrison is that he seems to have enjoyed the untrammelled power he had to keep

181

people locked up rather more than is healthy for a minister in a free society. But he was also subject to pressure from MI5 and his own civil servants. Their notion of the liberty they were defending seems to have been pretty sketchy, and their spitefulness considerable.

It has to be remembered that, throughout the war, Morrison was the government's leading enthusiast for locking people up and suppressing newspapers. All his colleagues seem at one time or another to have urged less draconian measures. He kept the communist *Daily Worker* closed long after most people thought it was no longer justified. Even Churchill was rebuffed when he wrote to Morrison asking for the release of the German-born Prince of Pless whose family he knew well, and offered personally to guarantee the man. Morrison wrote back huffily saying no: 'I note you say you have only met him twice.'

Morrison did not necessarily require personal animus to keep people inside, and MI5 seems to have been determined to ensure that John Beckett should stay locked up.

Does any of it matter? I have heard it argued that the 18B internees did not believe in freedom, so should not benefit from it; and that in any case their sufferings were nothing compared to what was going on in Germany. The second of these statements, at least, is incontestable. But to justify internment on the grounds that the Germans were doing far worse things is to make a mockery of everything Britain was supposed to be fighting for. In the summer of 1940, when invasion was thought likely and a well-organised fifth column was thought to be in place, rounding up dissidents in a panic is at least understandable. Later, as the immediate danger receded, you could still justify some detentions. Ramsay had been associated with spying activities, and Mosley was Britain's fascist leader.

The trouble was that people in key positions – not just Morrison, but also his civil servants and the faceless men from MI5 – grew to enjoy that sort of power. It is a considerable tribute to the Attlee government which took office after the war in 1945 that it managed to make a break, more or less, with the wartime attitude towards freedom. It could have poisoned our democracy for decades.

This account has been put together largely from the documents which the government has released. There are gaps where papers are still with-held, allegedly for security reasons. More than half a century after the event, it is most unlikely that there could be any valid security reasons. It is much more likely that these papers contain material which would damage even further the reputations of ministers, civil servants and security services.

Whatever the rights or wrongs, John remained a resentful and difficult prisoner in Brixton and Stafford jails and in prison camps on the Isle of Man and at Huyton near Liverpool. 'His conduct in all places of detention except Brixton have been the subject of adverse reports', Morrison's permanent secretary wrote primly.

'He taught me to play chess in Stafford prison,' recalled one old Mosleyite. 'He organised a chess competition there. I was with Mosley and he was not, so we did not talk politics.'

On the Isle of Man they were accommodated in old-fashioned boarding houses on the seafront at Peel, behind barbed wire. Each house elected its own 'house leader' and was issued with rations. The inmates were responsible for cleaning and cooking. John was house leader for the house containing the non-BUF people.

He joined an ambitious escape attempt organised by BUF and IRA internees. A tunnel was built under a road at the back of the camp, with the intention of finding a fishing boat to take them to neutral Ireland. John seems to have opted out at the last minute because each escapee had to get money brought in. He could only ask Anne to do this, and that would put her in danger. The organiser of the escape attempt, Arthur Mason, writes: 'John stood up to internment very well, except he was worried about Anne.'

The escape attempt went badly wrong. The fishing boats in Peel had had their spark plugs removed to immobilise them, and the men were arrested after they had rowed several miles out to sea. Three days later, a rumour spread that they were being ill-treated by the guards, and a riot began, with John as one of the leaders. The guards started shooting, and he claimed that one of them shot directly at him, missing him by a whisker. A few days later he and several others were returned to Brixton as punishment.

In Huyton, rations were short, says Mosleyite Bob Row who was also interned there. John's 'spirits and gift for repartee had not been diminished despite months of incarceration'. All the same, something very odd happened to him at Huyton.

Rations were short and we were all more or less permanently hungry. Long before meals were due there was a steady procession three times a day to join the cookhouse queue. Having nothing to do when we reached it, we talked, and often there were arguments because there were various factions in the camp apart from mainstream BUF ...

A rumour was put around in the queue ... firstly that your father's mother was Jewish and her name was Salmon or Salaman, and later in the day that his grandmother was Jewish and her name was Silver. Naturally he blew his top about all this.

The rumour, says Mr Row, was started maliciously by a small group of anti-Semite extremists from the East End of London. It was also, of course, true, and it seems likely that a group of obsessive Jew-haters from the area knew perfectly well that it was true. I wonder what John thought as he angrily denied it.

Outside the prison Anne conducted a relentless letter campaign for her husband's release, and worked closely with Tavistock, the Duke of Bedford. The duke may have helped her a little financially, but not much, because she was also forced to find secretarial work in London. His ancestral seat, Woburn Abbey, had been taken over by the Special Operations Executive, and several times a month Anne travelled to his almost equally opulent Scottish home.

It seems likely that she was left at liberty mainly so that MI5 could follow her, note the names of her associates, and record her visits to the duke. She found that a member of the BPP and of the National Socialist League, Major Harry Edmonds, seemed remarkably often to be travelling in her direction. John became convinced that Edmonds was spying; and also, I think, suspected him of taking a predatory sexual interest in Anne.

Edmonds was a friend of Major General Fuller, and seems to have fancied himself as a ladies' man. During the thirties, he founded the Wagner Society while involved with the German Zeppelin Company and coming into contact with the Wagner family. The Wagner Society continued well into the 1950s, and was always concerned with much more than musical appreciation. Edmonds had written a few novels in the thirties, too – sub-Bulldog Drummond stuff. One was called *Red Invader*, and its title tells you all you need know about the plot.

In August 1943 John wrote a remarkably intemperate letter to Herbert Morrison. Headed 'John Beckett, Political Prisoner', it ended:

In several cases lately you have caused this type of enquiry to be made by a 'Major Edmonds' and last week my wife received a most unpleasant letter from this man asking her to see him. Ever since my arrest he has pestered her in every possible way and plagued her with improper and indecent proposals. This letter is written mainly in the hope that it will supply you with sufficient information to avoid the necessity of exposing my wife to further worry and insult from this nasty piece of work whom you employ to obtain information.

I have found no evidence that Edmonds was MI5 (though that does not prove he was not) and Anne felt less animosity towards him than John did. Years later, after John's death, she was willing to have meals with him, and spend weekends in his splendid Sussex home. Those who knew him say he was less a spy, more a Walter Mitty character. But of course, the two aren't incompatible, in fact they go rather well together.

Perhaps John's imprisonment had made him paranoid. The petty restrictions of prison life, and the complacency and occasional vindictiveness of those who had him in their power, were certainly jangling his nerves. This must have aggravated his heart condition, which had been with him since his wartime service and which was to remain with him for the rest of his life, and which was eventually diagnosed as angina.

Jimmy Maxton visited him in hospital, this time in secret so as to avoid the political storm which his first visit provoked. Anne remembered arriving at the hospital bed to find Maxton already sitting on it, and John turning to her and saying, half humorously, 'Jimmy doesn't believe I'm ill.' In October 1943 John was delivered into the care of Dr Forgan, and forbidden to stray more than five miles from Forgan's home near Brentwood in Essex. Anne stayed there with him at night, but had to travel to central London to work as a secretary during the day, because they still had no money.

He hated living with Forgan. He had no work and nothing to do. He did not get on with Forgan's second wife, and loathed her large army of cats. He bitterly resented the five-mile restriction, pointing out that all the other former detainees had a ten- mile radius, except Mosley who had seven miles: only he had five miles. One day Anne came home from work and found him sitting on the bed looking as miserable as she had ever seen him. 'If I had £5 in my pocket I'd get out of here,' he said. She produced the £5 and they went illegally to London together and lay low in a tiny flat in Victoria. John grew a moustache to make recognition harder, and seldom or never went out. They were very happy for a few days.

Their idyll must, I think, have been interrupted by a call from Forgan to say that the police were searching Essex for John, and that Mrs Forgan had been unwise enough to tell the police that he was in London. John returned in haste to the Forgans' home and denied that he had been out of Essex. 'During the interview,' the Essex detective wrote to MI5, 'Beckett appeared very agitated; in my opinion his demeanour showed that he had been caught out, but realising he had his freedom at stake he very cleverly avoided the issue.'

Finally Anne went to the Duke of Bedford for help. He provided a cottage in the village of Chenies, on the border of Hertfordshire and Buckinghamshire, and the Home Office gave John permission to move there. Anne got some commissions to write theatre criticism for *The Queen* magazine, and had a couple of short stories accepted by the *Evening Standard* under the pseudonym Anne Stone. John fretted under his five-mile restriction, but started slowly to recover his health.

He started going for very long walks several times a week, something he did for the rest of his life. Partly, I am sure this was a reaction to being locked up for nearly four years. Partly, too, it must have been where he did his thinking, and his dreaming.

It is not hard to imagine what he might have been thinking as he walked the Buckinghamshire countryside in the summer of 1945. His old friend Clem Attlee was forming a new government, making his one-time friend Hugh Dalton Chancellor of the Exchequer and putting his old enemy Herbert Morrison in charge of the government's nationalisation programme. The army was bringing another friend, William Joyce, back from Germany and putting him on trial, and John was stirring himself to draft letters asking for clemency to go over the names of everyone he knew with a title. I think he took a very long walk on the morning they hanged William Joyce.

That year – 1946 – Jimmy Maxton died too. John must have felt that his place was following the coffin through the streets of Glasgow, as he had followed Wheatley's. But of course, it was out of the question.

Unlike Mosley and Chesterton, who disowned Joyce entirely, John never afterwards spoke of him without affection and admiration. Joyce's defence, that he was an American citizen, failed because he had obtained a British passport. When his friend John McNab asked if Joyce would return to the Catholic Church and see a priest, Joyce replied in words which John always quoted to show the man's bravery: 'I've got into enough trouble with false passports without trying to get one into heaven.'

Anne became pregnant, and that was when they started to think seriously about their lack of money. Most of what Anne could earn during the war had been spent on the campaign to get John out of prison, and on travelling around the country to see him and take him food and cigarettes. Now she felt her pregnancy was taking everything away from her, even draining her brain of its normal power. She could no longer find the eloquent flow of words for theatre criticism, the imagination which enabled her to write stories. Being pregnant was bad enough. Being pregnant and poor was unbearable. I was born on 12 May 1945, four days after VE Day.

John, I suspect, felt keenly his inability to keep her properly. He did not want to go back to politics. But who else was going to employ the notorious fascist John Beckett, 51 years old, whose main skill was propaganda, and who was not permitted to travel more than five miles from a tiny Buckinghamshire village?

Anne suggested that John should revive his childhood ambition and train for the bar, but he answered that he was too old. She suggested that they should set sail and start a new life in New Zealand. She still had relatives there who would surely help them get settled and find a home and some work. But John had turned down the chance to accompany his friend Ernest Mander to New Zealand when he was a young man with his life before him and the world at his feet. He was not going to set sail now, and struggle in a strange, harsh land through his declining years.

He had various surprising ideas. When another advisory committee met to consider his appeal against the five-mile restriction, he told them that the only work you could get in Chenies was farm labouring, and his health meant that he was not up to that. But if he were allowed to travel the six miles to Watford, he could get a job. Maybe in advertising, or newspapers. Maybe in factories, fire-watching. Maybe driving heavy lorries. He got quite enthusiastic about the idea of driving heavy lorries, and the committee cross-questioned him as to why he could drive a heavy lorry, but was not up to being an agricultural labourer.

MI5 was opposed, naturally. 'We regard Beckett as a potentially dangerous fascist and enemy sympathiser and are anxious that he should not have any chance of resuming political activity,' wrote Mitchell. So the committee turned him down, and it was not until 1945 that he got his radius extended. For a few months he earned his living as an administrator at Watford General Hospital. One day, learning that a baby in the hospital required bananas, he used hospital money to obtain them on the black market, and was fired.

And so, inevitably and sadly, John went back to earning his living in the only way that he knew he would be able to earn it: running a tiny, doomed political splinter on the far right of British politics. The Duke of Bedford had always assumed that John, on his release, would put his talents into reviving the British People's Party. The BPP was nothing at all without John. It wasn't a very great deal with him, either, but that little was enough for the duke.

They relaunched the BPP in December 1945 in Holborn Hall. 'Opening the meeting in typical style,' reported the communist *Daily Worker*, 'Beckett addressed the audience as "friends, Londoners, countrymen" and went on to say, "we are here not to praise victory but to analyse it." ' The next month the *Daily Worker* was able exclusively to report that the BPP was planning another meeting. The censor had opened a letter addressed to John and another addressed to *Daily Worker* news editor Douglas Hyde, and had put them back in the wrong envelopes by mistake. John, reports Hyde in his book *I Believed*, sent on Hyde's latter with a courteous note, but 'communists do not send courteous notes to fascists'.

In came quite a few of the old ranters, like the right-wing economist Professor Frederick Soddy. The chairman was Air Commodore Gerard Oddie. John said, truthfully in every sense, that his party had attracted all the oddies and the soddies.

The far right was splintering, just as it had done before the war. Mosley's former supporters formed three separate groups, which only came together in 1948 under Mosley's own leadership. Major Edmonds helped to found something called the Constitutional Research Association, of which Major General Fuller was vice president. At their inaugural meeting at Browns Hotel, Fuller 'foresaw disaster after disaster for the world until it acknowledged that there were superior men and inferior men, and saw to it that the superior men were permitted to take their natural place in the leadership of the world'. That's probably a pretty fair summary of the sort of constitutional research that this collection of arrogant and dim-witted army officers and Right Honourables had in mind.

In later years Edmonds's associates included Michael de la Bedoyere, editor of the *Catholic Herald*, and, apparently, Denis Thatcher. Increasingly this was the political ground occupied by John Beckett, though of course he was never acceptable in these circles. It was strange company for a former firebrand socialist to be keeping, but imprisonment seems to have damped down John's socialism and given him a new respect for the old establishment. Richard Griffiths has noted that many of the internees came out of prison with their own opinions exacerbated, and that was certainly true of John.

A. K. Chesterton started a short-lived organisation called the National Front for Victory, whose only long-term significance was its name: years later Chesterton was to re-use it when he founded the National Front. He then became deputy editor of *Truth*, which had been discreetly controlled by Neville Chamberlain before the war, and was now the magazine of the Conservative Party's far right. For ten years Chesterton was almost a mainstream figure, with a regular salary and a nine-to-five life, and John must have envied that, and envied the respectability that went with never having been interned.

Chesterton's wife, Doris, was always believed to have psychic powers. John was profoundly superstitious at heart. Many fascists are – it goes with the mystic belief in leaders. Doris Chesterton, so John's story goes, once read his palm, then refused to tell him what she had seen there. Some months later AK (as my parents always called him) said to him: 'We didn't expect to see you again. Doris thought that by now you'd have killed someone and be waiting to be hanged.' And in that intervening period John reckoned he had been closer to killing another human being than ever in his life, before or since. William Joyce used to tell the same story about Doris and himself.

The BPP, of course, could not replace the ILP of Maxton or the BUF of Mosley in John's life. It did not answer his need to have something he could believe in with all his heart. But he had that in hand. While in prison he had asked to see the Catholic chaplain, and was now being instructed with a view to being received into the Church. Catholicism was the faith of John Wheatley, and like fascism, it offered a total answer, which is why, throughout the twentieth century, there has been a constant coming and going between the Catholic Church and the Communist Party. And the Catholic Church was also mildly, carefully, patronisingly, but unmistakably, anti-Semitic. The *Catholic Herald* had been much admired in anti-Semitic circles before the war.

John was still a witty, fluent, compelling speaker, but he had lost the passion that electrified his pre-war speeches. He now often included diversions about people he had known, Attlee and Mosley in particular.

In addition to the old faces, the BPP attracted an undergraduate of 23, just demobilised from the army, who quickly rose to prominence while gaining a double first at Cambridge. His name was Colin Jordan, and he started his political career by writing articles for the *People's Post*, the BPP organ, and organising the Cambridge University Nationalist Club, a front for the BPP and controlled by the BPP secretary John Beckett. Today, more than half a century later, Jordan, rather disconcertingly, says: 'Next to Arnold Leese, my prime political mentor, I rate John Beckett the most impressive political figure I then met.'

Jordan soon started to fret at the BPP's moderation and cosiness. Council meetings were held over a weekend at the Duke of Bedford's ancestral seat in Woburn Abbey:

> I can picture the evening meal with the duke at the head of the table, and doing the carving – I have an idea we may have had bison and not just venison – and your father sitting next to him. In the lounge where the discussions took place, steered by John Beckett, I can picture the gentle gentleman, the duke, with his slippered feet resting on a footstool by the log fire. It was all very cosy and amiable, if, in the outcome, hardly productive in the advancement of the party.
>
> On the Sunday mornings the duke led a walk through the grounds, the rest of us following in pairs behind ... I remember your father, probably out of earshot of the duke, telling some of us of the connecting doors between many of the principal bedrooms, affording facility for liaison between guests of different sexes.

It was not what the obsessional young nationalist had gone into politics for, and Jordan was soon out of the BPP and mixing with German and American Nazis, as well as being courted by Mosley's supporters. His real hero was always the obsessive anti-Semite Arnold Leese, who put up the money that kept him in politics.

The BPP rented offices at 33 Maiden Lane, WC2, and held a series of meetings, some of which were broken up by the 43 Group, a militant group of Jewish ex-servicemen. John's primary task at the time seems to have been to make the BPP the strongest party on the fascist right, and his main efforts were directed at siphoning off Mosley supporters.

'A great part of my work since 1937 has been acting as a stretcher bearer and medical orderly behind the progress of the Mosley juggernaut,' he wrote in June 1948 to one disillusioned Mosley supporter, Michael McLean, suggesting that McLean meet Colin Jordan, who was also in Birmingham, and discuss his future. Presumably the appeal did not work, because a month later he was writing to McLean: 'Surely you can see that you could not help Mosley more than by allowing him to represent your sincere disgust with his movement as being a Jewish-Communist stunt.' McLean eventually passed the correspondence to the Board of Deputies of British Jews, where I was shown it.

As well as running the BPP and editing its regular publication, in 1948 John began to publish a fortnightly which he called *Fleet Street Preview*. This was not fascist or anti-Semitic at all, claiming to be simply well-informed, and aimed at an intellectual closed-circulation readership. '*Preview* does not pretend to give all the news – only that which is unobtainable through ordinary channels', it said on its news pages.

It had some well-informed comment and a few genuine scoops, especially on Labour Party affairs. It predicted Clement Attlee's move of constituency and the TUC purge on communist trade union officials, as well as the dismissal of Soviet Foreign Minister Molotov. These may have been largely intelligent guesswork; its September 1948 assertion that Stalin intended to retire cannot have had any very authoritative source. The revelation that Hugh Dalton was going to replace Ernest Bevin as Foreign Secretary was an intelligent guess given Dalton's ambitions but, as it happens, wrong. Its interview by 'our correspondent in Madrid' with Myriam Petacci, sister of Mussolini's mistress Clara Petacci, who was killed with Mussolini in 1945, was probably a genuine exclusive. But one cannot say the same for the unnamed 'socialist veteran' interviewed in August 1949, who remembered Herbert Morrison as a mean and vindictive leader of Hackney council in 1920. John Beckett's name was nowhere to be found in any issue of the magazine for the six years in which it appeared.

In those six years, 1948 to 1954, John and Anne had their only years of comfort and peace and freedom from financial worry together, and they were very happy. They had two more children. The duke paid the bills, and John may have felt that *Preview* was the beginning of his road back to respectability. In 1949 Anne persuaded the duke to buy a large and splendid house near Rickmansworth in Hertfordshire, so that her family could live in the main part of the house, and the rest could be rented out as flats to provide them with an income.

The house was called The Firs because of some wonderful fir trees dotted around the thirteen acres of ground, but John at once renamed it Thurlwood House after the farm which had once been leased by his yeoman ancestors (but which the Becketts had lost in the years between the wars). An ample driveway swept round a small spinney, lush if overgrown, to a pillared front porch in front of a very big flat-fronted Georgian house. John Beckett walked leisurely around his thirteen acres of ground, a shotgun in his hand, potting the occasional bird which might otherwise have gorged itself on his strawberries, or the apples from the small orchard in one corner of his estate. He looked like a real country gentleman. I did not know then that it was the latest of many parts he had played.

One day he saw a small bird perched near the fruit, and shot it dead, and then looked at it. He was so mortified to have destroyed that tiny, noisy piece of vibrant life that he went out and sold the gun that very morning. His daughter Lesley from his first marriage came to visit him at Thurlwood, bringing her son Patrick, who was born in 1945, the same year that I was born. She reported back to her mother Helen that John seemed at last to have fallen on his feet, and could perhaps help them financially – Lesley was having a thin time. Helen knew her man, and advised caution. And she was right.

He lived, as I suppose he must always have lived in his brief periods of affluence, as though money were never the slightest obstacle. When his Harley Street dentist told him that the biggest Rolls Royce in the world, the Phantom Three, was 'a poor man's car' because it never needed servicing, he seized on the excuse and bought a second-hand Phantom III that very day.

'We are aware of the existence of Thurlwood House and in the past this has been given attention,' wrote David Cohen of the Board of Deputies of British Jews in a memorandum in October 1950. The Board of Deputies liked to know where potentially anti-Semitic gatherings were taking place, and its informants had received notice of a BPP social to take place in November, with Air Commodore Oddie and the Duke of Bedford.

AK was a regular visitor to Thurlwood House. I remember him as a tall, dignified, rather distant and patrician figure with what seemed to me, as a child, to be an almost ducal disdain for the lower orders. I would travel with John in the car to Rickmansworth Station to pick up AK and Doris for Sunday lunch. Once at the station, a porter accidentally ran his big luggage trolley over AK's foot. AK made a huge scene about it, everyone gathered round to see what the fuss was, and even John was a little embarrassed. The station master came out, and after finding out what had happened, turned to AK and said: ''E said, mind yer backs, dinne?' AK explained at some length that saying 'mind yer backs' was not, in his view, good enough.

In 1953 Chesterton went to work for Lord Beaverbrook as 'literary adviser' and journalist on the *Daily Express*. 'Literary adviser' meant, partly, that he had to ghost-write Beaverbrook's autobiography. Tom Driberg, who had worked for Beaverbrook for years, was already working on a biography, and perhaps Beaverbrook wanted to make sure that the authorised version hit the streets first, although Driberg was very much Beaverbrook's creature. More likely it appealed to Beaverbrook's sense of humour to have the ex-communist Driberg in one pocket and the fascist A. K. Chesterton in the other.

The finished book, *Don't Trust to Luck*, was 'a terrible book, which nevertheless received sycophantic reviews from the Beaverbrook papers', Chesterton wrote afterwards, no doubt quite truthfully. Having been at Beaverbrook's beck and call for months, he wrote in a chapter on 'Man Management' that anyone who had the power of patronage over someone else's bread and butter, and who used that power to make the man the victim of his own caprice, committed an unforgivable sin. He handed the chapter to Beaverbrook and awaited the explosion. There was none. Beaverbrook simply added in brackets: ('I commit this sin.')

Perhaps working for the man whom John regarded as the personification of evil was the cause of falling out with AK. More likely it was because the next year, after his work with Beaverbrook ended, Chesterton founded the League of Empire Loyalists and John refused to join. Whatever it was, the break was complete and irrevocable, and I do not think they ever met again. John was a very unforgiving enemy, and I imagine Chesterton was too.

John would explain afterwards that the kink that made Chesterton an alcoholic was always there, and when he was dry, it came out in other ways. During their last disagreement, he said, he wrote AK a long, careful letter, and the letter came back to him with the one word FUCK scrawled over it in huge capitals. I was shocked because it seemed so unlike the dignified figure who used to turn up on the weekend closest to my birthday and solemnly take me to a shop to buy a present.

The brief years of comfort and relative security in John and Anne's life was coming to an end. They were never to know freedom from financial worry again. In 1953 the Duke of Bedford was killed in a shooting accident, and at once there was no more money.

In the next issue of the BPP paper John wrote an extraordinary obituary which tells us more about the writer than about the duke:

> The British aristocracy very occasionally produces a unique character, who does odd, courageous and independent things ... He was surrounded by every circumstance of training likely to turn out another well-behaved, well dressed nonentity. Instead he became the last representative of the traditions of aristocratic radicalism and nonconformity ...
>
> He never deserted his friends. My wife telephoned to Scotland on May 16 1940 to tell him I had been taken to Brixton prison that morning. He came from Scotland overnight to visit me and see if help could be obtained.
>
> James Maxton was my second outside visitor. These two men had much in common. Of all those I have known in 30 years of public life they were the only two completely honest men that I have met ... I like to believe that today they sit together in some pleasant part of Purgatory happily knowing that the Lord, whom they served by their lives, has not turned his face from them ...

It would of course have to be Purgatory. John was now a Catholic, and accepted the orthodoxy that non-Catholics cannot go to heaven.

It was one view of the duke. His son, the present duke, has another: 'My father (was) the loneliest man I ever knew, incapable of giving or receiving love, utterly self-centred and opinionated. He loved birds, animals, peace, monetary reform, the park, and religion. He also had a wife and three children.'

In the thirties the duke had been the centre of a sensational court case, when his wife sued for 'restoration of conjugal rights'. She called him 'the most cruel, mean and conceited person she had met'. He wrote to her: 'My health has been seriously affected by the strain, and as for a long time you have made it very clear that you do not wish to live with me as my wife, there is really nothing you want from me but my money.' Summing up, Mr Justice Bucknall said:

Lord Tavistock takes a rigid and austere view of life and dislikes many things, some of which he calls 'pagan', but which most men do not actively dislike. He dislikes boarding schools for boys, alcohol, tobacco, playing cards for money, and betting. He does not play games, and said he took very little interest in his wife's dress.

I think what concerned him is that his wife has completely turned away from his work and his ideals. Is that treatment a sufficient reason for Lord Tavistock refusing to go back to his wife? In my judgement it is.

John, who loved tobacco and alcohol and dreamed of sending his son to a top boarding school, was an odd companion for this austere figure; he thought the duke considered him a likeable rogue.

The BPP was wound up. *Fleet Street Preview* lasted another year. The hope that the duke might have left John and Anne money was quickly dispelled: he had left John just £600, which was not going to last very long in the hands of a man of 59 with three children under nine, expensive tastes, no income, no home, no work, no prospect of work, and a name and a face which people stubbornly declined to forget.

Everything we owned, including the roof over our heads, and every penny my parents had, was the duke's. They were now the property of the new duke, who had a thoroughly low opinion of his father's fascist friend, and wanted to sell our home to help pay his £4.5 million death duties.

My mother was beside herself with worry. My father carried on as though nothing had happened, but I think the turmoil beneath the calm exterior was intense. His own father had become bankrupt when he was fourteen, forcing John to leave school and abandon all his hopes for the future. John had himself been declared bankrupt at the age of 38, forcing his daughter Lesley to leave school.

It was John's very last chance, and once again someone came along to tell him what to do with it. This time it was A. K. Chesterton, who had a new patron, a reactionary millionaire living in South America.

For the first time, John said no. He really had changed at last, but it was too late. He had had enough of politics, and he could not take the League of Empire Loyalists at all seriously. He was feeling his age. He did not want to put Anne through any more hardships and dangers. He yearned for a kind of quiet conservative respectability which neither his history nor his character would ever allow him to attain.

With the BPP out of the way, Chesterton's Empire Loyalists and Mosley's Union Movement fought for the soul of the far right. More extreme groups sprang up, but most of the old BPP people decamped into the League of Empire Loyalists, and were still with Chesterton when he merged the far right neo-fascist groups together in 1967 to form the National Front. New racial minorities, immigrants from Africa and Asia, started to replace Jews as the necessary fascist enemy. Mosley's powers of self-deception were undimmed: he appears genuinely to have thought he was going to win North Kensington in the 1959 general election, when he lost his deposit.

Colin Jordan joined the Empire Loyalists; left to form the White Defence League; advanced (as he himself puts it) from British nationalism to pan-Aryan National Socialism in the 1950s; held 'Hitler Was Right' meetings; was crowned 'world Führer' with American Nazi Lincoln Rockwell designated as his successor; and married Christian Dior's niece Françoise Dior in a blood-mingling ceremony, using an SS dagger to spill their blood over a copy of Hitler's *Mein Kampf.*

Jordan has hovered uneasily all his life between being a sinister Nazi Jew-baiter and a figure of fun. John felt sad for him when he read about his antics. He was angry when he heard that Jordan had been fired from his teaching post for his political activities. But he wanted nothing more to do with neo-Nazis. Slowly and painfully, he was starting to accept that the Holocaust was not an invention of British warmongers, or Jewish international capitalists, or anyone else; it had really happened.

Jordan contacted him in the late 1950s to ask him to speak at one of his meetings. 'He declined', Jordan told me 'in words which, while I cannot precisely quote them, amounted to saying that he was thoroughly disillusioned with the British public and thought that activity designed to appeal to that public and solicit its support was a waste of time. He was not prepared, he intimated, to waste more of his time in this way, and urged me not to also; advice which obviously I ignored.'

CHAPTER TEN

THE OUTCAST

The new duke's trustees demanded vacant possession of Thurlwood House, which was not only the roof over John's family's head but also, with the old duke dead, his only source of income. John faced the possibility of his second bankruptcy.

He and Anne stalled the trustees. The duke, they said, had given them Thurlwood House to live in for their lifetimes. True, he had not left it to them in his will. But that was only because he had died unexpectedly. He would have revised his will and left them their home. He would not have had them homeless. They trawled their correspondence with the duke to find letters that suggested this. But the trustees were trying to raise £4.5 million to pay death duties. John, who knew a thing or two about death duties – he had been a strong advocate of them in his socialist days – had advised the duke to create a trust, so that death duties would be avoided, and John had been one of the trustees. If the duke had lived five years after creating the trust, it would have worked, but he died a few months too early. Death duties were payable on everything the duke owned, including, of course, Thurlwood House. The trustees had already sold the whole of the village of Chenies, which had belonged to the Dukes of Bedford since 1526.

While the argument was going on, some money had to be earned, and if it was not to come from A. K. Chesterton's new political party, where was it to come from? John thought quickly, and in 1954, the year after the duke's death, created a business for himself.

He had been (anonymously, of course) the stock exchange tipster for *Fleet Street Preview*, and still had the *Preview* and the BPP mailing lists. Both of these lists contained several men with a fair amount of money and not much brain. He wrote offering an investment advisory service, calling himself J. Barclay (Financial Consultant) so as to be able to attract subscribers who would not have anything to do with the notorious fascist John Beckett. For a modest subscription, just £5 a year, you could have a fortnightly stock exchange newsletter and a certain amount of free advice on your investments. He called it *Advice and Information*. A few fivers rolled in – enough to provide hope that all was not lost.

Then he tried to expand it beyond the very small circle of people who had joined the BPP or subscribed to *Preview*. His method was simple, and he showed it to me when I offered to help one day. He handed me the Bournemouth telephone directory, and told me to go through it picking out anyone with a senior military rank, or a title, or anyone who lived in a house with a name and no street number. These then received his promotional material. Former military officers, John explained, were his best market. They had a lump sum from the army and little experience of the world outside it, and they needed someone like him to guide them about what to do with their money.

Politically, the newsletter ran with the sort of respectable right-wing Conservatism which John was adopting for what he hoped might be a comfortable and respectable old age. The first issue, in November 1954, talked of 'Mr Butler's businesslike control of the national finances' (R. A. Butler was the Conservative Chancellor of the Exchequer) and asked: 'Will his firm adherence to the welfare state, with its high taxation, prevent a swing of the have-nots to the opposition? ... Experts think that Mr (Nye) Bevan will just succeed in keeping his party out at the next election. The danger is the futility of Sir Anthony Eden as Conservative leader ...'

That established the tone. *Advice and Information* was going to sound rather like a *Daily Telegraph* leader, with a few share tips thrown in at the end. John now sometimes said that if he could do it all over again, he might not be a lawyer after all: he would like to be a leader writer on a newspaper. A few issues later he was writing: 'It is time that the solid middle class people of this country made a little money for themselves as well as for the welfare state and I do sincerely hope to assist you in this endeavour.' The man who had disrupted Parliament because of the low rate of unemployment pay had travelled a very long way indeed.

Like *Fleet Street Preview*, it made the most of the qualifications of its author, and then added a few, though always obeying John's golden rule: stay as close to the truth as possible. 'For many years,' he wrote in January 1955, 'I was connected with the investment office of one of our few remaining very wealthy men.' This was one way of expressing his role in the Duke of Bedford's life.

In February he claimed that he had 'consulted associates in Paris and Washington'. His Washington contact was, apparently, 'one of the few men who really knows both President Eisenhower and world communist politics'. I do not know who this remarkable man was, but I expect it was

Ulius Louis Amos, known to his friends as Pete, a chancer from Maryland who produced some sort of newsletter rather like *Fleet Street Preview*, and claimed to have several rich contacts. He liked *Preview*, and when it closed, John wrote to him to see whether he could obtain commissions. Amos commissioned John to write a monthly *Letter from London*, for which, in the event, John was never paid, Amos's rich contacts apparently having let him down.

In March 1955 he made the most of another old friendship. 'Like everyone else who has enjoyed the personal friendship of Mr and Mrs Bevan I am very fond of them ... Together with charm, intelligence and wit, they both have a complete lack of commonsense. ' His small band of faithful subscribers thought he was a well-connected genius, some of them demanding that he should send his newsletters to Downing Street so that the nation might be better governed. Few things embarrassed John: in March 1956 he reassured them that he had 'the best of grounds for believing that *Advice and Information* is studied in Downing Street'.

Advice and Information was good value. John was able to boast that all the shares he mentioned in his first three months showed a profit, most of them a substantial profit. He made them some more money by correctly predicting a Conservative election victory in 1955, and advising them to buy in anticipation when Fleet Street financial editors were counselling caution; but he made no money for himself because he had none to invest. He found that one or two of his subscribers were willing to hand their whole share portfolio over to him to manage, in return for a modest percentage, and that produced a little extra income.

Then he had one of those really clever ideas which are often the foundation of enormous wealth.

He took it to lawyers and accountants, and they all said the same thing. It was so simple and beautiful that there must be something illegal about it, or someone would already be doing it. But they could not find anything wrong. So John wrote to all the subscribers to *Advice and Information* offering £10 units in the Thurlwood Investment Fund. He would invest the lot, and everyone would share in the fruits of his expert husbandry.

The idea of unit trusts is well established now, and fortunes have been built on them. But in 1954, they were unheard-of. The Thurlwood Investment Fund would have been the first.

The money flowed in. The fund had tens of thousands of pounds within a few weeks. And then came a letter from the Board of Trade. I do not know exactly what it said, but there was, apparently, no way round it. The Thurl-wood Investment Fund had to be wound up, and all the money sent back. I think John thought that the security services were watching him, and had had a word with the Board of Trade, and perhaps he was right. His MI5 file stops abruptly in mid-1945; the Home Office will not allow the rest to be seen. In any case, it was his last chance to make sure that he and Anne were permanently free of financial worry, and it was gone.

Negotiations with the duke's trustees dragged on for four or five years, and for most of that time it looked as though they would end up in court, a battle for which, of course, John could not pay. *Advice and Information* did not expand much beyond the tiny base provided by *Preview* and the BPP. To save money, John and Anne took to typing and duplicating it them-selves, and even despatching it. They got hold of a remarkable steel machine, and the children operated it twice a month. You passed a metal address label through it, placed an envelope over it, and banged the heavy handle down, and with luck a blurry and just about legible name and address appeared on the envelope. The family moved out of the house and into the small gardener's cottage at the gate, so that a very wealthy Amer-ican colonel and his family could rent the front part of the house.

It was a fretful time. John's heart murmur grew worse and was diagnosed as angina, and I remember him fainting fairly spectacularly a couple of times, while Anne's nerves were shredded to pieces. But it was in those years, between 1953 and 1958, that I learned about the extraordinary char-acters who had populated his life. I never met any of them, though. It was odd, having in your mind vivid descriptions of real people, who still lived, but whom I never met and would never meet.

He talked more about actors than politicians. One day, on holiday in the West Country, he and I went to the local theatre in Minehead, Somerset, to see a play starring his old theatrical friend Leslie Henson. As we drove from our caravan a few miles down the coast, John was casually wondering aloud whether he should go round to the stage door and see Henson after the play.

He told me his Henson stories. I'd heard them before, more than once, but I never minded my father's stories being repeated. I remember nothing about the play except that it was gently amusing and I enjoyed it, and that Henson, like every actor and writer my father recommended to me, lived up to his billing. He had the rich, fruity voice and the comic timing that I had been promised.

Afterwards I asked if we were really going backstage to see Henson. I badly wanted to be an actor. Perhaps this famous actor friend of my father's could help me? I know that was in my father's mind too, but he said no, he thought not, and we drove back in silence, my father speaking gently and levelly as he usually did with me, smoking cigarettes and throwing the butts out of the car window, and I could sense the depth of the despair and regret he was hiding. He could not be sure of his welcome, even from Henson.

Soon afterwards, he read that Henson had died. My mother never knew Henson, and my father had no one to mourn with but me. He brought me the obituary, told me he he'd always liked Henson, and sauntered back to the room he kept as an office. Years later I saw, in the *Guardian*'s birthdays column, that Henson's son, the actor Nicky Henson, was born on the same day in 1945 that I was born. I don't suppose my father knew that.

He watched from afar as Clem Attlee deliberately hung on to the leadership of the Labour Party until Herbert Morrison's chance of succeeding him had gone. To someone who knew the people and the politics, Morrison's frustration was evident, and John laughed loudly and shared the joke with anyone he thought might appreciate it, which, sadly, did not include most of the Catholic community in Rickmansworth who were his principal companions now.

Attlee finally retired in 1955. J. Barclay in *Advice and Information* told his readers that 'Many years ago I shared a house in Limehouse with him.' Perhaps subscribers were puzzled about how a story of a cowardly attack by Herbert Morrison on the imprisoned George Lansbury might be relevant to their investment portfolios. The point turned out to be that Attlee had 'resigned at the precise moment when it would be most difficult for Morrison to assume the leadership. After 34 years the chickens have come home to roost. Although the markets have been quiet they have been firm ...'

A year or two later John wrote to Attlee. He received back a chatty letter about his health and similar matters. Attlee took a risk to write that letter, even though he was no longer leader. It would have earned him ferocious condemnation from some of his colleagues if it had been known. I remember seeing the letter and being surprised that a former Prime Minister should type his own letters, inaccurately, with a typewriter whose margins were clearly not working.

I never even met the fascists and neo-Nazis, except for AK, whose visits abruptly ceased in the mid-fifties. One of them, Lady Domvile, the wife of

Admiral Domvile, was apparently my godmother – rather typically, my father thought that my life would be improved by having a titled godparent – but as far as I know, I never met her or heard from her in my entire life.

My father carefully introduced me to the authors he considered vital for the intellectual development of a young boy: Kipling, G. K. Chesterton, Belloc, G. A. Henty, Evelyn Waugh and the like, of course, but also Conan Doyle and Somerset Maugham, as well as his old friend Hugh Ross Williamson, Whittaker Chambers (the man who shopped Alger Hiss to Senator Joe McCarthy) and Douglas Hyde (the *Daily Worker* news editor who joined the Catholic Church) to show me what he considered to be the true nature of communism; more surprisingly, the autobiography of British communist leader Harry Pollitt; and a book which, at ten, I disappointed him by finding simply boring and lacking in style or elan. This was *My Struggle* by Adolf Hitler, and to this day I do not know what he expected me to say. My mother introduced me to Shakespeare, and transmitted her own enthusiasm. I was easily the best-read twelve-year-old I knew.

Of them all, G. K. Chesterton was the most important, and I spent happy hours with my father's copy of his collected works, and remembered his imposing, patrician cousin AK, who no longer came to see us. Forty years later I put the two together, in an article for the *New Statesman*:

> G. K. Chesterton wrote cheerful ballads about the pleasures of wine and beer. His cousin A. K. Chesterton was an alcoholic. G. K. was full of noisy, jolly pre-First World War imperial jingoism: 'The earth is a place on which England is found / And you find it however you twirl the globe round.' A. K. founded the League of Empire Loyalists in 1954.
>
> G. K. was languidly anti-Semitic in the 1920s. A. K. wrote anti-Semitic diatribes in the 1930s as chief propagandist for the British Union of Fascists, and became the first chairman of the National Front in 1967. Yet A. K. was not a monster, any more than his more famous cousin. The line between writing jolly little verses about races you dislike, and writing vitriolic attacks on them, is remarkably indistinct.

Even at twelve, I think I saw how G. K.'s dislike of Jews littered and disfigured his poetry. My father recommended, among others, a poem in which

Chesterton's dog Quoodle laments the lack of a sense of smell in humans. It's a happy little poem until you get to the jarring, gratuitous second verse:

They haven't got no noses,
They cannot even tell
When door and darkness closes
The park a Jew encloses,
Where even the law of Moses
Will let you steal a smell.

John, though, was returning to the values of his own childhood and his own boyishly jingoistic father, carefully introducing me to the authors he had once loved before 1914, before the war and the world of labour movement politics scarred his soul. To these he was adding what he saw as the humour and gallantry of the Catholic church. John, who had once seen himself as a sort of Henty swashbuckler, now, I think, started to see himself as a sort of strong, wise Catholic Chestertonian hero. He even had a Father Brown to play opposite his Flambeau, in Father Brendan Fox, the Irish parish priest in Rickmansworth.

Father Brendan fitted the bill rather well. He had a sophisticated taste in wine developed while training for the priesthood in Normandy, and was a kindly, devout, charming and essentially simple man who was renowned all over Hertfordshire for his skill at tipping the winners in horse races. He had also, as it happened, been at school in Ireland with William Joyce. I think he was John's last real friend, in the end the only friend who remained to him.

I could see that my father was different from the fathers of my friends. He was older, for one thing. He was also much, much noisier. In Hertfordshire's middle-class green belt, his loud laugh and emphatic speech were noticeably out of place. The local women's institute asked him to be a panellist on their brains trust, probably because they had heard he was a former MP. He must have sent them a sort of brief cv, because when we arrived the male chairman apologetically asked him what he meant by writing: 'Six years in Parliament and four years in Brixton'. 'The prison,' John cackled at once. The man looked so crestfallen that he took pity on him. 'You don't have to mention that if you'd rather not.' It wasn't mentioned.

My parents, in a sense, were in hiding. My mother was constantly terrified that we would be found – by the press, by the communists, by the people who had attacked his platforms as he spoke at open-air meetings.

I knew, from my mother's frightened face, that the appearance of the daubed words FASHIST BASTARD on our ample garden wall was a calamity. It destroyed her fragile feeling of safety and security. She had to see the words, with their threat to her and her children, every time she drove out of the house, until they were washed away. The police were called, but I do not know what was said to them, or what they said.

I knew too that my parents loved me with an overpowering love that had caught them by surprise. For the first nineteen years of my life I was constantly warmed, and sometimes scalded, by their love.

In 1958, an agreement was reached which enabled my parents to buy Thurlwood from the trustees for less than its real market value, and a bank loan to do it was secured. In the event that made things worse, but John, typically, was immediately sure that his financial future was assured, and at once put into effect his cherished, and expensive, plans for my education.

These had been made a decade earlier. When he first became a Catholic, he went on a retreat – the Catholic name for a period of quiet religious contemplation – at a very splendid and expensive Jesuit boarding school called Beaumont College, just outside Windsor, in Old Windsor, where many of the oldest and poshest Catholic families sent their sons. It was not until years later that I found out where he must first have run across it. In the 1930s just four public schools had fascist cells, and Beaumont was the only Catholic one. The other three were Stowe, Winchester and Worksop. William Joyce, of course, had been educated by Jesuits, at St Ignatius College in Galway, with Father Brendan.

They did a wonderful selling job on him during the retreat. He was terribly impressed. Beaumont had splendid buildings and an air of unobtrusive gentility, and called itself 'the Catholic Eton'. When it was founded, so the rector told John in his beautifully modulated vowel sounds, the head boy at Eton had written to the head boy at Beaumont: 'Harrow we know, Winchester we know, but what is Beaumont?' And the head boy at Beaumont had written back: 'Beaumont is what Eton used to be: a school for the sons of Catholic gentleman.'

Of all the dreams John ever dreamed, only one remained to him in the closing years of his life. He had left school when he was fourteen and regretted it all his life, and his son was to go to a top public school, no matter the cost.

This was to be John's gift to his older son, his way of making sure that the mistakes of his own life would not be repeated in mine. John had been in the army as an ordinary soldier, and knew how much better army life was if you had a commission. Beaumont had a compulsory College Cadet Force, and John was sure that no Beaumont boy went into the army as an ordinary soldier, to be kicked around and treated like dirt. There was still conscription in 1958, and old Beaumont boys became officers. The bar, that most snobbish of professions which my father had wanted so badly to join, was stuffed full of old Beaumont boys – and he was sure that the old school tie would be a great help if I decided to fulfil his dearest wish, and read for the bar.

He had felt patronised in Parliament by men from rich backgrounds and public schools; he wanted his son to do the patronising. He wanted to ensure that I would not end up with foolish notions of socialism, in the pursuit of which I might ruin my life as he had ruined his. He repeated the adage: 'Every man with a heart is a socialist before he is 30. Every man with a head is a Conservative after that.' I do not know whether he believed this rubbish, but he wanted me to believe it. He adopted, then preached to me, ideas which he thought would ensure a comfortable life for me.

It was the sort of conservatism that was confined to grumpy colonels in the corner of the Athenaeum, or the fringes of neo-fascist groups, until long after John's death when Margaret Thatcher made it respectable. Low unemployment, John wrote in *Advice and Information* in 1956, 'may seem a desirable state of affairs, but it means that, in present circumstances, the "workers" are in a position to dictate what wages they will accept, irrespective of economic facts ... Discounting miracles, there must either be a showdown with the unions, something on the 1926 model, or there will be a heavy fall in the value of the pound.'

He wanted to convey to me the desirability of behaving conventionally and not rocking any boats; to give me a comfortable and respectable right-wing conservatism to follow. It didn't work, but the love in the effort is enormous.

He discovered for himself, what he must have known theoretically as a socialist, that capitalism has its own contradictions. After Suez he told his subscribers: 'It is ironical that this final degradation of our national prestige will probably be accompanied by substantial profit for those subscribers who took our advice to buy Suez Canal Company shares at around £58.'

After the duke's death, Beaumont had been shelved. I passed the eleven plus and went to the local grammar school, Rickmansworth Grammar School, less than a mile from Thurlwood House. This was a monument to the Attlee government: purpose-built and newly opened at the start of the 1950s to cope with the new customers created by the swift implementation of the 1944 Education Act and the raising of the school-leaving age, and typical of its kind: light, airy and modern, with young and idealistic teachers who enjoyed what they did. It was a progressive and thoroughly civilised place which took care to bring out the best in all its pupils. I loved it.

But John had set his heart on Beaumont, and as soon as he had a deal with the duke's trustees, I was taken out of the grammar school and sent for a term to a crammer in Hampstead, because the Jesuits had convinced John that their academic standards were much higher than those of the despised state education system. This, I discovered as soon as I arrived at Beaumont, was an appalling lie. I had been well taught at Rickmansworth Grammar School, and in most subjects, was well ahead of what Beaumont's chalky pedagogues had to offer.

It was the last example of my father's style of decision-making, that style which led him to take his battered idealism to Oswald Mosley in 1933 and William Joyce in 1937. In 1958 he took me away from an excellent local grammar school where my education was free, to a virtual prison where a thoroughly inferior education was provided at an enormous cost, thus ensuring a poverty-stricken old age for him and my mother.

In the first year, my short, stout, emphatic class teacher, Father Bamber, made us learn three questions and answers from the Catechism every day. Failure to reproduce them word for word incurred a visit to Father Brogan, whose melancholy duty it was to spend morning break hitting boys' hands between three and eighteen times with a flat instrument made of whale-bone and rubber, called a ferrula.

After my first visit to Father Brogan I ran about for twenty minutes, clutching my hurt hands and vowing I would never do anything again that would bring this misery upon me. But I couldn't keep it up, and I collected ferrulas most weeks for the next four years. After a while they didn't hurt so much.

I was always being beaten, by somebody, for something. Miss CCF (College Cadet Force) without permission, as I did several times, and you were caned by Major Roddy. Cheek a seventeen-year-old monitor and you would find yourself bending over a chair to be caned by the head boy – the school captain, as he was called – who held court in the captain's lounge every morning after mass, examining offences and deciding how many strokes to administer.

A frequent offence for younger boys was to fail to march properly down the 'higher line gallery', a corridor reserved for older boys who were in the 'higher line'. When younger boys' business took them down it, for example to go to the library, they had to button up their coats and march down the centre, making a neat right or left about-turn at the door they needed. Older boys lounged along the walls, inspecting marching styles, languidly abusing their marching juniors, and making them go back and start again. But the real terror was called a panning. Apparently after lights out, two Jesuits, in their long black robes, collected the condemned boy silently and took him downstairs to be ceremonially laid out and beaten on his pyjamaed bottom. I believe someone said a prayer. The mere threat of it caused me nightmares for a week.

Every Thursday afternoon we shined our army boots and paraded to the clipped but perfectly formed vowels of Major Roddy, a sort of military caricature, with the handlebar moustache which I had seen in war movies. The major also taught history and art. By the end of my first year I had detailed maps of the dispositions at the battles of Hastings, Agincourt, Crécy and Bosworth, but little idea of what happened between these events.

He had a theory that wars were caused by the straight edges of the houses in which we lived, and could be ended if all rooms were round. You never find straight lines in nature, he pointed out. I told my father this theory, and he said that he had noticed how naïve military men were.

We slept in tiny cubicles, each furnished with a steel bed, a bowl and a jug of freezing water. Almost never seeing women, and never seeing young women, older boys became obsessively interested in younger boys, and we kept lists of our favourites. Generally it stopped at that, but in my year there was a circle about whose activities in the woods we all sniggered. Eventually most of them were expelled. Shortly afterwards my class was taken by coach to a museum in London, and we saw one of the expelled boys on the pavement as we climbed into the coach. My classmates set up a cry of 'homo' and 'Oscar' (two films about the life of Oscar Wilde had just been released.) I sat unusually silent. I was thinking: when the coach has pulled out, the boy who was expelled is free. I must return to prison. How I envied him.

I learned quickly that my grammar school background was not something to boast about. I was the only boy who had seen the inside of a state school, and it led to awkward questions. An older boy asked how much my father earned. I did a quick sum in my head and came up with a figure which I knew would provoke derision, so I doubled it. 'My God, the boy lives in penury,' he shouted, and departed to spread the glorious news.

Coming from a state school ensured that I was placed in the bottom stream. In spite of coming regularly at the top of it, I stayed there while others leap-frogged, until after five terms I gave up trying, and did no work whatsoever until I left. My classmates propped up the rugby scrum and acquired such skills as city gents and estate agents require. Our class, unlike the other streams, was taught double entry book-keeping. There was no attempt to disguise the fact that we were considered failures.

I learned quickly that the most cherished ambition of my life was sternly frowned on by the Jesuits. I wanted to be an actor. At the grammar school they had given me the lead in the school play, and I loved every minute of it. At Beaumont they refused to allow me to be in the school play, saying that I spent too much of my time reading plays, producing them and press-ganging my classmates to act in them. I begged to be allowed out to audition for the National Youth Theatre, but the rector turned me down. My parents told a lie for me, and collected me and delivered me at the interview, but I couldn't act that day. I thought that Beaumont had destroyed my confidence.

Boarding school is a means by which rich people can use their wealth as an alternative to parenting. The father of one of my classmates promised him a sports car at the age of eighteen if he did not smoke until then. He then sent him to Beaumont, which entirely absolved him from policing the promise. The other boys' fathers were vast, remote figures, their mothers fashionable and semi-detached. Parents had parted from their offspring with a sigh of relief, and seldom came to take them out.

My parents were completely different. They wanted, with every fibre of their being, to be real parents. They came to see me at Beaumont on the smallest excuse. A play I wasn't in, normally attended only by the relatives of the cast, brought my parents' car (increasingly an elderly and unreliable heap of junk, picked up for next door to nothing at a local second-hand car lot) wheezing from Hertfordshire to Berkshire.

One day, on one of the three days in the term when our parents could take us out, the car simply refused to make the journey, and the parents of another Hertfordshire boy were asked to collect me and drop me at a café in Rickmansworth. I remember his enormous father with his deep voice and his rich public school accent, who I think was a Harley Street doctor, turning round heavily in his car seat and pointedly saying, 'Good morning'. I had, I realised, not spoken to him since I was beckoned to his car and told to get into the back seat. Towards the end of the journey he said that to go round the one-way system in Rickmansworth 'would be a work of super-erogation'. 'What does that mean? What is the Latin root?' he demanded of his son, who did not know, and he explained sternly that it came from *rogo,* I ask. I have never been so relieved to get out of a car in my life.

The next time my father picked me up at Beaumont, in a tiny, elderly, battered Fiat 500, which he nursed along the road with all the care that he had once taken driving racing cars round Brooklands, John told me carefully that he had a new job and it involved working nights. He would, he said, be working for a big security firm, watching their investments overnight so that he could take instant action if their value looked likely to decrease. It was not until the holiday, when I saw him set off from the house in the early evening wearing a uniform, that I realised the truth. He had by then, I imagine, a pretty shrewd idea of the sort of school he had sent me to, and the misery that would be visited on me if it were known that my father was a night security guard for Securicor.

After I left school the pretence was dropped. He told me how Securicor had demanded an account of how he had earned his living for the previous 25 years, and he had to invent something for the years 1940 to 1943 because they would never employ a man who had seen the inside of a prison. And he told me what he would do if his van were attacked. 'I would put up the fiercest token resistance,' he said, and laughed his loud, cracked, full-hearted laugh.

By then the gardener's cottage was also rented out, and long before I left Beaumont in 1962 we moved to a few draughty rooms at the back of Thurlwood House, which had been the servants quarters when the house was built. Anne brushed up her secretarial skills and found a job, and that was how Beaumont's enormous fees were paid.

The main part of the house, where we had lived in the good times, was let to a Dutch embassy official and his kindly horse-mad wife, Mr and Mrs Binkhorst, whom my mother called The Binkles. This had the advantage that they paid rent, not just for the house, but also for the field, in which Mrs Binkhorst kept her horses.

Advice and Information was still coming out, but the number of subscribers was dwindling. There was a serious effort to talk about stock markets instead of politics, but its author's knowledge was decaying and his touch for good share tips seems to have become rather shaky. J. Barclay had disappeared in May 1959, to be replaced by J. W. Beckett. Servicing the mortgage on Thurlwood and paying Beaumont's fees must have absorbed all the income they could generate: the electricity was cut off for several months because the bills were not paid. Our rooms had access to the cellar where in happier times my father had kept his wine, and after a while we discovered that the electricity was still on in there, because its supply was charged to the Binkhorsts, not to us. Guiltily, we ran electric fires and lights from it for weeks.

The two younger children were told that there was an electric fault. I was told the truth, but I forgot as soon as I went back to boarding school, and when I returned for the next holiday and my younger brother proudly switched the light on and said it had been repaired, I simply looked at him blankly.

In 1962, the year I left Beaumont, Thurlwood was at last sold. It paid the debts and bought a new Triumph Herald. We rented a succession of South London flats. My father still took care never to be seen in his Securicor uniform. He feared meeting old friends, or, even worse, old Beaumont boys whom I might know. He left the house in the Triumph Herald wearing a sports jacket over his uniform trousers, and put on the cap and jacket when he got to work. Somehow he scraped up the money to buy me life membership of the Beaumont Union, the old boys' association. I had one letter from it, asking for money for something or other, and a couple of years later, the Jesuits closed Beaumont. Today few people have heard of the Catholic Eton.

Beaumont boys, when they left before taking A-levels, went to Davies Laing and Dick, the posh crammers in London. I was spared that. There was no more money, and I went to the City of Westminster College, a state further education college off Victoria Street. It was like being allowed back into Rickmansworth Grammar School. I rediscovered history. Instead of a dreary parade of long-dead martyrs and Catholic propaganda, Dr Warren taught us, methodically but with humour and passion, about Canning and Castlereagh, Napoleon III and Bismarck. There too, N. F. Simpson, just on the verge of his theatrical success with *One Way Pendulum* and *A Resounding Tinkle*, reminded me of the joy of

210

reading Shakespeare which my mother had given me as a child, and Beaumont had squeezed out of me.

Dr Warren was short and plump and had an accent which I loved but could not place. Now I know it was that middle European accent which suggests that he was probably a Jewish refugee who had come to Britain in the thirties, perhaps on the *kindertransport,* and who had that passion for history which often engages intelligent Jews who have seen persecution. Perhaps that was why, in this intense one-year course, he stopped in 1914; for European history in the years between the world wars might have been very close to home for him. He knew he had taught us enough to find questions on our A-level papers which we could answer.

Because Dr Warren stopped short, I asked my father to give me the interwar years, and, impromptu, he gave me the most accomplished lecture I had ever heard, better even than those thoughtful, precise lectures of Dr Warren's, with their clear starting places and ending places. But it was a meeting of strangers. I knew him well until I was thirteen. Then I lost him. His relationship with me, which mattered terribly to him, was one of the many things he sacrificed for Beaumont, in addition to his peace of mind and his precarious financial stability.

He still believed that, most of his life, his crime had been to be right at the time, while everyone else caught up with him a few years later. 'There may have been good grounds why Napoleon and Hitler should have been liquidated,' he told his few, no doubt bemused, subscribers in March 1963. 'They were not, however, destroyed because they were bloodthirsty dictators or immoral men. They were destroyed because they sought to organise a united European economy which would make Europe independent of the money magnates.' General de Gaulle, he said, was now doing that, and this meant that the general was courting danger.

The year I left Beaumont, 1962, his second wife Kyrle died. So one day in 1963, my parents quietly left the flat in Wimbledon to get married at the registry office in neighbouring Morden. I wonder how they managed to make sure that I and my brother and sister never found out.

It probably wasn't hard. I was too busy enjoying myself to worry about what they did. I had come out of the stifling atmosphere of an English public school into London, to find the sixties waiting for me. It seemed to me as though I had come from a prison into a new world, cleaner, fairer, fresher, freer, and infinitely more fun. I was filled with wild optimism – for me and for the world. Things could only get better. It was as though the hopes of the generation of 1918 had been transferred to that of the sixties: 'Proud of having conquered our inherited inhibitions, in our innocence we believed there was little else to conquer.'

By 1963, his 69th year, John was in more or less constant pain with what turned out to be stomach cancer. He was still dragging himself to Securicor most nights, until the husband of an old friend of Anne's, who owned a Savile Row tailor, had a heart attack, and John was drafted in as temporary manager. It was strange to see him welcoming customers with a passable effort at the proper obsequiousness. He doubled the wages of the elderly cutter and had him make me by far the finest suit I have ever possessed.

It was the last work he did. By the beginning of 1964 John was taking herbal remedies and could eat nothing more than Complan, a revolting sort of mush for invalids. For a hearty carnivore, never happier than when he had a steak and a glass of red wine or a pint of ale in front of him, it was torment. He took me out to dinner once and bought me a steak, and watched hungrily as I ate it.

My mother's concern was tinged with a sort of guilty relief. Increasingly as he had got older, the noise his false teeth made chewing on his meat had shredded her nerves, especially since he always talked loudly with his mouth full. The noise was never to be heard again.

The doctors told him he must have an operation. He never trusted doctors and never liked the idea of operations, but he wrote to Bob Forgan for advice. 'If I am ever able to eat a decent lunch again it would give me great pleasure to buy you one,' he added wretchedly. Forgan wrote back: yes, he should have the operation. A few months later, after his death, Forgan wrote to Anne:

'Perhaps you don't know that some months ago John wrote asking my advice, and from his letter I was certain that – short of a miracle – his time on earth was nearly over. Should I have told him so? He wished to save you worry, and his question was whether he should seek (and act on) orthodox advice ...

'Of course he depended on you in so many ways; and he talked of you a lot on the occasions when he and I met for lunch – three times, I think, in the last six years ...'

John carried on trying to get *Advice and Information* out, but it is clear from looking at their style that great chunks were now being written by Anne. He was growingly appalled by the idea of a Labour government led by Harold Wilson, for whom he had conceived a distant loathing so intense that I think Wilson must somehow have reminded him of Ramsay MacDonald. But his political antennae were no longer as sharp as they had been – perhaps they were masked by pain. At the start of October 1964, now dictating his newsletter to Anne from a hospital bed, he was predicting a Conservative victory. Harold Wilson narrowly won the general election that month.

Two incoherent *Advice and Information* newsletters appeared in November. Just before Christmas we brought him home to die. On Christmas Day we gave him a drop of brandy drowned in a glass of water. He was looking forward to it, but he choked on it. On 28 December he died. He had asked to be cremated. He said it was because he dreaded the thought of being buried alive, and partly it was. But he had never forgotten Arthur Bouchier's funeral pyre in South Africa, where the mourners were ushered away as the flames roared towards the sky and consumed his friend. He would quote G. K. Chesterton:

> If I had been a heathen
> I'd have piled my pyre high
> And in a great red whirlwind
> Gone roaring to the sky.
> But Higgins is a heathen
> And a richer man than I
> And they put him in an oven
> Just as if he were a pie.

I am afraid that putting him in an oven was the best we could manage.

'He might have become a great personal force and it was sad to see him wasted,' said Brockway. It's a generous assessment. It may be true. Labour movement politics at times of crisis become bitter, vicious, unforgiving and supremely dishonest. It filled him with such blind rage that he could no longer see clearly, and he exchanged the friendship and companionship of Brockway and Jimmy Maxton for that of William Joyce and A. K. Chesterton. Maxton was the best man for his second marriage, and Joyce for his third. It was the worst exchange I have ever heard of anyone making.

Briefly, between 1979 and 1984, I found myself somewhere near the heart of Labour movement politics, and saw the Party's two armed camps at close quarters. I look at the twenties and thirties through the window of the seventies and eighties, and I think that I can glimpse the despair that made fascists. It makes fascism no less dreadful – in fact, it makes it perhaps more dreadful – to see that it is sometimes the product of abused and distorted idealism.

One senior Labour politician seemed to feel as I did, and that was John Silkin, Agriculture Minister until 1979 and shadow defence spokesman after 1979. We became friends, and I helped to run his campaigns for the leadership and deputy leadership of the Labour Party. One day, rereading my father's autobiography, I discovered that John Silkin's father Lewis Silkin was the man sent by Labour Party headquarters to drive my father out of Peckham, and who eventually inherited the Peckham seat. The dispute between him and my father was obviously personal as well as political, and very bitter.

I resolved to tell John Silkin next time we lunched together. But before I could launch into my tale, he had one of his own. Had he ever told me, he asked, the reason he always stayed in an elderly, inconvenient hotel in the centre of Brussels when he was Agriculture Minister, when all the other ministers stayed in the modern hotels conveniently situated just by the Berleymont building? The reason, he explained, was that during the war the Nazi gauleiter in Brussels used that town centre hotel. Silkin always demanded the same suite that the gauleiter had. He liked the idea of a Jewish cabinet minister lording it in the room, dancing on the murderer's grave.

I left the restaurant without telling him about my father. I resolved to do so next time. But a few weeks later John Silkin died suddenly, so I never did tell him.

Yet I did benefit from my father's experience. Briefly in the early 1980s, under the intoxicating influence of the young Neil Kinnock, I started to believe that individuals could change the world. One day, working in the House of Commons on the shadow cabinet corridor, (I had been employed as a publicist for the shadow industry spokesman, Stan Orme), I caught myself making plans to get into Parliament, and knew that it would be the most terrible mistake. It would make me more unhappy than anything else I could do. If I did it, I would one day find a way to destroy my life, as my father had destroyed his: not his way, but something just as effective.

Today you can once again hear Labour politicians talk about the immorality, greed and fecklessness they find among the poor. Often they are talking about people who have committed no crime which is not motivated by the daily terror that tomorrow they may be unable to give food to their children. I recognise the rage I feel: I read about it in my father's unpublished autobiography written in 1938.

John Beckett was of the generation of 1918, the generation that fought the First World War. After I finished writing this book, I read the newly published diaries of another of that generation, Collin Brooks: editor of the *Sunday Dispatch* in the late 1930s, then editor of *Truth* after the war broke out and Henry Newnham resigned the job. Brooks lived and died an establishment figure.

His diaries reveal that he was a member of English Mistery, one of the nuttiest of the pro-Nazi groups; and that he and Rothermere remained pro-fascists and anti-Semites long after Rothermere formally broke away. In 1939 Brooks celebrated the elevation of 'the first Mistery Man to take cabinet office' (Dorman Smith.) As war approached, his diaries are full of meetings with leading fascists, and of Rothermere's freelance attempts to prevent war by placating Hitler.

His crude racial taunts make startling reading. Here's a pretty typical extract. He's writing in 1939 about the Secretary of State for War, Leslie Hore-Belisha: 'On his visit to the front ... he arrived arrayed like a Bond Street bum-boy, even wearing spats. They took him through all the mud they could find and tired him out. At the château there were two privies, one upstairs which was civilised with running water and one outside which was primitive. They concealed from His Majesty's Secretary of State the existence of the civilised one, so he excreted in extreme discomfort. He repeated some remark that Winston, he said, had made in a cabinet ... which annoyed somebody, coming from this pushing Jew-boy.'

John Beckett's anti-Semitism didn't have that, crude, cruel, snobbish edge. But it was there, all the same, even though he claimed (and perhaps, sometimes, even believed) that he simply disliked international finance which happened to be run by Jews.

He wasn't a traitor, or a fifth columnist, or any of the things for which he spent nearly four years in prison. For a time he called himself a fascist, but he had a clearer conception of democracy than the men who kept him locked up, or many of those, like Brooks, who spent the war years in respectable comfort. He was an anti-Semite, but he was not locked up for that, for the very good reason that, if anti-Semitism had been an offence in 1940, the prisons would have overflowed with many of the greatest in the land.

He would not have thought much of this book. Introspection wasn't his style. 'The study of human nature,' he wrote, 'is an evil drug which brings much unnecessary unhappiness. 80 per cent of people are slightly varying replicas of types one knows by heart; but in the other 20 per cent there is incalculable interest, repulsiveness or charm. Sometimes I offend most of the 80 per cent because I find it almost impossible to simulate interest, and I have never acquired the politician's art of tolerating fools gladly.'

Perhaps a little time spent contemplating human nature – his own and that of others – might have shielded him from some of his grossest errors. The academic historian Richard Griffiths, author of several recent books about 1930s fascists and pro-Nazis in Britain and France, certainly thinks so, because he justifies his work like this:

> Most people, when they wake up in the morning, look in the mirror and say to themselves 'I am all right; my attitudes and actions are justified.' And then some of those people go out and do, or get involved in, dreadful things. My aim, throughout, has been to try and work out such people's reasons for action, or the justifications they make to themselves. Only thereby can we learn how to deal with such people and attitudes in the future.

Exactly.

A NOTE ON PRIMARY SOURCES

The key sources for this book are John Beckett's memoirs, covering the period 1918–1938, and my own memories of his conversation.

After completing this book I deposited his memoirs, most of his remaining books, the small number of papers he left, and his bound volumes of some of the publications he edited, in the library of Sheffield University, where any serious writer or researcher will be able to look at them. With them I have left all my own research for this book, including my notes, and copies of documents from the Public Record Office and other places.

MI5 and other Home Office material is in the Public Record Office in Kew. A great deal is still held back by the Home Office, even though half a century and more has elapsed. Material is often reserved for what are said to be security grounds, when the real reason is that they will show top politicians and civil servants in a bad light. The material I have been able to see is bad enough, so when in the middle of a run of documents I find a file 'closed for 75 years' I shudder to think what it might contain.

Most of the information used in this book from the PRO is in classes HO 45, HO 144 and HO 283. Within those, I mention in passing that HO 144/21040 is closed until 2039. HO 283/26 is 'retained under Section 3 (4)' on the authority of one A. Booth, and is apparently so sensitive that there is no date given for its release. Both deal with state surveillance on individuals.

I have also had access to material collected by the Board of Deputies of British Jews and the Friends of Oswald Mosley.

I have interviewed or corresponded with as many of the people who populate this book as I could find. The interviews are acknowledged in the text when they are quoted.

BIBLIOGRAPHY

I make no attempt to provide a comprehensive bibliography. Here are some books I think are useful.

There are some excellent biographies and autobiographies of the main Labour Party people in this story.

Beckett, Francis, *Clem Attlee*, Richard Cohen Books, 1997

Brown, Gordon, *Maxton*, Mainstream, 1986

Brockway, Fenner, *Towards Tomorrow*, Hart-Davis MacGibbon, 1977

Dalton, Hugh, *Call Back Yesterday*, Frederick Muller, 1953

Davies, Paul, *A. J. Cook*, Manchester University Press, 1987

Donoughue, Bernard and Jones, G. W., *Herbert Morrison*, Weidenfeld and Nicholson, 1973.

Howell, David, *Labour's Lost Left* (for John Wheatley)

McGovern, John, *Neither Fear nor Favour*, Blandford Press, 1960

Silkin, John, *Changing Battlefields*, Hamish Hamilton, 1987

There are also some excellent books about British fascism.

Colin Cross's *The Fascists in Britain*, is out of print now, but still the best introduction to the subject. It was written by a journalist with an eye for the colour, while the events it describes were still fresh in the mind, and before the Mosley machine painted its own gloss over the history. Richard Thurlow's *Fascism in Britain* is much more up to date and contains a great deal of information unavailable to Cross, so it is vital for the serious student. If you are to understand anti-Jewish agitation, you need Colin Holmes's authoritative *Anti-Semitism in British Society*. For post-1945, there is now no up-to-date book, but I have high expectations of the work being done by Graham Macklin.

Beckman, Morris, *The 43 Group*, Centerprise Publications, 1992

Benewick, Robert, *The Fascist Movement in Britain*, Penguin, 1972

Boyle, Andrew, *The Climate of Treason*, Hutchinson, 1979

Cross, Colin, *The Fascists in Britain*, Barry and Rockill, 1961

Griffiths, Richard, *Fellow Travellers of the Right*, Constable, 1980

— *Patriotism Perverted – Captain Ramsay, the Right Club and British anti-Semitism 1939–40*, Constable, 1998

Holmes, Colin, *Anti-Semitism in British Society*, Edward Arnold, 1979

Linehan, Thomas P., *East London for Mosley*, Frank Cass, 1996

Simpson, A. W. Brian, *In the Highest Degree Odious: Detention without Trial in Wartime Britain*, OUP, 1992

Thurlow, Richard, *Fascism in Britain 1918–1935*, Blackwell, 1987

Todd, Nigel, *In Excited Times – The People Against the Blackshirts*, Bewick Press, 1995

There are biographies of some of the key fascists. Those of Mosley require a health warning. Robert Skidelsky seems to have accepted Mosley's own unsupported explanations of events rather too easily. And Nicholas Mosley made an honourable attempt to come to terms with his father's life and not gloss over it, but I do not think he succeeded. David Baker's *Chesterton* frustratingly starts grinding to a halt around 1945, just as Chesterton's life starts to be significant. Cole's *Joyce* is good but a new biography of William Joyce by Colin Holmes is likely to end up as the definitive work, with extensive and sometimes startling new information.

Baker, David, *Ideology of Obsession – A. K. Chesterton and British Fascism*, I. B. Tauris, 1996

Cole, J. A., *Lord Haw-Haw – The Full Story of William Joyce*, Faber and Faber, 1987

Crowson, N. J. (ed.), The Journals of Collin Brooks 1932–40, Royal Historical Society, 1998

Mosley, Nicholas, *Beyond the Pale*, Secker and Warburg, 1983

Skidelsky, Robert, *Oswald Mosley*, 1975

INDEX

Action, 133, 134, 146–7
Actors Association, 44, 108
Advice and Information, 197–200, 205, 210, 212, 213
Alderman, Professor Geoffrey, 122
Alhambra Theatre, Glasgow, 115
Allen, Clifford, 34–5, 38, 58
Allen, W. E. D., 88, 96, 120–2, 135, 139
Amalgamated Engineering Union, 133
Ambrose Applejohn's Adventure, 73
Amos, Ulius Louis, 199
Anderson, Garland, 109
Anderson, W. C., 21, 22
Anglo-German Fellowship, The, 155, 158
Anomolies Bill, 97, 99, 107
Anti-Semitism in British Society, 144
Appearances, 109
Ashcroft, Peggy, 110
Attlee, Clement, 9, 10, 24, 25, 30, 32–8, 39, 40, 41–2, 43, 49, 51, 55, 57, 58, 63, 80, 87, 88, 97, 105–6, 107, 110, 134, 137, 144, 155, 156, 159, 162, 163, 182, 186, 189, 192, 201, 206

Baker, David, 143, 144
Bailey, Sir Abe, 61
Baldwin, Oliver, 88, 96
Baldwin, Stanley, 45, 68, 69, 70, 87, 88, 97, 101, 103, 140, 141

Ball, Sir Joseph, 161
Bamber, Revd H., S.J., 206
Barclay, J., 197, 201, 210
Bauer, Dr Christian, 169–70
Beamish, H. H., 53–4
Beamish, Tufton, 53
Beaumont, Captain, 104–5
Beaumont College, 204–5, 206–9, 210, 211
Beaverbrook, Lord, 162, 193
Beckett, Anne (JB's wife), see Cutmore, Anne
Beckett, Cecil (JB's brother), 14
Beckett, Dorothy (JB's mother), see Salmon, Dorothy
Beckett, George (JB's uncle), 15
Beckett, Helen (JB's wife), see Shaw, Helen
Beckett, John (JB's grandfather), 14
Beckett, John (JB's uncle), 15
Beckett, Hannah (JB's grandmother), see Billington, Hannah
Beckett, Joe, 168
Beckett, Kyrle (JB's wife), see Bellew, Kyrle
Beckett, Lesley (JB's daughter), 9–10, 41, 85, 100, 115, 192, 195
Beckett, Patrick (JB's grandson), 192
Beckett, William (JB's father), 13, 14, 15, 16
Bedford, Duchess of, 194–5
Bedford, 12th Duke of, 11,

156, 158, 159, 160, 161, 162, 167, 170, 179, 184, 186, 188, 190, 191, 192, 194–5, 197, 198, 200, 206
Bedford, 13th Duke of, 194, 195, 197
Bellamy, Richard Reynell, 146
Bellenger, F. J., 173
Bellew, Kyrle, 11, 44, 65, 71, 74, 76, 79, 91–2, 109, 111–2, 114–5, 116, 119, 123, 147, 211
Belloc, Hilaire, 81, 144, 202
Bevan, Aneurin, 88, 198, 199
Bevin, Ernest, 60, 144, 155, 191
Binkhorst, Mr and Mrs, 209, 210
Billington, Hannah, 15
Birkbeck College, London, 135
Birkett, Norman, K. C., 169–72
Black House, 131
Blackshirt, The, 133, 134
Board of Deputies of British Jews, 122, 191, 192
Borodaile, Viscount, 105
Bottomley, Horatio, 15
Bourchier, Arthur, 11, 42–4, 49, 65, 70, 73–4, 76, 108, 109, 111, 114, 213
Box, F. M., 139
Bradford Pioneer, 50
Bride, The, 114, 124
British Council Against

European Commit-
ments, The, 153–6
British Council for a Christian Settlement in
Europe, 160–1, 162
British Fascists, 134, 135,
140
British Legion, 24, 25
British People's Party, 11,
157–9, 160, 161, 164,
170, 184, 188, 189–91,
192, 194, 195–6, 197,
198, 200
British Union of Fascists,
11, 115–6, 120, 121, 122,
126–152, 161, 189, 202
British Vigil, 155
Britons, The, 53, 155
Brockway, Fenner, 24, 26,
34–5, 38, 42, 71, 72, 82,
83, 86, 90, 92–4, 101,
106, 108, 116, 118, 122,
125, 128, 131, 213
Brogan, Revd. J., S.J., 206
Brooke, Rupert, 35, 54
Brooks, Collin, 215
Brooks, Fred, 83–4, 95, 116
Brown, Gordon, 90, 101
Brown, W. J ., 90, 92, 96–7
Buchanan, George, 90,
91–2, 102, 104, 105, 107,
161
Bucknall, Mr Justice, 194–5
Butler, R. A., 198

Caine, Derwent Hall, 77
Callaghan, James, 42
Campbell, John Ross, 46
Camrose, Lord, 146–7, 168
Castle, Barbara, 116
Chamberlain, Neville, 63,
154, 159, 161, 163, 189
Cambridge University
Nationalist Club, 190
Catholic church, 189, 202,
203
Catholic Herald, 188, 189
Chambers, Whittaker, 202
Chesterton, A. K., 126,
130, 132, 134, 135–7,

139, 143–4, 145, 150,
151, 154, 155, 156, 161,
163–4, 165, 186, 189,
192–3, 195–6, 197, 201,
202, 213
Chesterton, Doris, 143,
189, 192
Chesterton, G. K., 136,
144, 202–3, 213
Christian, John, 139
Churchill, Winston, 64, 82,
95, 125, 157, 162, 163,
172, 182
City of Westminster
College, 210
Civil Servants Association,
96
Clynes, J. R., 39
Cocks, Seymour, 31, 91
Cohen, David, 192
Communist Party of Great
Britain, 22, 24–5, 26, 34,
48, 57, 63, 65–6, 70, 89,
104–5, 106, 116, 117–8,
127, 189
Comrades of the Great
War, 23
Connolly, James, 80
Constitutional Research
Association, 188
Cook, A. J ., 59–60, 66, 88,
102
Corvinus Press, 150
Cripps, Stafford, 79
Cromwell, Oliver, 10, 91
Cross, Colin, 30, 124, 127,
128, 132, 146
Crowley, Aleister, 132
Cutmore, Anne, 9, 11, 123,
129, 147–50, 154, 155–6,
159, 161, 164, 165, 174,
177–8, 183, 184–6, 187,
191, 194, 195, 197, 200,
204, 211, 212, 213
Cutmore, James, 149–50

Daily Express, 82, 193
Daily Herald, 22, 31, 52, 88
Daily Mail, 48, 93, 110,
127

Daily Telegraph, 146, 198
Daily Worker, 117, 131,
162, 182, 188, 202
Dalton, Hugh, 41, 49, 52,
53, 54, 55, 56–7, 58, 63,
76–8, 79, 80, 87, 88, 90,
95, 102, 103, 105, 106,
144, 163, 186, 191
Dalton, Ruth, 87, 163
Davies Laing and Dick, 210
Day, Colonel Harry, 48–9
Decline and Fall of the
Labour Party, The, 128
De Gaulle, General, 211
De la Bedoyere, Michael,
188
Dior, Christian, 196
Dior, Francoise, 196
Domvile, Admiral Sir Barry,
155, 158, 160, 161, 175,
180, 201–2
Domvile, Lady, 201–2
Donovan, B. D. E., 142
Don't Trust to Luck, 193
Doyle, Arthur Conan, 202
Driberg, Tom, 117, 193
Dundas, Ian, 134, 148

Eadie, Denis, 109
East London Pioneer, 34
Eden, Sir Anthony, 198
Edmonds, Major Harry,
184–5, 188
Edward, Prince of Wales
(King Edward VIII), 50,
140–2, 167–8
Eisenhower, Dwight, 198
Elliott, Bertha, 47
Engels, Friedrich, 21
Englander, David, 23
English Array, The, 153,
155
English Mistery, 153, 215
Equity, 108
Eton College, 204
Evening News, 127
Evening Standard, 175, 186

Falck, Lionel, 73–4
Fascism in Britain, 133

Fascists in Britain, The, 124, 127
Fascist Quarterly, 126
Fascist Week, 126
Firebird, 112
Fleet Street Preview, 191, 195, 197, 198, 199, 200
Follow My Leader, 39
Forgan, Robert, 96, 106, 116, 122–4, 125, 128, 132, 148, 164, 176, 180, 181, 185–6, 212
Forsyte Saga, 33
Fortescue, Vernon, 111
43 Group, 190
Fox, Fr Brendan, A. A., 202, 204
Francis-Hawkins, Neil, 134–5, 139, 140, 142–3
Friends of Oswald Mosley, 139
Fuller, Major General J. F. C., 132, 139, 155, 156, 158, 164, 184, 188

Gabbitas Thring, 152
Galsworthy, John, 33
Gandhi, Mahatma, 92, 120
Gandhi, Manilal, 71
Geddes, Sir Eric, 34
George V, 101
Gill, Eric, 161
Gilley, Sheridan, 81
Glasgow Evening Standard, 80
Glasgow Observer, 80
Goebbels, Dr Josef, 133
Gordon-Canning, Captain Robert, 160, 180
Grayson, Victor, 31
Greene, Ben, 155–6, 157, 158, 160, 161, 164, 167, 170–1, 179
Greene, Charles, 155
Greene, Graham, 155
Greene, Katherine, 164
Greenwood, Arthur, 61, 87, 156
Griffiths, Richard, 157–8, 216

Groves, Reg, 31
Guardian, 201
Gwenn, Edmund, 109

Haig, Earl, 25
Hale, Sonny, 112
Hamilton, Mary Agnes, 39
Hardie, Keir, 26, 30
Hastings, Sir Patrick, 68, 70
Henderson, Arthur, 45–6, 78, 81, 94, 102, 105
Henson, Leslie, 110, 114, 200–1
Henson, Nicky, 201
Henty, G. A., 13–14, 20, 120, 202, 203
Hiss, Alger, 202
Hitler, Adolf, 9, 138, 142, 151, 153, 154, 156, 157, 160, 172, 196, 202, 211, 215
Holmes, Professor Colin, 26, 83, 86, 93, 94, 144
Hope, John, 140, 171
Hore-Belisha, Leslie, 88, 215–6
Horrabin, Winifred, 66, 67
Housman, Laurence, 161
House of the Arrow, The, 109
Howard, Sidney, 112, 114
Hughes, James McGuirk, 139–40, 171, 172, 173, 179
Hunter, Ernest, 31, 39, 48
Hyde, Douglas, 118, 188, 202

Independent Labour Party (ILP), 10, 22, 26–7, 38, 44, 45, 81, 86, 92, 94, 101, 115, 117–8, 128, 162, 189
International Class War Prisoners Aid Society, 66

Jackson, Tommy, 66
Jenkins, Roy, 56, 87
Jerome, Jerome K., 154
Jews Who's Who, The, 54

John Bull, 52
Jordan, Colin, 54, 190, 191, 196
Joss, Detective Sergeant, 164–5
Journey's End, 136
Joyce, Frank, 167
Joyce, Hazel, 160
Joyce, Heather, 135, 146, 160
Joyce, Margaret, 135, 160
Joyce, Quentin, 167
Joyce, William, 11, 26, 122, 125, 127, 132, 134, 135, 139, 140–1, 142, 143, 145–6, 147, 148, 150–2, 155, 157, 158, 160, 167, 169, 172, 180, 186, 189, 202, 204, 206, 213
Joynson Hicks, Sir William, 63–4

Kaufman, Gerald, 62
Keen, Malcolm, 114
Kennedy, Joseph, 163
Kent, Tyler, 163, 167
Kinnock, Neil, 214
Kipling, Rudyard, 13, 18–19, 72–3, 202
Kirkwood, David, 90
Knight, Maxwell, 135, 140, 160, 171
Kurtz, Harald, 171–2, 179

Labour Representation Committee, 27
Labour Party, 23, 24, 27, 38, 45, 69, 83, 101, 117, 118, 126, 155
Labour Weekly, 52
Lanchester, Elsa, 39
Lansbury, George, 29–30, 52, 71, 72, 105, 107, 201
Laski, Neville, 122
Latymer School, 16
Lauder, Harry, 39
Law, Andrew Bonar, 35, 36–7, 45
League Against Imperi-

alism, 71
League of Empire Loyalists, 193, 195–6, 202
Lee, Jennie, 102, 106, 156, 199
Leese, Arnold, 155, 167, 175
Lenin, Vladimir, 82
Leese, Arnold, 54, 190
Liberal Party, 27
Limehouse Election News, 36–7
Link, The, 155, 160
Lloyd George, David, 10, 22, 35, 36, 63, 82, 95, 101, 167
Lobster, 171
Lymington, Lord, 153, 156, 167, 179

McCarthy, Senator Joe, 202
MacDonald, Ramsay, 9, 22, 24, 25, 27, 30, 32, 38–9, 46, 48–9, 50, 52, 64, 65, 74, 77, 79, 80, 81, 82, 85, 86–7, 88, 95, 97, 98, 99, 100–1, 102, 103, 116, 118, 137, 154, 156, 213
McGovern, John, 98, 99, 104, 105, 106, 107, 129, 131, 161, 162, 164, 177
McLean, Michael, 191
Maclean, Neil, 52
McNab, John, 146, 148, 151, 152, 160, 167, 180, 186
MacNeill Weir, L, 156
Major Barbara, 108
Mander, Ernest, 23, 24–6, 27, 187
Marx, Karl, 21
Mason, A. E. W., 109
Mason, Arthur, 183
Mathews, Jessie, 112
Maugham, Somerset, 202
Maxton, James, 25–6, 47, 65, 79, 81, 82, 83, 84, 88, 89, 90, 91–2, 95, 96, 97, 98, 99, 100–2, 103, 104, 105, 106, 115, 118,

121, 125, 128, 130, 155, 161, 162, 164, 169, 185, 186, 189, 194, 213
May, Sir George, 98, 100
Mein Kampf, 196, 202
Mellor, William, 88
Melville, J. B., K.C., 77–9
Mikado, The, 156
Militant Christian Patriots, the, 155
Mill, John Stuart, 21
Minority Movement, 85
Mitchell, G. R., 177–80, 187
Molotov, Vyacheslav, 191
Mond, Sir Alfred, 51–4, 144
Montague, Fred, 80
Morrison, Herbert, 10, 27–30, 57, 77, 78, 87, 102, 104, 105, 106, 144, 172–3, 175–83, 186, 191, 201
Mosley, Lady Diana, 142, 168
Mosley, Nicholas, 127, 137, 143, 145, 148
Mosley, Sir Oswald, 10, 11, 26, 35, 76, 82, 95–7, 105, 106, 110, 115–6, 121, 125, 126, 127, 130, 131, 132–3, 136, 137–147, 155, 156, 157, 158, 160, 161, 163, 165, 166, 167–8, 169–70, 171, 173, 175, 176, 179, 180, 182, 185, 186, 188, 189, 190–1, 196, 206
Mussolini, Benito, 9, 119, 121, 133, 137, 143, 148, 153, 191

Naismith, Paddy, 77
National Front, 189, 196, 202
National Front for Victory, 189
National Socialism Now, 125
National Socialist League,

11, 150–2, 160, 184
National Unemployed Workers Movement, 117
National Union of Ex-Servicemen, 23–5, 134
National Youth Theatre, 208
Nehru, Jawaharlal, 92
Neilson-Terry, 108–9
Newcastle Journal, 130
New Leader, The, 94
Newnham, Henry, 161
New Party, 95–7, 115, 121, 122
New Pioneer, 156
New Statesman, 131, 156, 202
New World, 24
Nice Goings On, 114
Nicholson, Harold, 101
1917 Club, 32, 38, 39, 41, 43, 44, 48, 108
Nordic League, The, 155
North Mail, 75, 78

O'Connor, Terence, 69–70
O'Connor, T. P, 64
Oddie, Air Commodore Gerard, 188, 192
O'Riordan, 108
Orme, Stan, 214
Othello, 44, 110
OUDS, 42
Owen, Frank, 87, 175
Oxford University, 42

Palace Theatre, 114
Palace Theatre, Newcastle, 130
Patriotism Perverted, 157–8
Peace Pledge Union, 160, 161, 163, 179
People's Post, 190
Petacci, Clara, 191
Petacci, Myriam, 191
Philby, Kim, 121, 158
Philby, Harry St John, 158, 159, 160, 167
Pilsudski, Marshal, 66, 67
Pimlott, Ben, 53

Pirates of Penzance, The, 59
Pless, Prince of, 182
Pollitt, Harry, 131, 202
Pollitt, Lieut. Col, 52
Portrait of a Leader, 126
Postgate, Raymond, 52
*Protocols of the Learned
  Elders of Zion*, 53–4
Purcell, Fred, 60

Ramsay, Captain Archibald
  Maule, 158, 161, 163,
  166, 167, 171, 175, 182
Red Aid, 66
Representation of the
  People Act, 1918, 35–6
Rickmansworth Grammar
  School, 206, 210
Right Club, 158, 161, 163,
  171
Robeson, Paul, 109–10
Rockwell, Lincoln, 196
Roddy, Major, 206, 207
Roosevelt, Franklin, 163
Rothermere, Lord, 97, 127,
  144, 215
Row, Bob, 183–4
Ruskin, John, 21
Russell, Bertrand, 35
Russell, Dave, 116–7

St Ignatius College, 204
Sally Who, 112
Salmon, Dorothy, 10, 13,
  15, 16, 120, 125, 144,
  149, 184
Samuel, Sir Herbert, 61,
  101, 103
Scanlon, John, 128, 155,
  156, 157
Scrimgeour, Alexander, 150
Securicor, 209, 210
Shakespeare, William,
  43–4, 202, 211
Shaw, George Bernard, 23,
  28, 108
Shaw, Helen, 11, 20, 32,
  41, 57–8, 74, 85, 91,
  109, 115, 159, 192
Shaw, Tom, 80

Shepherd, Arthur, 66, 67
Sherriff, R. C., 136
Silkin, John, 214
Silkin, Lewis, 77, 104, 116,
  118, 214
Simpson, N. F., 210–1
Simpson, Wallis, 141–2
Skidelsky, Robert, 137, 143
Slaughter, Tod, 111
Smillie, Bob, 110
Smith, Dorman, 215
Snowden, Philip, 64, 95,
  98, 100, 102, 125
Socialist Workers Party, 105
Soddy, Professor Frederick,
  188
Soper, Revd Donald, 161
Stalin, Joseph, 146, 191
Stephen, Campbell, 102,
  162
Stokes, Richard, 161
Strachey, John, 96, 106,
  116
Strand Theatre, 11, 43, 44,
  108, 109, 112–4
Strauss, George, 90
Sturt, G. W., 181
Sunday Dispatch, 127, 215
Swales, Alonzo, 60

Tavistock, Marquis of, see
  Bedford, Duke of
Taylor, P. G., see James
  McGuirk Hughes
Taylor, Valerie, 109
Tebbitt, Norman, 54
Thatcher, Denis, 188
Thatcher, Margaret, 68,
  205
Thomas, Jimmy, 50, 61, 97
Thompson, Paul, 14
Thompson, Raven, 143
Thorndike, Sybil, 108
Thurlow, Richard, 133,
  134, 138, 163
Thurlwood Farm, 14–15,
  192
Thurlwood House, 192,
  197, 204, 206, 209, 210
Thurlwood Investment

Fund, 199–200
Tillett, Ben, 60
Trades Union Congress, 60
Treasure Island, 111, 114
Trevelyan, Sir Charles,
  44–5, 55, 63, 77, 99
Trotsky, Leo, 146
Truth, 161
Truth About This War, The,
  161

Union Movement, 196

Vaudeville Theatre, 109

Wagner Society, 184
Waldorf Hotel, 113
Warren, Dr., 210, 211
Watson, Selwyn, 148
Waugh, Evelyn, 202
Webb, Beatrice, 76, 100
Webb, Sidney, 76, 100
Wheatley, John, 25, 64–5,
  76, 80–3, 84, 88–90, 91,
  95, 98, 101, 106–7, 110,
  116, 118, 119, 120, 158,
  186, 189
White Defence League, 196
White Knights of Britain,
  The, 155
Wilkinson, Ellen, 57, 58,
  59, 66, 80, 84–5, 93
Williamson, Henry, 160
Williamson, Hugh Ross,
  160, 162, 202
Wilson, Harold, 212–3
Wise, Frank, 125
Wolkoff, Anna, 163

Zinoviev, Grigory, 48
Zinoviev letter, 48